April
1991

ECONOMIC POLICY A European Forum

Senior Editors
GEORGES DE MENIL
RICHARD PORTES

Managing Editors
DAVID BEGG
CHARLES WYPLOSZ

Assistant Editors
JOHN BLACK
DAMIEN NEVEN
PAUL SEABRIGHT

Board of Governors
GEORGES DE MENIL *Co-Chairman*
RICHARD PORTES *Co-Chairman*
FRANÇOIS BOURGUIGNON
JEREMY HARDIE

Cambridge University Press and
Editions de la Maison des Sciences de l'Homme for
Centre for Economic Policy Research and
École des Hautes Études en Sciences Sociales

Panel

Richard Baldwin
Columbia University

Charles Bean
London School of Economics

Pierre-Andre Chiappori
DELTA, Paris

Nicholas Crafts
University of Warwick

Henrik Horn
University of Stockholm

Alexis Jacquemin
Commission of the European Communities

Arie Kapteyn
Tilburg University

Mervyn King
London School of Economics

Jean-Paul Lambert
Facultés Universitaires St Louis

Edmond Malinvaud
College de France, Paris

Maurice Obstfeld
University of California at Berkeley, Harvard University and NBER

Marco Pagano
University of Naples

Jean-Charles Rochet
University of Toulouse

Horst Siebert
Kiel Institute of World Economics

Guido Tabellini
University of California at Los Angeles

Anthony J. Venables
University of Southampton

John Vickers
Nuffield College, Oxford

Statement of purpose

Economic Policy provides timely and authoritative analyses of the choices which confront policy-makers. The subject matter ranges from the study of how individual markets can and should work to the broadest interactions in the world economy.

Edited in London and Paris, *Economic Policy* offers an independent, non-partisan, European perspective on issues of worldwide concern. It emphasizes problems of international significance, either because they affect the world economy directly or because the experience of one country contains important lessons for policy-makers elsewhere.

All the articles are specially commissioned from leading professional economists. Their brief is to demonstrate how live policy issues can be illuminated by the insights of modern economics and by the most recent evidence. The presentation is incisive and written in plain language accessible to the wide audience which participates in the policy debate.

Prior to publication, the contents of each volume are discussed by a Panel of distinguished economists from Europe and elsewhere. The Panel rotates annually. Inclusion in each volume of a summary of the highlights of the Economic Policy Panel discussion provides the reader with alternative interpretations of the evidence and a sense of the liveliness of the current debate.

Financial support from the Esmee Fairbairn Charitable Trust, the SPES programme of the Commission of the European Communities, and the Scaler Foundation is gratefully acknowledged.

Subscriptions: *Economic Policy* (ISSN 0266-4658) is published in April and October, volume 6 (issues 12 and 13) subscription prices, which include postage, valid until 31 December 1991, are per volume £27.00 UK, £29.00 elsewhere (US $43.00) for institutions, £15.00 (US $22.00) for individuals ordering direct from the publisher† and certifying that the journal is for their personal use. Single issues cost £14.00 (US $22.00) plus postage. US dollar prices apply to USA and Canada. Copies of the journal for subscribers in USA and Canada are sent by air to New York to arrive with minimum delay. Orders, which must be accompanied by payment, may be sent to a bookseller, subscription agent or to the publishers: Cambridge University Press, The Edinburgh Building, Shaftesbury Road, Cambridge CB2 2RU, UK or 40 West 20th Street, New York, NY 10011-4211, USA.

† When exchange control regulations permit, individuals may pay by any of the following methods: Cheque (made payable to 'Cambridge University Press'), UK Postal Order, International Money Order, bank draft. Post Office Giro (a/c no. 571 6055 – *advice of payment should be sent with the order to the Press*), Barclaycard/Visa/BankAmericard or Access/MasterCard/Eurocard.

Advertising: Apply to Cambridge University Press, UK or North American branch.

12

Contents

Editors' introduction

The five papers in this issue were presented at the 12th meeting of the Economic Policy Panel in London on 18–19 October 1990. Each paper is preceded by a summary of the argument and principal conclusions. In this Editors' introduction we place the papers in context of the wider debate.

The international debt crisis remains one of the most intractable problems in the world economy. Encouraging debtor countries to help themselves by adopting prudent macroeconomic policies and microeconomic reform, the essence of the Baker plan, did not prove a great success. The Brady plan goes further by linking debt relief to a commitment by debtors to the pursuit of such macro and micro policies.

Yet the provision of debt relief may not always have the consequences intended. Suppose there is a practical ceiling on the amount of external transfers a debtor can make, and that these transfers fall short of the amount initially required to service the outstanding debt in full. Debt will then trade at a discount in secondary markets. Complete debt relief would of course benefit the debtor by removing the need to make continuing transfers. But partial debt relief, unless it alters the debtors' ability to pay, may leave debtors making the same transfers as before, and simply raise total payments to creditors and the value of debt in secondary markets. In such circumstances, the benefit of debt relief is entirely captured by the creditors, frequently the commercial banks of the rich industrial countries.

This possibility has led many to be sceptical about the likely success of the Brady plan. However, once the danger is recognized, it may be possible to formulate a debt relief plan in which the benefits do indeed accrue to the debtor as intended. Such considerations were uppermost in the design of the Mexican package of 1990, and the significance of this deal therefore goes far beyond the implications for Mexico itself; it sheds vital light on the prospects for the Brady plan in the 1990s.

We asked Sweder van Wijnbergen of the World Bank to evaluate the success of the Mexican debt deal.

Van Wijnbergen describes the evaluation of the financing gap, the difference between what Mexico could credibly pay and its inherited external commitments. This defined the debt relief required. He then discusses at length the negotiation which took place and the way in which the package was designed to ensure that capital gains did not accrue entirely to creditors. The key was the *compulsory* exchange of previous claims for new claims, ruling out free-riding behaviour by existing creditors. Readers will be intrigued by the legal and other threats mounted to achieve this outcome. Using the sophisticated tools of modern finance theory, van Wijnbergen evaluates the impact of the deal on the market value of debt, and concludes that a substantial part of the relief did indeed accrue to Mexico and not to its creditors. Thus, his conclusion is that, with careful design, the Brady plan is capable of success.

Our second paper deals with credibility, the buzzword which has dominated the analysis of monetary policy in recent years. It is often argued that credibility is the prism through which the EMS must be viewed, and it lies at the heart of the continuing debate about the constitution of a possible European Central Bank. But what does the notion of credibility actually mean? Much of the literature of the last decade has been devoted to providing a theoretical answer, but as yet the corresponding empirical research lags behind. We asked Axel Weber whether credibility is a practical and measurable concept, and if so whether it can fruitfully be applied to the analysis of the EMS. It has become conventional wisdom that the EMS has operated as a greater Deutsche Mark area: other Member States have used the EMS to borrow the reputation of the Bundesbank as a resolute fighter of inflation. Yet evidence for this contention has usually been indirect, for example, the extent of convergence of interest rates to German levels. Weber offers the first direct estimates of central bank credibility. That is why his paper is so interesting.

His results are startling and at odds with the accepted view. He finds that the EMS is not a uniform DM area; rather it has contained two zones. Germany did indeed provide a hard currency option, but the option was so hard that only the Dutch guilder could live with it. The others, particularly previous members of the snake – for example Belgium and Denmark – initially forsook the DM zone for a softer option around the French franc. Only recently have the two zones dissolved, converging on a middle ground. This coincided with the hardening of policy in Ireland and Belgium, possibly also in Denmark, probably forcing France to follow suit. At the same time, the stance of the

Bundesbank has mellowed. Weber dates the unification of the EMS as occurring during 1985–87. And in the most inflation-prone country, Italy, he confirms that the monetary authorities' credibility was never high, though it has been improved in recent years.

These conclusions are based on actual measures of the credibility of monetary policy announcements: how far the market believes what the central bank promises to do. Such measures are problematic since nobody directly observes what the public really expects. Weber's results necessarily depend on his technique for inferring what expectations must have been. Obviously, there is scope for further research in this area.

Even so, the results deserve careful scrutiny. If Weber is right, we must reconsider some commonly held views about the EMS. The first is that membership immediately and automatically confers credibility; rather, it has to be earned, albeit within an EMS framework which may provide greater incentives for discipline than a single country can achieve on its own. Thus, in the current context, full UK membership of the EMS will not be an instant panacea for inflation control. Second, as we contemplate a common European currency, the EuroFed may have to earn its credibility afresh, even if the Bundesbank remains *primus inter pares.* This in turn may suggest, as Weber would advocate, that Europe should accelerate the implementation of the Delors Report.

As elsewhere in advanced economies, the Europe of the next few decades will have an increasingly aging population. In virtually every country, the consequences of aging are being debated, often with alarmist undertones. The paper by Axel Börsch-Supan is an important contribution to this debate. His article has two distinctive features. First, his cross-country comparison using data from Germany and the US allows him to begin to separate out institutional features and individual behaviour, the precondition for an intelligent policy response to the challenge of an aging population and possible changes in institutions and incentives. Second, his research relies on detailed survey data enabling a much more complete analysis of how individual behaviour depends on economic and demographic conditions.

He focuses on three aspects of the economics of aging. The first is the age of retirement, which affects not only individual incomes but public finance. The fewer people work, the greater the pressure for tax increases, less generous pensions, or a reversal of trends for an earlier retirement age. The second issue is savings, and the fear that as the population ages aggregate saving will decline, threatening capital accumulation and future living standards. The third issue is housing. As people live longer, a given population needs more homes. There are also important implications for the way in which elderly people live, the role and financing of retirement homes, and the social and economic impact of having elderly people live with their children.

The topic is vast and complex. In his extensive analysis, Börsch-Supan explodes a number of myths. For example, he finds that on average elderly people keep saving after retirement. One obvious interpretation is that they wish to build up bequests for their children, but he rejects this view, showing that the elderly cannot spend all their income, because of either changing tastes or declining health. If true, this might imply we could reduce retirement benefits or tax bequests more heavily. A second example is the effect of benefit provision and legislation on individual incentives. Public policy in Germany provides striking incentives to retire at the age of 60, 63 or 65. Few people work beyond the age of 65. Thus, a simple change in policy *could*, if it was desired, have a major effect on the retirement age chosen by Germans. As the postwar babyboomers move slowly but inexorably towards retirement age, we believe Börsch-Supan's evidence should be influential in the emerging policy debate.

In the next three issues of *Economic Policy*, we shall turn our attention increasingly to the remarkable events in Eastern Europe and their consequences for Europe and the world. The reforms have been dramatic and economists have not been shy in offering advice to the infant market economies of Eastern Europe. What should we be telling them?

Some advice quite properly is purely theoretical, but evidence is worth its weight in gold. What can Eastern Europe learn from similar experiments elsewhere? Perhaps the most telling case study is the experience of China, which began to abandon rigid central planning in 1978. How did China fare in the decade after reform? We asked Athar Hussain and Nicholas Stern to draw out the lessons of the Chinese reforms.

Even now China is by no means a full market economy. But partial reform of agriculture in the late 1970s and enterprises in the early 1980s have been remarkably successful: per capita real growth averaged nearly 10% a year in the 1980s. Inflation, initially modest, began to get out of control in the late 1980s until the brakes were sharply applied.

Hussain and Stern focus chiefly on the consequences of the enterprise reforms for public finance and macroeconomic control. Prior to reform, enterprise profits were a major source of government revenue. The decentralization of enterprise decision-making, coupled with inadequate control of credit, led to a collapse of government revenue which was not properly foreseen. Nor is there any clear dichotomy between the public and private sector when the state banking system provides credit on soft terms to enterprises. Hussain and Stern draw out important implications for investment, for public finance and for monetary policy. The theory of the second best alerts us to the importance of the sequencing of reforms when reform is only partial. The authors repeatedly demonstrate the significance of this point. Freeing up some decisions when important distortions still remain elsewhere may be a recipe for undesirable outcomes, and valid arguments for continuing intervention during the process of reform are easy to construct. The Chinese experience carries crucial lessons for Eastern Europe, and we believe Hussain and Stern's analysis provides important insights for that process.

The final paper examines an example of continuing reform in a developed market economy, namely the lessons of the UK privatization of electricity. Privatization became increasingly popular throughout the world in the 1980s, and the UK pioneered many of these developments. Yet the 1990 privatization of electricity was in many respects the most radical, and involves issues whose significance extends well beyond the energy sector. Unlike telecommunications or gas, electricity generation was not privatized as a single entity, but broken up into competing suppliers. Of equal significance, competition was introduced into the wholesale market for distribution and transmission. Many of the interesting issues concern the effectiveness of markets when networking is important, raising questions about the need for, and potential effectiveness of, regulation of this area.

We asked John Vickers and George Yarrow, who have been influential commentators on the entire programme of privatization, to examine the special features of electricity and the generic issues to which it gives rise. They provide a comprehensive assessment of the types of market failure which can occur, and the possible policy responses. Novel features of their discussion include a study of the spot market for electricity, almost as if by a Walrasian auctioneer, in a framework where inadequate supply at any point would impose massive externalities on the rest of the transmission system; and the possible role of *financial* contracts (options and futures) in the intelligent behaviour of an energy supplier under such circumstances. Interestingly, they tend to conclude that the major payoff to the shift in policy may not be more efficient pricing – electricity pricing has always been amongst the most sophisticated in the public sector – but in greater competition and control in the future *construction* of power stations.

Economic Policy April 1991 Printed in Great Britain

The Mexican debt deal

Sweder van Wijnbergen

Summary

When a debtor cannot repay in full, debt trades at a discount in secondary markets. Debt relief via injections of outside money may simply supplement payments to creditors, rather than reduce the burden of payments by debtors. For this reason, many have argued that the Brady plan will not help debtor countries. The Mexican debt relief package is a crucial test of whether this pitfall can be overcome.

Mexico has already shown the will to implement tough reform measures, but could not sustain growth given the debt she had accumulated. Official agencies were prepared to provide a measure of debt relief. Could Mexico prevent all the gains accruing to her creditors? Since individual creditors have an incentive to free ride on the debt relief provided by others, a key feature of the deal was the successful political and legal arrangement of compulsory surrender of existing debt for a range of new debt instruments embracing various forms of explicit debt relief. The paper investigates how official injections or 'enhancements' were in fact divided between debtors and creditors, concluding that most of the benefits did indeed accrue to Mexico, and discusses whether the consequent debt relief is sufficient to enable the resumption of sustainable output growth.

Mexico and the Brady plan

Sweder van Wijnbergen
World Bank and CEPR

1. Introduction

Mexico has throughout the 1980s been centre-stage in the debates and events shaping the sovereign debt problem. Caught between a sudden collapse of its terms of trade and rising world interest rates, Mexico suspended debt-service payments in August 1982 and ushered in what has since become known as the debt crisis. In the following years, lending to LDCs dried up and debtor countries were increasingly forced to run high trade surpluses to effect ever-growing transfers from poor back to rich countries.

In the face of falling growth rates and rising inflation in the high-debt countries; then Secretary of the Treasury Baker proposed the 'Baker plan': in return for economic reforms, high-debt countries would get new access to medium-term new loans, in addition to rolling over of amortization of old loans. New loans had to come both from commercial creditors and the official lending institutions. With access to capital markets restored, the economic reforms would, it was hoped, allow the debtors to grow out of debt.

But experience in the high-debt countries showed that the original hopes of the proponents of the Baker plan went unfulfilled. Net transfers out of the borrowing countries went up rather than down; as

I am indebted to my colleagues in the World Bank's Latin America Vice Presidency and the Mexico Division of the IMF for many helpful discussions and comments. I have, furthermore, benefited from discussions with Augustin Carstens and Manuel Galan of the Banco de Mexico, Angel Guria and Luis Tellez-Kuenzler of the Mexican finance ministry, Chris Mcloy of the US Treasury, Daniel Cohen of CEPREMAP and Stijn Claessens, Reuben Lamdany, Ricardo Martin and Sergio Pena in the World Bank. Finally Mervyn King, Santiago Levy and Richard Portes helped to sharpen many of the points made below. Much of the work presented here is based on joint work with Sergio Pena and with Stijn Claessens. But I alone am responsible for the views expressed in this paper. These views do not necessarily coincide with those of the World Bank or the Government of Mexico.

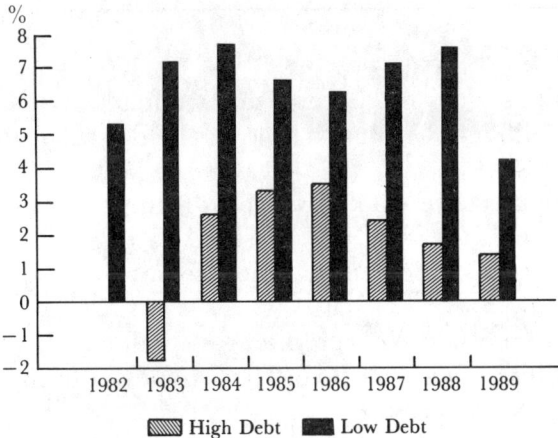

Figure 1. GDP growth (%)

Source: *World Economic Outlook*, IMF, September 1990.

countries could not or would not make matching adjustments in their public finances, inflation skyrocketed, investment fell behind and growth basically disappeared (see Figures 1 and 2).

In the years that followed its announcement, Mexico became the *de facto* paragon of the Baker plan; after initial retrenchment and consolidation, Mexico started a far-reaching process of structural reform, relying on international capital markets to support that process through rescheduling and new money in two consecutive debt restructuring packages (1983–84 and 1986–87). However, over the entire period of 1982–88, no real growth took place in Mexico at all. Mexico's experience bears scrutiny, as it vividly demonstrates the reasons for the eventual failure of the Baker plan.

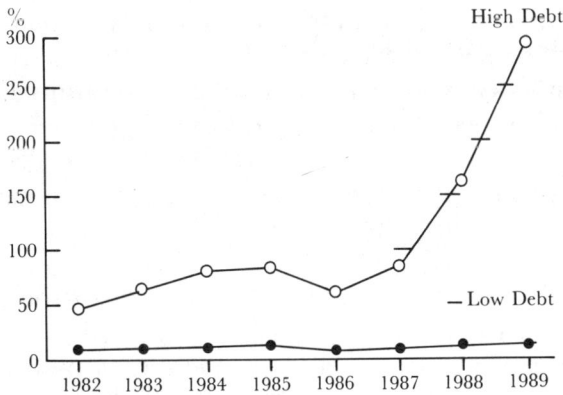

Figure 2. Inflation (%)

Source: As Figure 1.

Box 1. Glossary

Escrow Account: an account that does not become accessible to anyone until specific conditions are fulfilled. Until such time it is held by a third party.

Exit Bonds: exit bonds are bonds that will be free from future calls for new-money commitments.

Junior Debt: debt that will not be serviced until other, senior, debt has been serviced first.

New Money Commitments: a commitment by a creditor to actually provide new loans in addition to rolling over principal. New money commitments thus imply refinancing of interest.

Novation: debt renewal. A legal procedure by which a set of debt instruments is replaced by a new set of debt instruments.

Onlending Provisions: provisions under which a creditor is allowed to use moneys transferred to a debtor Government to extend a loan to a local borrower in the debtor country. Such provisions sometimes carry the restriction that the ultimate beneficiary has to be a Government agency or enterprise.

Reserve Financed Debt Buy-Backs: buy-backs of debt by the debtor from the creditor using hard currency reserves. This is effectively prepayment of debt and typically takes place at discount.

While the reform process at best promised tangible benefits over the medium term, reschedulings and new-money commitments came only on a short-term basis, and each time after tortuous negotiations. This inherently short-term process left continuing uncertainty as to whether similar accommodation would be available in future years. It thus failed to provide a medium-term framework within which the private sector could, with reasonable confidence, assume current policies to continue. The resulting uncertainty about exchange rates, future tax policy and financial regulation ruled out a return of flight capital and the recovery of private investment. As a consequence growth stagnated to such an extent that the social consensus behind the reform programme became increasingly frayed.

Towards the end of the de la Madrid administration, the view took hold in Mexico that a different approach had to be taken. This view was pursued with vigour by the Salinas administration that took power in 1988. On one hand, the reform process was accelerated beyond anybody's expectations, and a comprehensive, imaginative macro-economic stabilization programme skilfully put in place. On the other hand, President Salinas, in his inauguration speech on 1 December 1988, gave external creditors notice that, while Mexico wished to avoid confrontation, they were expected to contribute to a medium-term solution of Mexico's debt problem. At about the same time, the main international organizations took a considerably more flexible approach to debt management in their annual meeting in Berlin, September 1988.

But the real breakthrough came when Brady, Baker's successor as Secretary of the Treasury in the US, in a speech at the State Department, 10 March 1989, effectively legitimized the concept of debt relief, thus recognizing the failure of the Baker plan. In a departure from the Baker approach, it was recognized that new money, which had not been forthcoming in the amounts hoped for, could not be the backbone of a debtors' rescue plan. This speech opened the way for the negotiations between Mexico and its commercial creditors that, six months later, led to the agreement that is the subject of this paper.

The Brady plan has been a source of controversy from the day it was put forward. As to the answers to some questions, only time will tell. Widespread beliefs that the plan was not backed up by sufficient resources may come true, but for the time being, so few countries have actually travelled this road that the issue has not yet come up. Others have pointed out that the Brady approach, with its exclusive focus on commercial debt, is of little help to those debtors whose debt is held mostly by official creditors. This is clearly a valid point, and for those countries a different approach needs to be found.

A more fundamental criticism was that the plan amounted to little more than a bail-out of the commercial banks. Many argued that the type of debt restructuring envisaged under the Brady plan would simply benefit the commercial creditors at the cost of the official sector, with the debtor nations no better off (Bulow and Rogoff, 1988). This is a serious objection, and the main focal point of this paper. There is no doubt that such a creditor bail-out is a possible outcome. But is it an unavoidable outcome? Is there no way the Brady approach can work? To get an answer, there is no better way than to analyse the Mexican Brady exercise just completed. The main point of the analysis of the Mexican case presented below is that, in defence of the Brady approach, such a creditor bail-out can be and has been avoided. The Brady plan, while no panacea, provides a useful framework for those creditors whose debt is mostly in commercial hands.

2. The Mexican debt deal: economic background

In the years preceding the 1989–90 debt negotiations, Mexico had gone through a rather tumultuous series of macroeconomic developments and, towards the end, through an increasingly rapid process of structural reform. A better understanding of what happened in the years leading up to the negotiations explains much of the various parties' positions, and of the urgency with which Mexico and its official supporters in the international community approached the negotiations. We, therefore, provide a brief survey of this period.[1]

2.1. Macroeconomic developments

Between 1950 and 1973, Mexico enjoyed a remarkable period of high growth, low inflation and moderate external debt accumulation. Real growth averaged 6.4%, and inflation was in single digits throughout the period. This era came to an abrupt end in the early 1970s. Government involvement in the economy expanded rapidly, and increased public expenditure pushed up aggregate demand and the rate of economic growth. However, the higher government expenditure was not matched by rising public sector revenues. As a result, the inflation tax and external debt became increasingly important sources of public finance. At the same time, a decline in private savings incentives (real interest rates turned sharply downward) prevented a matching increase in private savings; external debt thus grew, increased oil revenues notwithstanding. The period of single-digit inflation ended in 1973, the real exchange rate started to appreciate and the accumulation of external debt accelerated above the GNP growth rate. A comparatively brief crisis in 1976 terminated following major oil discoveries in 1977. The ensuing prosperity lasted until 1982, when falling international oil prices, rising world interest rates, and massive capital flight led to a refusal by external creditors to roll over Mexico's short-term debt and a subsequent suspension of Mexican payments of interest on its external debt.

The onset of the financial and economic crisis of 1982 brought in its wake explosive inflationary and balance-of-payments difficulties. Initial strong fiscal and monetary adjustment efforts were undermined by external shocks such as the collapse of international oil prices in 1986. Inflation, rather than slowing down, accelerated, partially in response to the sharp real devaluation of the exchange rate necessitated by the 1986 downturn in the terms of trade. The subsequent *de facto* targeting of the real exchange rate, together with an increase in the frequency of wage and cost adjustments, introduced an element of inherent

[1] For details see Dornbusch (1988), Ortiz (1990) and van Wijnbergen (1989).

instability into the system, culminating in a run on the peso in the last quarter of 1987 and triple-digit inflation.

The Government responded with the 'Economic Solidarity Pact' (Pacto), an agreement between business, labour and government. This agreement called for accelerated structural reform, further tightening of fiscal and monetary policy, a freeze of minimum wages and of basic public- and private-sector prices, and, the cornerstone of the 'Pacto', a freeze of the nominal exchange rate against the US dollar. This partial freeze was extended at three-month intervals through the end of 1988, and renewed, with some modifications, by the new Mexican Administration under the name of 'PECE' (Pact for Stabilization and Growth). The main change under the PECE was a daily adjustment of the exchange rate of about one peso against the US dollar.

The fiscal measures, backed by the temporary exchange rate freeze and an array of formal and informal wage and price controls, had a dramatic success in reducing the rate of inflation, from 159% in 1987 to 20% in 1989.

2.2. The process of structural reform

Mexico has, throughout this period of macroeconomic turmoil, transformed itself into one of the most open economies in the world through an extensive trade reform. Trade liberalization, most of which took place between 1985 and 1988, has lowered the percentage of domestic (non-oil) tradeable production covered by import quotas from 100% in 1984 to less than 17% at present. Maximum import tariffs were cut by similar magnitudes. Non-oil merchandise exports, which represented less than one-third of total exports in 1984, have doubled their share since then.

These 'core' reforms have been complemented by many others. In May 1989, foreign investment regulations were considerably relaxed and made more transparent. The tax system underwent a series of reforms bringing marginal tax rates more in line with levels in major industrial countries, encouraging the repatriation of flight capital and increasing the sanctions for tax evasion. The impact of inflation on the (corporate) tax system was eliminated by eliminating purely inflationary gains from the tax base. The Government initiated a parallel process of financial market liberalization. Ceilings on commercial banks' deposit interest rates were removed; forced allocation of commercial credit towards favoured sectors has been abolished, too, and credit subsidies through official development banks have been reduced. Most recently, privatization of the commercial banks, which were nationalized in 1982, was announced.

2.3. The case for debt relief

Despite the far-reaching reforms implemented in Mexico, international
capital markets have not provided the resources needed to bridge the
period between the current costs and the future benefits of the reform
programme. Continuing high external transfers generated uncertainty
about whether the rapidly growing transfer burden could be met. This,
in turn, generated increased uncertainty about future exchange rates,
taxation and financial regulation. Thus, to forestall further capital flight,
Mexico had to pay unsustainable interest rates on its domestic debt. *Ex
post* real interest rates were almost 50% in the months before the debt
accord was reached.

Real interest rates so far above the real growth rate of the economy
are explosive under any circumstances; in Mexico, however, there was
an additional complication in that the government, at the time debt
negotiations started, was in the middle of a stringent economic stabilization programme in which fiscal retrenchment played an important
role. High real interest rates were mostly due to credibility problems
with the exchange rate component of the Pacto. Local currency rates
were around 30 percentage points above the rates on dollar-denomi-
nated Government debt while the exchange rate was fixed against the
dollar during 1988. The uncertainty caused by future transfer problems,
through its impact on perceived sustainability of the exchange rate
regime and from there on domestic real interest rates, thus became a
direct threat to the survival of the stabilization programme.

Beneficial domestic effects of the debt package could, therefore, be
expected to follow as much from reduced uncertainty and improved
expectations about future policies as from the direct fiscal impact of
any reduction in net transfers to foreigners. But for such expectational
factors to come into play, the deal needed to be of a medium-term
nature. Hence, the imperative not only of a solution, but a solution that
would likely forestall debt problems for the foreseeable future. Year-to-
year deals would have kept the possibility of impending balance-of-
payments crises open. A deal for, say, two or three years only would
have cast a large shadow over Mexico's adjustment programme.

This is in particular an issue for the revival of private investment,
because of the irreversible nature of capital accumulation. Uncertainty
about the future will bias private savers towards more liquid assets,
including foreign ones, until such uncertainty is resolved (van Wijnbergen, 1986). Also, with the possibility of balance-of-payments crises still
looming on the horizon, a major reduction in domestic real rates would
seem unlikely: nominal rates would first of all reflect higher expected
depreciation, raising *ex post* real rates; second, private investors would
almost certainly require continued high premia before accepting

exchange rate risk, raising *ex ante* real rates too. This suggests that a short-term deal would not only have precluded recovery of private investment, but it would also have perpetuated the fiscal problems created by high real interest rates on domestic debt.

The need for debt relief needs to be seen from this perspective. It was not so much the level of the country's debt, as the current flow of debt-service payments that was too high and caused too much uncertainty to allow growth and sustainability of adjustment. Debt relief offers the most certain way to reduce future net transfers for a long time to come, New money commitments, if credible and stretched out far enough into the future, could in principle have served equally well; however, they were unlikely to come in sufficient amounts and sufficiently far into the future to do more than postpone the problem while in fact adding to it.

There was another, more political, argument for debt relief rather than new-money commitments: political because Mexicans have accepted such a large reduction in living standards that any package without an extensive and visible contribution by external creditors would not have been acceptable domestically.

The conclusion should be clear. Mexico had the structural policies and domestic fiscal measures in place for sustainable growth to take off. What was missing was a sufficiently long period during which external creditors would allow this inherently sound economic programme to get off the ground. The only way of obtaining a credible commitment to such medium-term international accommodation is debt relief.

3. The debt agreement between Mexico and the commercial banks

To put the debt package in perspective, it helps to know how much debt was involved, who the creditors were, and how big, under reasonable assumptions, was the financing gap that Mexico would have faced without such a deal. So before describing the deal, I first provide an overview of size and structure of Mexico's external debt and the financing gap it has led to.

3.1. Structure of the debt and the pre-deal financing gap

3.1.1. Structure of the debt. At the end of 1988, Mexico's external debt stood at $100.4 bn. (all debt figures are in US dollars). Of this total, most was held by commercial creditors (see Table 1), with the remainder held by official creditors, mostly the World Bank and the IMF. Of the commercially held debt ($70.6 bn.), a small amount ($5.1 bn.) has never

Table 1. Mexico's external debt, end 1988, $ bn.

	Debtor	
Creditor	Public sector	Private sector
Commercial banks	65.1	5.5
of which: rescheduled	37.9	
new money	14.8	
non-rescheduled	5.1	
interbank	7.3	
Other creditors	28.8	1.0
of which: IBRD	7.4	
IMF	5.0	
Bilaterals	8.7	
Bonds	3.7	
Other	4.0	
Total	100.4	

Source: Debt Reporting System, World Bank.
Notes: Rescheduling occurred in 1983–84 and 1986–87; new money
loans were also part of these agreements.

been rescheduled. The bulk of this $5.1 bn. consists of PEMEX liabilities
($3 bn.) that traditionally have been rolled over automatically.

The new financing package covers the sum of the $37.9 bn. that was
rescheduled during 1986–87 and the $14.8 bn. of new money that was
provided in the previous two rescheduling exercises (1983–84 and
1986–87). This total ($52.7 bn.) has since been reduced to $48.9 bn.
because of cross-currency exchange rate changes, debt-equity swaps
and cancellation of debt held by Mexican institutions. Thus, the basis
covered by the debt package was $48.9 bn. A certain amount of this
was held by Mexican-owned banks. Those claims were either brought
under the new-money option described below, or did not receive any
collateralization if debt or debt-service reduction options were chosen.

3.1.2. Financing requirements and financing plan 1989–94. Based on simulations
with an econometric macro model presented elsewhere (van Wijnbergen, 1990), Mexico's total gross financing needs over the 1989–94 were
estimated to amount to over $50 bn. (Table 2). This level of financing
would accommodate a growth target of an average 4% over the next
six years. At current interest rates and for the given 'pre-deal' structure
of the country's debt, this would require a cumulative current account
deficit of around $23 bn. (around 1.5% of GDP on average). In addition,
reserves were assumed to increase by $3.1 bn., as stipulated under the
IMF Extended Fund Facility that came into operation May 1989, raising
the total to around $26 bn. Total financing requirements include, in

Table 2. Mexico's financing needs and sources, 1989–94, $ bn.

Needs		Sources	
Current account deficits and reserve changes	26.3	Direct foreign investment	21.9
Net scheduled amortization	18.3	International agencies	3.4
Other capital outflows	6.5	Bilaterals	2.3
	51.1		27.6
Financing gap	23.5		

Note: Other capital outflows is imputed reinvestment of interest earnings on private assets held abroad.

addition, the scheduled net amortization payments to commercial banks, bondholders, suppliers and holders of private non-guaranteed debt. These amortization payments amounted to $18.3 bn.

To meet the above needs, funding will be available from net lending by bilateral creditors and the international financial institutions. In addition, substantial direct foreign investment (DFI) is projected to take place in response to the economic reforms described in the preceding section, including the recent liberalization of the foreign investment regime. Table 2, however, indicates that funds available from these sources were short of gross financing needs; thus a financing gap was projected of $23.5 bn. cumulatively over the period ending in 1994, or almost $4 bn. per year.

This scenario is sensitive to developments in the world environment. Every dollar decrease in world prices for Mexican oil costs Mexico $0.5 bn. in forgone export revenues per annum. Thus, if oil prices are two dollars lower than assumed, Mexico would lose up to $6.0 bn. over six years. The financing gap would increase correspondingly. Conversely, unanticipated increases in the price of oil would reduce the financing gap. Similarly, a one percentage point increase in international interest rates would increase the cumulative current account deficit by close to $6 bn. over the period, with a matching increase in the financing gap. This sensitivity to international interest rates highlights the potential benefits of fixed-interest debt instruments.

3.2. Economic considerations underlying the package

From the Mexican point of view, two considerations were important in judging any proposal: impact on cash flow and implied debt relief. At one extreme, rescheduling, capitalization of interest due and new money have a one-for-one positive impact on cash flow but imply no debt relief. At the other extreme are reserve-financed debt buy-backs in the secondary market: these imply debt relief equal to the amount of debt repurchased times the discount at which it is bought, but actually lead to negative cash-flow effects in the year of purchase.

An alternative way of looking at cash-flow effects is to recognize that, because of the external credit constraints, Mexico must have a higher discount rate than that suggested by world interest rates. In that case, packages with equal discounted value when evaluated at world interest rates may have a different discounted value when evaluated at the Mexican, higher discount rate. In particular, packages that give the debt relief early on would be preferred on that criterion. Thus, a reserve-based debt buy-back would be worse than an equal present value (evaluated at world interest rates) cut in interest rates when evaluated at Mexican discount rates because of the early negative cash-flow effect of such buy-backs.

The impact of Central Bank reserve losses on the precarious exchange rate situation made reserve-financed debt buy-backs ill advised. Any package thus had to come down to a combination of cash-flow oriented interest-capitalization/new-money schemes and debt-relief oriented debt exchanges. For similar reasons, debt reschedulings with onlending provisions, like those incorporated in Brazil's package in 1988, were not advisable on a significant scale. In an economy with open capital markets like Mexico, a relending provision is tantamount to instantaneous prepayment at face value. Such arrangements would thus not only involve no debt relief, but would also result in a major negative cash-flow impact. The only way to avoid this is to restrict onlending to public-sector agencies.

Debt buy-backs can be distinguished by the asset being sold (or type of new debt issued) to finance the debt buy-backs. These could be publicly-owned assets; examples are a reserve-financed debt buy-back or a debt-equity swap involving a publicly-owned company. When such schemes involve public assets, there are no fiscal problems since the public sector already owns the asset.

The case of public debt for private assets (for example, equity) is different: to execute such a public debt for private equity scheme, the public sector needs to acquire the asset first. Therefore, the government needs to raise the resources to acquire the private asset. For the evaluation of such public-debt/private-equity swaps it matters how the government raises the resources to acquire the private-sector asset. This can be done through increasing the primary budget surplus, inflation tax, internal debt issue or external (net) debt increase (i.e. reserve losses).

The primary surplus was already strained to the limit because of the fiscal retrenchment under the macroeconomic stabilization programme. Use of the inflation tax (through a change in exchange rate policy) goes against the grain of the current stabilization programme. Use of internal debt issue was ill advised as long as internal debt carried in excess of 30% real interest rates. Finally, I already mentioned that the use of reserves was not possible in the current precarious exchange rate situation.

These considerations ruled out public debt for private equity swaps. Anyhow, Mexico's experience in the 1987 programme suggests that such schemes reduce debt but not really foreign liabilities: the average discount was slightly over 10% only (Sanguines, 1989). One could conceivably use the privatization programme to engineer public debt for public equity swaps, but unless claims on future oil production are brought in, such schemes will never be big enough to have a major impact. Thus, while debt-equity swaps might play a small positive role in the government's privatization programme, they cannot and should not play a major role in any debt reduction operation.

That left as the only option exit-bond schemes and cash-flow oriented measures. Exit-bond schemes would require guarantees of principal and interest payments to allow significant debt relief. But any package also had to involve major cash-flow oriented measures, such as for example interest capitalization. An attractive option was reduced interest rates. Refinancing of old loans at lower interest rates implies debt relief because the discounted value of all future payment obligations falls; at the same time it provides early cash-flow relief because it does not involve any purchase of assets up front. Finally, since there is no need for the public sector to obtain ownership of private assets, no fiscal problems arise. Thus, interest relief combines the favourable cash-flow effects of new-money packages with the debt relief impact of discounted exchange offers.

But to maximize the amount of debt relief, Mexico had to offer its creditors a menu of choices. The reason why a single-option deal would have reduced the amount of debt relief lies in the differences in regulatory and tax environment that Mexico's commercial creditors face. For this reason, different schemes that would present equal debt relief to Mexico, could imply very different costs to its creditors. Thus, restricting the choice to one instrument only would, for given willingness to grant relief by the creditors, unambiguously reduce the amount of relief actually received by Mexico.

3.3. Negotiating Mexico's external debt: a chronology of events

Negotiations were extraordinarily complicated right from the outset. One complicating factor was the number of banks involved (more than 600). This problem was dealt with in what is by now a standard solution, through the formation of a Bank Advisory Committee with representatives of some 15 creditor banks. This committee conducted the actual negotiations with representatives of the Mexican Government, which were concluded with the 23 July agreement on a 'term sheet' containing the outlines of the agreement.

But there were more players in the act. Prior to any negotiations with commercial creditors, Mexico sought to reduce net transfers to its official creditors and, in addition, sought their support for the principles underlying subsequent negotiations with commercial creditors. An agreement was reached with the Paris club, representing creditor governments, covering $2.6 bn. of principal and interest payments falling due in the period 6.1989–5.1992. All amortization over the three-year period was rescheduled over 10 years with six years' grace. Also rescheduled were 100% of interest payments due in the first year, 90% of interest payments in the second, and 80% of interest payments due in the third. Access to import financing of up to $2 bn. per annum was also secured.

Even before this agreement, negotiations had started with both the World Bank and the IMF about a major package of support measures. In February 1989, Mexico and the IMF reached agreement on an Extended Fund Facility for SDR 2.9 bn. (about $4.1 bn.) covering three years and an optional fourth year. At around the same time, the World Bank and Mexico successfully concluded extensive negotiations covering three Structural Adjustment Loans for $0.5 bn. each, plus a commitment by the World Bank to a lending programme of about $2 bn. per annum for the period 1990–92.

Moreover, both institutions publicly supported Mexico's claim that reduction in Mexico's debt burden was called for in one form or another if growth was to recover in Mexico. Both the IMF and the World Bank allowed a portion of the resources extended to Mexico to be used for support of debt-reduction operations. In another first, both institutions made available to Mexico an additional, one-time sum for debt-reduction purposes (Interest Support Facilities of $0.6 bn. from the IMF and $1.26 bn. from the World Bank). At the same time, the Government of Japan, through its EXIM bank, offered financial support to Mexico to the extent of $2.05 bn., also to be utilized in the debt-reduction package with the commercial banks.

Once negotiations with the IMF and the World Bank were concluded, negotiations with the Bank Advisory Committee began in New York in early April. Although the negotiations were officially behind closed doors, the various proposals and counterproposals were widely reported in the press throughout the three months of negotiations. The initial skirmishing was about Mexico's financing needs were growth to recover, in which both the World Bank and the IMF played an advisory role, albeit an unofficial one.

When the negotiations moved on to debt relief, initial positions were far apart, with Mexico asking for 55% debt relief and the committee offering only 15%. Although various counterproposals brought the parties somewhat closer, negotiations in New York seemed to stall in early summer and were escalated towards a higher level. The final negotiations, in Washington DC, involved the Mexican finance minister, Mr Aspe, Secretary Brady, the chairmen of the most important banks involved and senior officials of the World Bank and the IMF. This phase was successfully concluded with the announcement of an agreement in principle on 23 July 1989. This agreement included a debt-relief option involving 35% debt relief, exactly halfway between the opening proposals of both parties. The structure of this agreement, which was further refined in subsequent negotiations between Mexico and its commercial creditors, is described in the next section.

3.4. Terms of the agreement

On 15 September 1989, the Government of Mexico and the Bank Advisory Committee representing the commercial bank creditors reached agreement on a financing package covering the period 1989–92, restructuring approximately $48.9 bn. of Mexico's external debt. The agreement consists of a menu of financing options which includes two debt and debt-service reduction facilities and four new-money facilities. On the same day, the Government of Mexico disseminated a term sheet to all of its commercial bank creditors and invited them to participate in the financing operation. The following are the summary terms of the financing options offered by Mexico to its commercial bank creditors under the 1989–92 Financing Package (details in the Appendix).

The agreement, implemented over the next eight months, offered creditor banks, holding altogether $48.9 bn., three choices. First, old claims could be exchanged for new claims carrying LIBOR plus 13/16%, like the old debt, but with the principal reduced by 35%. Second, old debt could be exchanged for new instruments at par, but these instruments carry a fixed interest rate of only 6.25%. Both instruments will be amortized fully in one final payment 30 years after issue. Their principal is fully collateralized, through a 30-year zero-coupon bond placed in escrow at the Federal Reserve Bank in New York. In addition, 18 months' worth of interest payments is covered by another escrow account also established at the FED in New York. But contrary to the principal collateralization account, interest accruing on this account is not ploughed back into the account but paid out to Mexico. Third, old debt could be exchanged for new debt at par and market rates, but banks choosing this option have to make additional loans over the next three years equal to 25% of the amount brought into this option. Also, banks that chose this 'new-money option' do not receive any collateralization of principal or interest payments. Finally, the two debt-service reduction instruments carry a *recapture* clause from 1996 onwards: if in 1996 or later years oil prices rise above $14 per barrel in real (1989) terms, 30% of the extra revenue so obtained from crude oil exports will be available for the creditors under this clause, with two additional restrictions: (A) if less than 100% of the creditors choose debt-reduction options, the amount available under this clause will be scaled back proportionally; (B) no creditor can receive more than 3% of the amount of old debt brought into the debt-service reduction options in any given year under this clause.

The escrow accounts, which eventually amounted to slightly over $7 bn., were funded from World Bank and IMF contributions, Mexico's own reserves and a loan from the Government of Japan. The World Bank and the IMF contributed $1.6 bn. and $0.6 bn. respectively through additional loans. Furthermore, they allowed Mexico to divert respectively $0.750 bn. and $1.09 bn. towards funding of the escrow accounts from loans already scheduled for different purposes. Japan lent $2.05 bn. The remainder was made up from Mexico's own reserves. Thus, of the total of $7 bn. 'enhancement money', about $3.9 bn. represents resources that would not otherwise have been available to Mexico.

3.5. Subscription by the commercial banks

This agreement, reached with the Bank Advisory Committee and supported by management of the major banks involved, the official creditors, the US Government and the Government of Japan, was in subsequent months presented to all creditor banks. Although the agreement also included a small early commitment fee expiring at the end of October, the majority of the commercial banks only submitted their preference towards the end of the year. This was partially due to the complexity of the deal, but partially also to lingering uncertainty about tax and regulatory treatment of the consequences of the various options in the different countries involved.

To become effective, banks holding at least 90% of the debt eligible for the exchange had to sign up. In the event of a shortfall, this threshold could be lowered to 80% if 50% of the creditor banks agreed to it. This

Table 3. The debt deal: choices by the creditors (percentages)

	Par bond	Discount bond	New money and others
Non-Mexican creditors	49.8	40.7	9.4
All creditors	46.7	40.2	13.1

Source: Mexican Finance Ministry.

arrangement was designed to avoid a small minority of banks exercising an effective veto right.

Table 3 summarizes the choices made (details are provided in the Appendix). As is clear from the table, par or discount bonds were the preferred options for most banks. Out of the non-Mexican creditors, most opted for one of the debt-reduction options, with only 9.4% choosing new money.

Since 67% of the Mexican creditors chose new money, the overall new-money option choice was higher, at 13.1%. The remaining 33% of the Mexican creditors (holding $1.02 bn. opted for the discount bond. Thus, with all creditors combined, the configuration of Table 3 comes out, with a total of $22.8 bn. for par bonds and $18.7 bn. brought under the discount bond option by non-Mexican creditors. In all the debt relief calculations that follow, Mexican banks holding claims and choosing discount bonds have been included in the category 'new money and others'; this yields the following percentages: Par Bonds 46.7%; Discount Bonds 38.2% and New Money and Others 15.1%.

Banks were explicitly denied the option just to hold on to their claims; in a process called 'novation', all eligible debt was to be exchanged for one of the new debt instruments created under the agreement. Mexico made it clear it would not recognize any remaining old claims covered by the agreement after a certain date. Legal experts widely expected this approach to hold up in New York courts (the venue where any legal proceedings would have to be settled), although precedents involving Costa Rica did not really support such views. The circumstances of that case (in particular the absence of any support by the US Government in that case) were apparently sufficiently different to warrant optimism this time around.

Mexico's extensive support was reflected in the fact that Governments in the major creditor countries publicly supported the approach early in the process during a G-7 meeting in February 1989. This official support very likely contributed also to the virtual absence of any serious attempt to free ride by simply holding on to existing claims. By the end of January 1990, all banks had made their preferences known, paving the way for the official signing of the agreement on 4 February 1990 during a public ceremony in Mexico City.

4. Evaluation of the agreement

Section 4.1 below assesses the amount of debt relief to which the 23 July agreement and the subsequent choices of the creditor banks have led. I then ask whether this amount is actually enough. This question can be approached from two angles. First, is it enough given the resources devoted to the package? In other words, have the enhancement moneys been used efficiently? Efficiency of use can be assessed in two different ways. In one approach, the operation is seen as a project on which a rate of return can be calculated. This rate can then be compared with the cost of financing of the enhancement funds. This Rate of Return approach is pursued in Section 4.1. An alternative approach takes more of a bargaining approach and looks at market values rather than face values. This approach comes down to asking whether, in the end, the enhancement moneys accrued to the creditors or to Mexico. The answer to this question requires an assessment of likely market valuation before and after the deal, and with and without enhancement moneys (the escrow accounts), which is attempted in Section 4.2.

The second angle from which to assess the amount of debt relief is not from the point of view of use of enhancement moneys, but from Mexico's point of view. Is it enough to allow efficient growth to take place without the fiscal and balance-of-payment problems that have stymied the process of growth over the past six to seven years? This question is taken up in Section 4.3.

4.1. How much debt relief?

Table 4 below summarizes the element of debt relief embedded in each of the three options the commercial banks can choose between. In addition, the table evaluates the impact of the actual subscription, a blend of 46.7% par bonds (IR), 38.2% discount bonds (PR) and 15.1% new money and others (NM). Discount bonds chosen by Mexican banks have been included in 'others' (NM), i.e. they are not counted in the measure of debt relief, because Mexican banks were Government-owned at the time.

Of course, new money implies no debt relief. The principal reduction option involves 35% debt relief, since the markup of 13/16 of one percentage point on top of LIBOR will not be changed under this scenario. Evaluated at current interest rate projections, the low interest

Table 4. Debt relief implied by the three options

	Percentage debt relief	
	Without recapture	With recapture
New Money	0	0
Interest reduction	28	26
Principal reduction	35	33
Actual mix	26	25

Note: Debt relief is defined as the reduction in the discounted value of debt service as a percentage of the face value of the outstanding debt. Debt relief granted by Mexican creditor banks is not counted in this table.

rate option implies 28% debt relief.[2] This results in a debt relief percentage for the mix chosen of 26.4% of the face value of $48.9 bn., or $12.9 bn.

Furthermore, the debt and debt-service relief options qualify for the recapture clause. The value of these provisions depends both on expected future oil prices and on the variability of these prices. Thus, any evaluation needs to incorporate explicitly the impact of uncertainty on the expected cost of this clause; evaluating the impact of the recapture clause on debt-service obligations at some point in the future based on projected future oil prices is not enough. One way of doing this is presented in Claessens and van Wijnbergen (1990b).[3] The method proposed there starts by formulating a series of call option contracts on the price of oil that will exactly reproduce the contingent payment stream resulting from the recapture clauses. These option contracts are then priced using standard option pricing techniques and an estimate of the anticipated variance of oil prices implicit in the price of existing oil options. This procedure suggests that the recapture clause is worth about 2% of the amount brought under the debt/debt-service reduction options. Thus, the debt relief would be reduced to around 24.8% for the mix chosen. In absolute amounts, this would imply almost $0.8 bn. less debt relief, for a total of $12.1 bn.

---

[2] This number is sensitive to the projections used for international interest rates. The table uses a LIBOR of 8.5% for 1990 and 8% for the remaining years. The two debt-relief options would be equivalent in terms of implied debt relief if LIBOR stayed at 9.1% for the coming 30 years. However, the interest-reduction option provides more than debt-service relief. Because the interest rate on this exit instrument will be fixed, it also provides insurance against interest rate fluctuations.

[3] A similar approach is presented in Galan (1990).

4.2. Is there enough debt relief?

4.2.1. Rate-of-return approach. The rate-of-return approach compares the implicit rate of return on the enhancement money with the cost of financing the $7 bn. Such a rate of return can be calculated by considering the whole package as a project with as net benefits the reduction in scheduled cash flow over the next 30 years that the deal will bring about. The gross benefits consist of (a) the old flow of debt service, including amortization, since old claims have been extinguished; (b) interest earnings on the interest collateral accounts; (c) amounts to be released from all collateral accounts in 2019, which at that time will include the face value of the discount bonds placed in the principal collateral accounts; (d) the new-money disbursements; (e) the back payment for excess payments in 1989 due to the fact that the deal was retroactive to 1 July 1989. The gross costs, to be subtracted from the gross benefits, include: (a) the debt service on the new debt instruments, including amortization and the new-money instruments; (b) The $7.04 bn. placed in the various collateral accounts at the time the debt exchange took place.

This calculation indicates a real rate of return of 36%, clearly well above the cost at which Mexico is borrowing the enhancement funds, or the rate of return it could expect to earn on the reserves Mexico itself has devoted to the package. Moreover, such a rate-of-return calculation, by concentrating on the net foreign exchange savings, ignores the favourable domestic impact of the deal and as such is an underestimate of the benefits of the deal. Using the rate-of-return approach, the answer to the question of efficient use of enhancement moneys would thus seem to be unambiguously positive.

4.2.2. Market valuation of the new instruments. Among the many factors influencing market valuation of the package, three are likely to dominate. First, remaining Mexican credit risk and the extent to which different instruments are affected differently. Second, for given credit risk, the amount of debt relief (and hence capital loss for given credit risk) associated with the choice of any of the three options. Third, the tax and regulatory treatment of the income and balance sheet consequences of any swap.

The impact of credit risk and debt relief on the value of the new instruments is evaluated in Table 5. This table summarizes the projected secondary market valuation of the different instruments, assuming the actual mix chosen between interest reduction, principal reduction and new money. The table lists the value, as a percentage of face value, with and without enhancements. This valuation is based on an option

Table 5. Projected secondary market valuation of the new instruments

% chosen	Without enhancements % of new face value	With enhancements % of new face value	% of old face value
	Cents per dollar	Cents per dollar	Cents per dollar
IR 46.4	34	44	44
PR 38.2	49	59	39
NM 15.4	27	NA	27

Notes: IR: Interest Rate Reduction; PR: Principal Reduction; NM: New Money; NA: Not Applicable.

pricing model of secondary market valuation (Claessens and van Wijnbergen, 1990a). The table suggests that as a percentage of the new face value and without any enhancement, the principal reduction exit bond would be quoted at the highest price, because it receives market interest rates as opposed to 6.25% fixed. With collateralization of principal and 18 months of interest, as stipulated in the tentative agreement, the value would increase further, from 49 to 59 cents on the dollar. The low-interest instrument would trade for less, simply because it carries a lower interest rate (and, something that is not incorporated here, because the interest rate is fixed).

However, the unit value of the new claims is not the only factor entering the decision on which option to choose. After all, with principal reduction, old claims are exchanged at a 35% discount for new claims, while the low-interest bond would be exchanged at par. To incorporate that discount, the secondary market valuation needs to be compared to the old face value; in this way any discount at the time of the exchange of the old debt for the new instrument is taken into account. This reverses the outcome of the comparison: the low-interest option would remain the same with enhancements, since old and new face values are the same; but the value of the discount bond, inclusive of enhancements, would fall by 35%.

The second striking result in the table is the low valuation of the new-money option. This option has clearly been presented as junior debt by the Mexican authorities, junior to the exit instruments. This has a major impact on valuation. Without subordination, the new-money option would have traded at close to the unenhanced, new face value quotation of the principal reduction deal, since it carries market interest rates but no guarantees. Its junior status reduces the valuation to 27 cents, however. This is the *marginal* price of Mexico's debt, 60% of the *average* price of 45 cents, the price the model predicts if the majority indeed goes for interest rate reduction. 45 cents was in fact the secondary market price immediately after the closing of the deal.

It is not possible to perform a similarly general analysis of the consequences of tax and regulatory aspects, since they are different for each country; they could even depend on the particular balance sheet and profitability situation of individual creditors. In addition they have not fully been clarified in all countries. In the US both instruments will be treated similarly for financial disclosure and accounting purposes. But for regulatory capital purposes it is likely that banks will have to recognize the 35% loss with the discounted bond, while apparently banks opting for the par bond may be able to avoid the capital loss recognition, thus reinforcing the attractiveness of the interest-reduction option over the principal-reduction one. The Bank of England has recently increased mandatory provisions to levels close to 50%. The increased provisions are out of regulatory capital but are not tax deductible. Tax deductions can only be taken when the loss actually occurs. Hence, British banks have an incentive to take the discounted bond. Japanese banks were unclear about the treatment of the different options for tax purposes. Clearly, the tax impact depends on the country the creditor is located in, and on any individual creditor's tax position; therefore no attempt was made to incorporate tax aspects in the evaluation attempted here.

This analysis does suggest, however, that the choice between par and discount bonds is a close call, and even more so once one takes into account the insurance value extended to Mexico through the fixity of interest rates on the par bond. With such small price differences, particular tax circumstances become important determinants of the choice made. Based on this fact, and the low value of the new-money option, the actual choice made should not come as a surprise: of the foreign creditors, almost 90% opted for the discount and par bonds, in roughly equal amounts for each of the two exit instruments.

4.2.3. A market view: did Mexico strike a good bargain? One view on how to evaluate the debt package focuses on the pre- and post-deal market value of the claims under negotiation, and the voluntary character of the Brady plan. Since, in such a voluntary approach, creditors always have the option not to negotiate, one cannot really expect the market value of the claims to go down as a result of the negotiations. This would rule out debt relief unless a third party is willing to offset the impact of debt relief on market value by enhancing, in one form or another, the market value of the new claims to be created after the negotiations.

In the views underlying this approach, there is a reduction in the burden of the debt (discounted value of expected payments) if the market value of the claims without the enhancements goes down; if the market value of the claims goes up by the full value of the enhancements, however, there is by implication no debt relief, thus defeating the purpose of the third party's enhancement effort. In that case the creditors have walked off with the third party's resources. The relevant question to ask, then, is to what extent the value with enhancements went up versus the degree to which the value without enhancement went down. Some bargaining models predict an equal split between equal parties (Rubinstein, 1982); this would, therefore, seem a reasonable benchmark.

Evaluating the pre- and post-deal market value is more complicated than it sounds. This question cannot really be answered by simply reading off secondary market quotations of the various instruments traded before and after the deal. International events did not stand still over the six months of the negotiations, and it is thus difficult to disentangle the impact of the deal from other events influencing market evaluation of Mexico's credit risk. To separate out the impact of the deal, we use the same option-pricing approach that was used in the previous section. One way of benchmarking it is to price the debt before the deal using the same model that was used in the previous section and that predicted correctly the value of the discount bond within 1%. The same model can also be used to evaluate the new package, with and without the credit enhancements provided by the World Bank, the IMF and the Government of Japan.

This exercise yields a unit price for Mexico's debt before the deal of 39.3 cents, at the high end of, but within, the range observed in the six months leading up to the Brady speech. This would yield a total pre-deal market value of $19 bn. We can assess the market value of the set of new claims using the values listed in Table 5. This yields a full market value with enhancements of only $19.1 bn., almost the same as the pre-deal market value. Evaluating without the enhancements, however, yields a much lower value of only $15.6 bn. (Figure 3). The market value of the enhancement moneys is thus $3.5 bn., most of which did indeed go towards debt relief.

The conclusion is very clear: Mexico managed to obtain almost the complete value of the enhancement moneys and must thus be judged to have struck a remarkably good deal. Even if the full face value of the recapture clause (i.e. not corrected for credit risk) is added to the post-deal market value, we obtain $19.9 bn. for the value with enhancements and $16.4 bn. for the value without. This would give Mexico 75% of the market value of the enhancement moneys, still a good result,

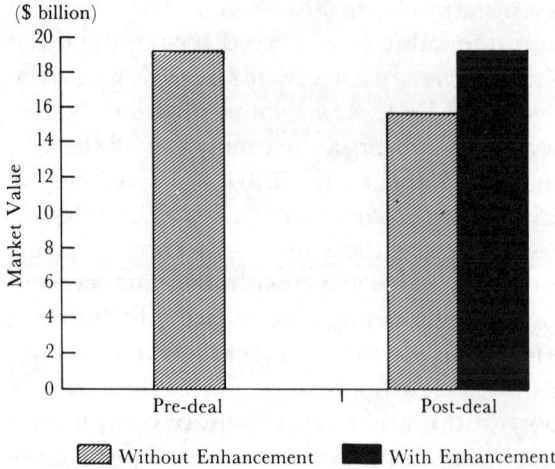

Figure 3. The market value of Mexican debt ($ bn.)

and an underestimate of the actual number, since the recapture clause has been evaluated without incorporating credit risk.

Some have argued that the infra-marginal benefits of debt relief would unavoidably accrue to commercial creditors. The conclusion would be that mechanisms that assure such an outcome, such as auction based reserve buy-backs, are the best one can do and might as well be used. What this analysis shows is that Mexico has succeeded in avoiding such an outcome.

4.3. Impact of the deal on the financing gap, creditworthiness and growth

4.3.1. Impact on the financing gap and creditworthiness. The impact of the debt package on Mexico's financing needs has been a source of much confusion. There is little argument about the direct impact of the debt exchange itself. All remaining amortization on the discount and par bonds has been shifted to the year 2019, and the amortization on the debt exchanged for discount bonds has been reduced by 35%. Interest payments have been cut; by 35% on the discount bond and on the par bond commensurately with the cut in the interest rate to 6.25%. All this is estimated to yield an annual saving in interest payments of almost $1.3 bn. per annum from 1990 onwards (there will also be a retroactive payment covering excess payments between 1 July 1989 and the implementation date of the agreement; this will yield about $800 mn. just for 1989).

Where the confusion arises, however, is with the financing package for the enhancements, the $7 bn. Some have mistakenly argued that

Table 6. Cumulative financing gap ($ bn.)

	Pre-deal	Post-deal
1989–91	12.0	2.1
1989–94	23.5	2.0

the just-quoted figure for interest savings ($1.3 bn. per annum) over-estimates the gains because of the financing costs of the contributions by the World Bank, the IMF and Japan (see for example Castaneda, 1990). This is, however, a mistaken view because it ignores the fact that the enhancement moneys are used to buy assets, the return on which will accrue fully to Mexico. The 3.5–$4 bn. to be used for establishment of interest collateralization escrow accounts will earn market rates of interest, all of which will instantaneously be transferred to Mexico. Similarly, the moneys to be used for collateralization of principal, which will be invested in zero-coupon bonds, will earn a competitive rate of return. This return may be in the form of capital gains, but it neverthe-less represents income accruing to Mexico. The fact that it is earmarked for future debt reduction is irrelevant for the issue discussed here.

A full accounting of the interest and principal savings should incor-porate the direct effects mentioned above, as well as the full financing costs of the foreign contributions to the enhancement moneys *and* the interest income forgone on Mexico's own reserves used for these funds; *but also the income generated in these collateral accounts.* Because all foreign loans are priced at market rates, and the assets in the collateral accounts will also earn market rates, the latter two factors more or less cancel out over the 1989–94 period.

Table 6 shows, for the options actually chosen, the net impact of these three factors, plus the new-money contributions, on Mexico's financing gap. The 'pre-deal' base case is also shown without the rescheduling of $12.7 bn. of amortization payments to the commercial banks for 1989–94.

As a result of the debt deal there will be a gap of only $0.3 bn. per annum on average, a number that is well within the margin of error of the estimates. Moreover, for such a small number, it is not unreason-able to count on return of flight capital in response to the renewed confidence in government macroeconomic policies to which this deal has already led and the favourable tax treatment the Mexican Govern-ment has accorded to Mexican citizens repatriating capital from abroad. In fact, substantial return of flight capital has taken place already ($2.5 bn. in 1989 and most likely around $5 bn. in 1990).

Table 7. Creditworthiness indicators (%)

	Pre-deal		Post-deal	
	1989–91	1992–94	1989–91	1992–94
Debt/GDP	49.2	42.1	46.5	37.5
Debt service/GDP	7.9	6.2	6.7	4.7
Debt service/exports	42.5	31.7	35.8	24.3

Table 7 above lists the impact on creditworthiness indicators and, for comparison, the corresponding pre-deal 'base case' projections. By assumption, in the base case the financing gap is filled by new money at LIBOR plus 13/16% so that planned output growth indeed does take place. Thus, the improvement shown in the table is a conservative estimate of the favourable impact of the debt deal; in reality new money would not have been forthcoming and hence growth could not have taken place. Nevertheless, all the indicators show substantial improvement in Mexico's creditworthiness indicators as a consequence of the package. Also, these measures take gross debt rather than net debt in that they do not incorporate as offsetting items the moneys in the collateral accounts; reducing the debt by the amounts contained in these accounts, which arguably leads to a more appropriate measure of public-sector indebtness, would lower the indebtness indicators further.

4.3.2. Impact on economic growth. The debt relief package will thus reduce the net transfer Mexico needs to make to its creditors by almost $4 bn. per annum over the 1989–94 period. Half of this amount would come from traditional rescheduling of amortization. The reduction in required external transfers will have a direct beneficial impact on Mexico's fiscal situation and its likely output growth. At least as important, however, would be the indirect, 'secondary' effects through renewed confidence. A reduced net external transfer means reduced pressure on the exchange rate. Also, because this is a medium-term deal, the uncertainty about future exchange rates, financial regulation and taxation has been reduced considerably. This greatly reduces the risk associated with Peso-denominated public-sector debt. One should, therefore, expect a reduction in domestic interest rates. Developments since the details of the package became known in July 1989 support this argument. Nominal interest rates fell from 56% to around 36% on an uncompounded basis immediately after the details of the package became known. At the same time, the maturity structure of public debt has widened considerably, another indication of private confidence.

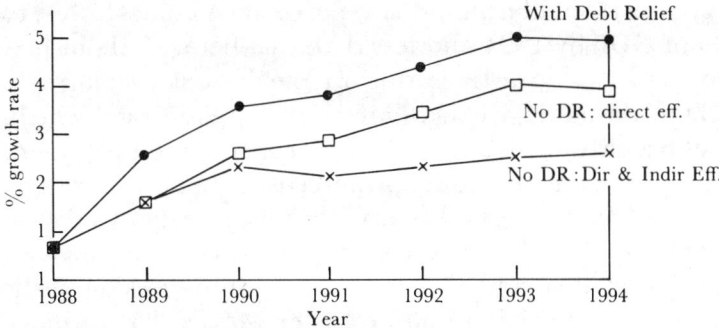

Figure 4. Impact of debt relief on growth

Figure 4 shows the impact on economic growth of the direct transfer effect and of the secondary effect through restoration of confidence and reduction of uncertainty. This is done by using an econometric model for Mexico to simulate what would happen without a debt package.[4] The difference between this simulation and the base scenario based on the availability of the subscribed debt package, indicates the macroeconomic impact of Mexico's debt package.

In the absence of the debt package, Mexico would have to service fully interest and amortization on all public commercial debt. This would need to be met out of an already severely cut back budget. Therefore, the Government would be forced to cut back public investment in line with the decline of 'allowable' external net borrowing. The drop from the top line to the middle line in Figure 4 indicates the direct impact on growth of this cut back in public sector investment.

Moreover, it is assumed that the Government would, even under such stressful circumstances, attempt to maintain its stabilization effort. It would then be highly unlikely that domestic interest rates would come down without a debt package. Therefore, domestic real interest rates stay at 30% in this simulation; 30% is the value that prevailed on average in the year preceding the debt accord. Thus, private investment would decline because of higher real interest rates, compounding the negative impact on growth caused by the fall in public investment. This secondary effect causes the further decline in growth from the middle to the bottom line in the Figure 4. Both effects have a major impact on growth. Output growth would be lower by one percentage point initially; as time goes by the difference in growth deepens to more than 2% by 1994, as both private and public investment decline. Over the next six

---

[4] The model is presented in detail in van Wijnbergen (1990).

years, average growth would be almost two percentage points lower, to reach only 2.6% of GDP by 1994 and less than that before. About half of the final slowdown in growth is due to the impact a failure to implement a debt deal would have on domestic real interest rates which, in turn, would reduce private investment. Not surprisingly, employment growth would slow down too, by about one percentage point on average.

In this scenario, without access to external funds, a real devaluation would be unavoidable. This is, of course, the main channel through which uncertainty over the external debt situation influences domestic real interest rates. By reducing the net transfer Mexico has to make over the coming years, debt relief is likely to take pressure off the exchange rate by raising the real exchange rate compatible with planned policy settings (see van Wijnbergen, 1990, for a quantitative assessment).

If, instead of full service of existing debt obligations, one takes as an alternative the case where all principal is rescheduled but interest is fully paid, the net marginal impact of the debt package on growth is still substantial. In that case, the direct transfer effect is halved, for a total of less than 0.5% per annum in total instead of slightly under 1% per annum. But a pure rescheduling exercise would leave a substantial financing gap ($10.8 bn.), so no favourable domestic effects should be expected from rescheduling alone. Accordingly, the full secondary impact of the debt deal through its impact on domestic real interest rates and investor confidence would not be affected by the change in alternative against which the comparison is made. Thus, even judged against this less extreme alternative, one should still expect a net marginal effect of the debt deal on GDP growth of around 1.5% per annum over the 1989–94 period.

Such econometric results should be interpreted with caution; in a well-defined formal sense, however, they represent the best use of currently available information. Based on these results a clear conclusion emerges: the debt package does meet the minimum requirements for restoration of growth in Mexico. But without the debt package, growth cannot be expected to exceed 2% in any of the coming six years; with the debt package, a gradual restoration of growth towards 5% per annum is likely.

5. Conclusions

5.1. The Mexico package: a good deal for Mexico?

The purpose of the negotiations was to provide Mexico with financing on a medium-term basis, either through debt relief or through new money committed ahead for a sufficient number of years. With the package outlined above, Mexico's financing gap will in fact be almost covered. The package meets Mexico's financing needs as currently projected and is compatible with a gradual recovery of growth in Mexico over the next six years. Thus, the stage for renewed growth in Mexico seems set.

In addition, a substantial impact can be expected from renewed confidence in the economy by Mexicans holding assets abroad. Assumptions on return of capital flight are too hazardous to actually incorporate them in the quantitative projections underlying this assessment; the most recent developments in Mexico, however, suggest a strong response of both private investment and private capital inflows to the announcement of the new debt package.

Moreover, the low-interest option chosen by half of the non-Mexican commercial creditors provides Mexico with insurance against interest fluctuations on the part of the old debt brought under this option. Thus, in addition to the debt relief embedded in the package, Mexico has reduced its vulnerability to fluctuations in international interest rates.

Two final points. First, I have demonstrated in this paper that Mexico made very efficient use of the official funds available to it for debt reduction purposes. The market value of the claims before enhancement went down by close to the full amount of the value of the additional foreign official resources devoted to this package, indicating that a creditors' bail-out has been avoided. Alternatively, the rate of return on the use of the official resources far exceeds the interest rate at which they have been extended. Second, although it follows by implication from the first observation, the market value after enhancement was basically the same as the market value of the outstanding claims before the deal. Mexico's commercial creditors thus got a fair deal, with the credit enhancement by and large making up for the debt relief granted. Thus, most of the official creditors' money in the end benefited Mexico rather than its commercial creditors. Therefore, the World Bank, the IMF and the Government of Japan achieved their objective of helping Mexico; the additional resources did *not* accrue to the creditors, something that was widely feared in advance, and has been claimed as unavoidable by some.

Thus, to sum up, the package as it came out seems a reasonable compromise between the conflicting interests of Mexico and its commercial creditors. And, most importantly, on the available evidence, this package seems sufficient to establish a basis for sustainable growth in Mexico.

5.2. The Mexico package: a panacea for debtor countries?

The Mexico package may have been a successful arrangement for Mexico; is it also, as the first major 'Brady deal', a model for other debtor countries? Several arguments suggest some reason for caution. Arguably most importantly, the Brady plan only suggests official involvement in bringing about commercial debt restructuring. This implies that it is by and large an irrelevant framework for countries whose debt is predominantly held by official creditors. Thus, Sub-Saharan Africa requires a different approach, and so does, to a lesser extent, most of Eastern Europe, where a debt problem of Latin American proportions is building up.

But what about Latin America, where, at least in the bigger countries, most of the debt is in fact commercially held? Costa Rica suggests that Mexico may have been less of a special case than many thought at the time. In both cases, countries that either had in place or were implementing a programme of economic reform, negotiated a debt reduction package that promises to provide the necessary breathing space for the programme to succeed.

Questions remain, however; in many countries, the political situation is too fragile to push through the type of economic reforms that have become the *sine qua non* for official support under the Brady plan. But without such economic reforms, any official credit extended is likely either to accrue directly to commercial creditors or to allow continuation of the very policies that triggered the problem to begin with. Support of what are clearly unsustainable programmes would in turn jeopardize the creditworthiness of the official institutions themselves. The losers in such a process would in the end be those countries who borrow from institutions like the World Bank but have managed to stay out of the type of problems that have stalled economic growth in the high-debt countries. Thus, the Brady plan does not offer help to those countries that cannot muster the domestic consensus necessary for implementation of a sensible programme of economic reform. This is in my view no shortcoming; it is not obvious that such help should be extended before a consensus in support of economic reform has been obtained.

Another doubt can be laid to rest, however. Some have argued that the infra-marginal benefits of debt relief would unavoidably accrue to commercial creditors. The conclusion would be that mechanisms that assure such an outcome, such as auction-based reserve buy-backs, are the best one can do and might as well be used. Official support would in that case have been difficult to defend; why should creditor banks be bailed out, and, even if they should, why in such a convoluted way? What my analysis shows, however, is that Mexico has succeeded in avoiding such an outcome; the Brady plan has succeeded in shifting the relative bargaining power into a configuration that is less lopsidedly stacked against the debtor. The Mexico experience suggests that the Brady plan provides a negotiation environment where a creditors' bail-out can be avoided and real debt relief can be obtained. For those countries that have substantial commercial debt, plus a reform programme in place that merits the official support extended to Mexico, the Brady approach presents a feasible way out of the debt problem.

Discussion

Mervyn King
London School of Economics

During the 1980s the problems of third world debt loomed large in the world economy. Mexican experience illustrates well the broader history of third world debt. In 1982 Mexico failed to make interest payments on its external debt. From that time the issue of the 'debt problem' has overshadowed Mexican economic development. In the period 1982–88 the growth rate of GDP was negative (−2.2% a year), inflation averaged 83% and reached 114% in 1988 and over 6% of national income was transferred abroad each year (see Figure A.1). By 1988 the external debt had reached $100 bn., most of which was in the hands of commercial creditors. Nevertheless, substantial progress was made in reducing the public non-financial sector deficit. The reduction in the primary deficit between 1982 and 1988 was no less than 14% of GDP (see Figure A.2).

In late 1988 a stabilization package was implemented, including a pre-announced gradual depreciation (about 1% a month) of the peso against the dollar, and a continuation of the deregulation of the domestic economy and the reduction of trade barriers. An attempt to renegotiate the debt burden had begun. Over 600 banks were involved and the difficulty of organizing a collective agreement was clear. At the centre of this effort was an estimate of the 'financing gap' between the non-interest balance of payments and the requirements of debt servicing of $25.9 bn. over the period 1989–94. After lengthy negotiations an agreement was finally signed on 4 February 1990. It provided three options for creditors:

(1) New bonds offering market rates with a 35% write-down of face value;
(2) New bonds with a lower interest rate of 6.25%;

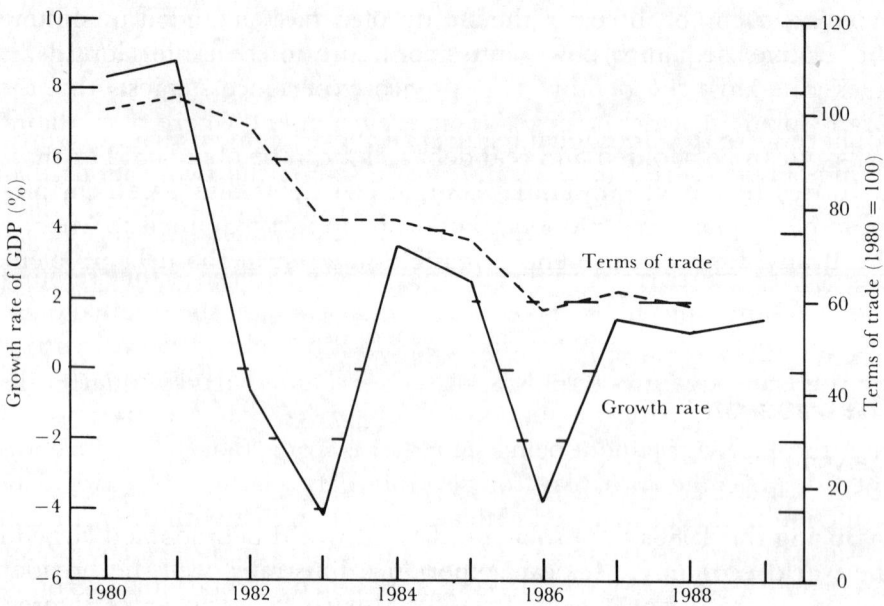

Figure A.1. Growth rate and terms of trade; Mexico, 1980–89

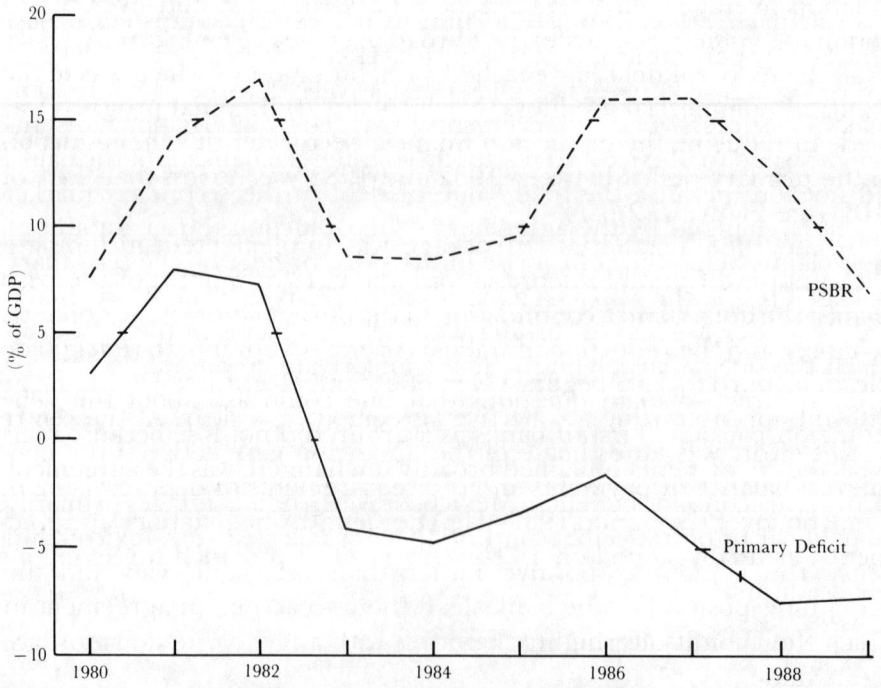

Figure A.2. Primary deficit and PSBR; Mexico, 1980–89

(3) Retention of the par claim but in return for the provision of new money (equal to 25% of the face value of the claim) at LIBOR plus 13/16%.

There were two additional features of the agreement that are worth noting. First, there was a recapture clause for the two options that involved debt reduction. If either the real oil price or the revenues from oil exports increased above a reference level then 30% of the excess of revenues from crude oil exports would accrue to the creditors subject to an upper limit of 3% of the dollar value of the original debt. The reference price level was fixed as $14 a barrel in 1989 prices and the reference quantity level was set at 113.75 mn. barrels a quarter. In view of the dramatic fluctuations in oil prices that occurred within months of the agreement being signed, it is ironic that this feature was not due to come into play for several years. Second, the two debt reduction packages involved 'enhancements' in that both the principal and also the interest payments for 18 months were guaranteed by money set aside by the IMF, World Bank and Japan (a total of $5.75 bn. – Mexico also dedicated $1.3 bn. of its own reserves to the funds providing the guarantees). The 'enhancements' are not gifts but loans.

Following this agreement 42% of the debt was exchanged under option (1), 47% under option (2) and 9% under option (3).[5] The deal was calculated to lead to a reduction in net external transfers of just over $4 bn. per annum over the period 1990–94.

Sweder van Wijnbergen argues persuasively that the Mexican debt deal was a success. The enhancements provided by international institutions accrued to Mexico and not to the commercial banks. But the banks did not lose because the total value of debt in the secondary market was little changed by the agreement – the reduction in the amount of their claims being offset by a rise in the price of debt on the secondary market. Hence, the Mexican experience suggests that the Brady initiative may offer a basis for dealing with debt problems in those cases in which the debt is largely in the hands of private creditors.

There are two main questions that one could ask about the debt reduction package. First, if banks as a group did not lose because total expected repayments remained broadly unchanged, was the agreement of any real economic benefit to Mexico, or were the advantages primarily of political importance? Second, if there was a gain to Mexico – and hence the game was positive rather than zero-sum – why did the bargaining position of the banks lead them to accept an agreement in which the benefits accrued to Mexico?

---

[5] These figures do not add to 100% because of debt in Mexican hands.

How important was the debt renegotiation to the development of the Mexican economy? Mexico certainly achieved its objective of lowering prospective net external transfers over the next five years. The Mexican government argued that 'Elimination of the debt overhang is a pre-condition for substantial capital repatriation and for renewed access to voluntary markets'. Its importance may, however, have been as much psychological as real – a seal of approval by the world economic establishment of the stabilization strategy of the Salinas government. The issue turns critically upon the relative importance of the two problems posed by the debt – the cash flow problem of financing the payments, and the wealth impact, and resulting incentive effects, of the burden. The potential of the Mexican economy suggests that the major issue was the financing problem. As far as external transfers are concerned, the estimated 'financing gap' could have been met by either debt forgiveness, rescheduling and/or new loans, repatriation of flight capital, or some combination of all three. The calculations cited above suggest that the reduction in debt servicing was adequate to cover the financing gap. But there appear to have been few new loans and clearly few creditors opted for the choice of retaining their claim and extending new money. The cost of servicing internal debt fell. After the announcement of the deal, interest rates in Mexico fell by almost 20 points (percentage *not* basis points!). Despite this the conclusion of the deal seems to have encouraged the return of flight capital. The potential for growth in the Mexican economy is large – if the reform efforts and a free trade agreement with the US proceed. An increase in oil prices to around $25 a barrel would have been sufficient to eliminate the 'financing gap'.[6] Events in the Gulf – still unfolding at the time of writing – led to prices in excess of this level for much of the second half of 1990. Future prices may well turn out to be much lower, but the point illustrates the sensitivity of the calculation of the alleged 'financing gap' to assumptions that may be invalidated within months. Nevertheless, the combination of the value of the official enhancements and the effect of a reduction in the debt overhang on the ability to adopt further growth-enhancing measures, suggests that there was a net gain from the exercise.

Why, then, were the banks unable to capture some of the gains from a restructuring? The paper argues that the commercial banks did not suffer from the deal because the reduction in the value of their claim was equal to the rise in the value of the remaining debt in the secondary market. But the use of 'novation' – the retrospective annulment of the

---

[6] On the assumption that an increase of one dollar a barrel in the price of oil increases export revenues by $400 mn. per annum.

terms of the original debt contracts – meant that, although the banks could choose among the three options described above, the removal of the status quo as a feasible option undermined the bargaining power of the banks. Such a solution could not have been achieved without the active support of western governments for this legal manoeuvre. It will not encourage new lending.

In conclusion, therefore, it would appear that the cash flow problems associated with the debt burden have largely been resolved. Indeed, the recent rise in the oil price would in itself have been more than enough to cover the financing gap. In the longer run the ability of Mexico to sustain its recent recovery will depend upon the structural reforms under way and in prospect, including a free trade agreement with the US. Whether the Mexican debt deal offers a blueprint for other cases in which debt is primarily in the hands of commercial banks is less clear.

Richard Portes
Birkbeck College, London and CEPR

Creditors have adjusted very slowly to the realities of the debt over-hang and the inability of sovereign debtors to meet their obligations. First, they resisted rescheduling and made its terms onerous; then they argued that any form of debt relief would harm the debtors' long-run interests, never mind the effects on creditors; and when the case for debt relief was finally accepted politically, they fought any real debt reduction, trying to confine debt relief to financial devices that did not reduce the present value of claims on the debtors. Meanwhile, the debtor countries laboured under an insupportable burden, at tremendous economic and political costs to themselves and with great damage to the world economy.

An alternative interpretation of these events is that creditors have simply been very successful in limiting their actual losses and enforcing debt service much longer than historical precedent would suggest. They have reconstituted their balance sheets, meanwhile taking profits on much of their LDC loan book. The result is that they are now able to absorb substantial real losses (ignoring other bad loans). Moreover, it is likely that whatever debt reduction may now come will still leave them with reasonable average *ex post* rates of return over the entire lives of the sovereign loans issued in the 1970s, just as lenders came out reasonably well on average from the loans of the 1920s (Eichengreen and Portes, 1990).

On either view, the stage is finally set – financially, economically and politically – for serious debt reduction. The indebtedness of the most seriously indebted countries is not improving of its own accord.

Econometric work gives empirical content to the costs of the debt overhang and the inefficiencies of the 'debt Laffer curve'. Despite domestic financial fragility, the international financial system appears able to cope with large writedowns. There is not, however, any 'clean' solution, in the sense of any analogy with 'Chapter 11' restructuring and protection from creditors; nor any 'global' solution, some international debt discount facility that would deal with most debtors following widely accepted, relatively simple and uniform procedures. As in the past, the outcome is likely to be settlements negotiated case by case that will provide enough debt reduction eventually to restore capital market access to those countries that do have growth potential. The continuing resistance of creditors and weakness of debtors may still make this a halting, unnecessarily painful process.

The question this paper poses is whether the Mexican case is one that has finally been treated properly, with lasting effect and lessons that can be generalized elsewhere. Sweder van Wijnbergen comes out broadly in favour of the 1989 agreement, the first major one under the Brady plan. He argues that the rate of return on the resources devoted to debt reduction was extremely high; that the deal was not a creditor bail-out or boondoggle; and that the results were sufficient to permit satisfactory growth, in the sense of eliminating the estimated external financing gap. The free rider problem was overcome by a device that effectively required all banks to pay part of the debt reduction cost.

I accept most of the analysis but am not convinced by the bottom line. First, the agreement covers only half of the total debt outstanding (slightly less, in fact). The proportion of debt reduction in those options offering it was 35%, precisely half way between the 55% that Mexico had asked and the 15% the banks originally offered. It is interesting that the lengthy, complicated bargaining process ended up with this simple solution; a game theorist might have predicted it, but those looking at a secondary market discount of 65% at the end of 1989 might have thought that Mexico should do a lot better. Second, the agreement leaves Mexico with a debt service ratio averaging 30% over 1989–94 and debt service projected at 5% of GDP at the end of the period. On van Wijnbergen's record, these estimates are probably as good as we can get: his option pricing model for the price of the par bonds issued in the agreement put their price at 44, and it has indeed been hovering around that level since mid-May. One might ask, however, why such a large secondary market discount persists if the agreement is so good. Flight capital appears to be coming back in significant amounts, but this may be due to tax concessions and real interest rates that are both excessive.

The agreement reduced the financing gap from $4 bn. to $0.3 bn. per annum, but this overestimates the effect of the debt reduction element in the agreement, since a simple rescheduling of principal would already have brought it down to $1.8 bn. The model simulations are interpreted similarly: growth at 2% with no deal, 5% with this deal – but we must suppose significantly above 2% with just a simple rescheduling.

In any case, I would argue that the financing gap and these simulated growth rates are not the appropriate criteria for assessing the agreement. Debt has been reduced sufficiently if and only if the agreed settlement restores normal capital market access for the debtor on a long-term basis. This is the key lesson of the interwar period and its aftermath. After decades of default, Mexico itself negotiated such an agreement in 1963, and lenders were delighted to welcome it back to the market then. It is not yet clear whether the 1989–90 deal has cleared the books anywhere near enough to give this outcome.

Nor is it clear that there was much alternative, except to be a lot more intransigent. I fully agree with van Wijnbergen's negative view of debt-equity swaps: in practice, they give little discount, offer little additionality, create financing problems, and are highly distortionary. Open market buy-backs on a large scale probably would not have given Mexico much benefit, and substantial secret buy-backs (Cohen and Verdier, 1990) were probably not feasible.

To me, the message of this excellent paper is that the best efforts of the international agencies coupled with the highest levels of political and economic commitment and expertise in the debtor country are still not enough. Creditor country governments – especially the US, but the others as well – must go much further in recognizing the need for very substantial debt reduction, and in a wider range of countries than have so far benefited from the Brady plan. At least we know much better now how to assess any proposed package, thanks to van Wijnbergen.

General Discussion

A number of panellists wanted further clarification about the incentives for commercial banks involved. Maurice Obstfeld wondered why any banks had chosen the new-money option when debt remained so heavily discounted even after the deal. Furthermore, it was unclear why the banks had an incentive to agree to the deal at all instead of continuing to negotiate. Sweder van Wijnbergen pointed out that the whole purpose of the agreement was to enable Mexico to issue new senior debt; this would be impossible unless all banks involved agreed to give up their old claims. The fact that it was an all-or-nothing deal meant there was a great deal of pressure on potential free riders.

Guido Tabellini asked about the use of debt Laffer curves in the argument. Debt overhang was presumably related to the market value rather than the face value of outstanding debt: if so it was hard to see why reductions in face value were of such importance, especially if they led to insignificant changes in market values. Richard Portes said each Laffer curve was dependent on a particular state of the economy. A shift to a better economic state would shift the Laffer curve, thus imposing an implicit tax on the gains from the improved state. If it was a country's own efforts that shifted the curve, that implicit tax would impose a problem of moral hazard. Tabellini was right to point out that debt overhang was due to the actual flow of debt repayments rather than the face value, but debt reduction was aimed at making sure that actual repayment flows did not increase too sharply when economic conditions improved.

John Black argued that taxpayers in industrialized countries were concerned about the operation of debt relief not just because they were averse to bailing out commercial banks. Many countries with a debt problem had also experienced capital flight, sometimes on as large a scale as the debt problem itself. He thought large-scale debt relief might for this reason be quite unpopular with taxpayers.

Appendix. The Mexican debt deal of 1989–90: a description

Terms of the Agreement. On 15 September 1989, the Government of Mexico and the Bank Advisory Committee representing the commercial bank creditors reached agreement on a financing package covering the period 1989–92, restructuring $48.4 bn. of Mexico's external debt. The agreement consists of a menu of financing options which includes two debt and debt-service reduction facilities and four new-money facilities. On the same day, the Government of Mexico disseminated a term sheet to all of its commercial bank creditors and invited them to participate in the financing operation. The following are the summary terms of the financing options offered by Mexico to its commercial bank creditors under the 1989–92 Financing Package:

Option A: Collateralized Floating Rate Discount Bond Exchange

Creditors may exchange eligible debt for new Collateralized Floating Rate Discount Bonds issued in a principal amount equal to 65% of the principal amount of the eligible debt offered for exchange. The new bonds will be in registered form, will mature in a single instalment on 31 December 2019 and will bear interest at a rate of 13/16% per annum over the six-month LIBOR rate for the currency in which the bonds are issued. Payment of the full principal amount of the Discount Bonds on 31 December 2019 will be secured by a pledge by Mexico of zero-coupon US Treasury obligations. Payment of interest will be secured by a pledge by Mexico of cash or permitted investments in the currency of the bonds in an amount equal to 18 months' interest (calculated at a constant interest rate of 10% per annum in the case of Discount Bonds issued in US dollars).

Option B: Collateralized Fixed Rate Par Bond Exchange

Creditors may exchange eligible debt for Collateralized Fixed Rate Par Bonds in a principal amount equal to 100% of the principal amount of eligible debt offered for exchange. The Fixed Rate Par Bonds will also be in registered form; and will mature in one maturity on the same day as the Floating Rate Discount Bonds. The interest rate payable on the Fixed Rate Par Bonds will be 6.25% per annum for those issued in US dollars and corresponding rates for those issued in other currencies. Principal and interest payments on the Fixed Rate Par Bonds will be secured in the same fashion as for the Floating Rate Discount Bonds, except that instead of using an assumed 10% interest rate, the interest payments on the Fixed Rate Par Bonds will be secured to their full contractual levels.

Option C1: 1989–92 New Money Credit Agreement

Lenders may elect to commit to lend up to 100% of their New Money Commitment (defined as 12.5% of Facilities 2 and 3 advances under the 1987 Multi-Facility Agreement and 25% of all other eligible debt) in the New Money Credit Agreement which will provide Mexico with a 15 year (seven years' grace) loan at an interest rate of (a) 13/16% over LIBOR, or (b) 13/16% over the three months Certificate of Deposit rate or (c) a fixed rate calculated to provide a comparable yield to maturity as the floating rate options. The loans will be made in the same currencies as the Debt and Debt Service Reduction Bonds, except that European Currency Units can also be lent under the New Money Credit Agreement. Amounts under this Agreement will be available for disbursement in six semi-annual tranches commencing on 1 December 1989 and concluding in July 1992. The first tranche will permit the disbursement of 40% of the loans and each subsequent tranche will permit the withdrawal of 12%.

Option C2: New Money Bonds

Each creditor may elect to purchase New Money Bonds in an amount
up to 50% of its New Money Commitment, although not more than
$500 million of New Money Bonds will be issued in total. New Money
Bonds will be in registered form, issued in US dollars; and will bear
interest at the rate of 13/16% over LIBOR. They will be issued on the
date of the borrowing of the first tranche under the New Money Credit
Agreement, and will be repayable in equal semi-annual instalments
beginning in 1997 and ending in 2004 (15 years' maturity, seven years'
grace).

Option C3: Onlending Facility

Up to a limit of 20% of its New Money Commitment, each creditor
may elect to make advances to a trust established by Mexico (with Banco
de Mexico as trustee) for the purpose of onlending funds to Mexican
public-sector borrowers with the guarantee of the United Mexican
States. These advances will have the same repayment schedule as the
loans made under the New Money Credit option (15 years' maturity,
seven years' grace), at an interest rate of (a) 13/16% over LIBOR or (b)
13/16% over the three months Certificate of Deposit rate. Advances
made under the Onlending Facility may be in any of the currencies
permitted under the New Money Credit Agreement; and the same
restriction on availability applies as the one on loans under the New
Money Credit Agreement.

Option C4: Medium-Term Trade Credit Facility

Up to a limit of 20% of its New Money Commitment, each creditor
may elect to make advances to a trust established by Mexico (with Banco
de Mexico as trustee) for the purpose of financing certain eligible trade
credits (e.g. unguaranteed portions of bilateral trade credits to Mexican
public-sector borrowers, or trade credits to Mexican private-sector borrowers for transactions approved by Mexico). The Medium-Term Trade
Credit Facility will have the same primary terms and conditions as the
Onlending Facility.

  Creditors holding claims in their home currency can, if that home
currency is not the US dollar, choose whether to maintain the original
currency denomination or switch into US dollars. If they choose to
remain in their non-dollar home currency, the total funds devoted to
enhancement will not exceed what would have to be provided for an

equivalent dollar claim.[7] Banks holding Mexican obligations contracted in the 1983–88 period will reschedule them to seven years' grace with 15 years maturity to the extent they are not swapped for Par or Discount Bonds. Mexico's external creditors would provide all the necessary waivers to make feasible the issue of new debt and debt-service reduction instruments with credit enhancement.

The Government would be entitled to buy back any of the newly issued Discount or Par Bonds if (a) it is current on interest payments and (b) the collateral account for interest support is either not drawn upon or replenished. This latter restriction lapses after the end of 1994.

Mexico would continue to service the interest on its existing loans on their contractual terms until the exchange takes place. However, the terms of the agreement would, upon signing, be implemented with retroactive effect from 1 July 1989. For the New-Money Commitments, this implies that at the time of the signing, participating banks would disburse immediately all the instalments due until and at that time, subject to the satisfaction of certain conditions precedent (which include the issuance of the Discount and Par Bonds). Similarly, once the Discounted and Par Bonds are issued, Mexico would deduct from the initial interest payments the amounts of interest paid on the exchanged loans in excess of the interest due on the new bonds, after July 1989. This clause was introduced to eliminate any possible perverse incentive on the part of the banks to delay the signing of the agreement.

Debt-equity conversion

Banks participating in the 1989–92 financing package will have access to a debt-equity programme which would be authorized up to $1 bn. per annum. This programme would be limited to public sector companies that are being privatized and to qualified infrastructure projects. The lower limit of discount would be 35% on Par Bonds, New Money and eligible old debt, and the conversion of Discount Bonds would not be higher than the face value.

Recapture clause

Banks that have chosen Discount or Par Bonds are eligible to recover some of the money given up through a 'recapture clause'. Under this

---

[7] There is one exception to this rule. Up to 5% of the Yen-denominated debt held by Japanese creditors is eligible for full collateralization of principal through zero-coupon bonds and 18 months of interest coverage.

clause, beginning July 1996, 30% of the additional oil revenues Mexico gets if the price of oil rises above $14 per barrel (to be adjusted for US inflation), will accrue to the banks that have granted debt and debt-service relief. The total amount to be recaptured, however, will not exceed in any year 3% of the nominal value of the debt exchanged for debt-reduction instruments at the time of the exchange (i.e. there is no indexation of this cap). Furthermore, the amount available under this clause will be scaled back by the percentage of the total debt brought under the two debt-reduction options. These recapture clauses, once attached to new instruments, can survive early redemption of such instruments by at most five years.

Credit enhancement

All Discount and Par Bonds will be repaid in a single instalment on 31 December 2019. The principal is secured by the pledge of zero-coupon US Treasury obligations with a maturity date matching that of the Mexican bonds. In addition, interest payments are partly secured by a pledge of cash or permitted investments in the relevant currencies for an amount equal to 18 months of interest payments due. The securities and cash pledged as collateral will be held in special collateral accounts, to be managed by the Federal Reserve Bank of New York, as collateral agent. Creditors' debt service would be paid out of these collateral accounts in case the Government failed to make interest payments for longer than 30 days, for as long as there are funds in the accounts. To enable establishment of the special collateral accounts, waivers of the negative pledge restrictions are necessary and have been received from Mexico's commercial bank creditors. Interest earned on the funds held in the collateral accounts is released to Mexico. The balance in the collateral accounts is released to Mexico. The balance in the collateral accounts, once the bonds for which interest support was provided have matured, will be returned to the Government.

To implement Mexico's credit-enhancement scheme for the Discount and Par Bonds, it was necessary for the Government to obtain limited waivers of the restrictions against giving security on other external debt – the negative pledge restrictions – contained in agreements that Mexico has entered into with the World Bank, IDB and other external creditors including the commercial banks. As the Morgan bonds were secured and had no negative pledge restriction, those bond-holders did not have to be consulted.

According to the term sheet agreed upon 23 July 1989, a total of at least $7 bn. is needed to secure the debt and debt-service reduction instruments subscribed by Mexico's commercial creditors, and more if,

Table A.1. Enhancement funds required ($ bn.)

	Discount Bond	Par Bond	Total
Principal collateralization:	1.18	2.22	3.40
Interest coverage:	1.82	2.11	3.96
Total:	3.00	4.36	7.36

Notes: Based on a six-months based 30-year bond yield of 7.925%, or a cost of 9.7 cents per dollar, a debt base of $48.9 bn., and a mix of 46.7% Par Bond, 38.2% Discount Bond and 15.1% New Money plus other categories receiving no enhancement moneys. In particular, debt held by Mexican banks is assumed not to receive any enhancement. Totals may not add up due to rounding errors.

Table A.2. Commitments made by creditor banks ($ bn.)

Non-Mexican banks	45.8
of which: Par Bonds	22.8
Discount Bonds	18.7
New Money (II/III)	3.8
II/III unenhanced	0.5
Mexican banks	3.1
of which: Par Bonds	0
Discount Bonds	1.0
New Money	2.1

Note: II, III refer to two loans (facilities II and III) with 50% World Bank guarantees from earlier debt negotiations. These loans were restructured into a 50% part with 100% World Bank guarantee (outside the current package) and a 50% part brought within any of the three new options.

at the mix chosen, $7 bn. is not enough for full collateralization of principal and 18 months' interest coverage. 49.8% of the debt not held by Mexican agencies has been committed to the Par Bond, and 40.7% to the Discount Bond, with the remainder going towards the New Money option and to other categories receiving no enhancements. Placing Mexican creditors in the New Money option for purposes of the calculations, results in a mix of 46.7% Par Bond, 38.2% Discount Bond and 15.1% New Money. This mix would require $7.36 bn. (Table 3), $0.36 bn. more than was committed by the World Bank, IMF, Japan and Mexico itself. The calculation is based on the long-term bond yield

at which the US Treasury has agreed to sell 30-year zero-coupon debt
instruments to the Mexican Government.

References

Bulow, J. and K. Rogoff (1988). 'The Debt Buy Back Boondoggle', *Brookings Papers on Economic
    Activity.*
Castaneda, J. (1990). 'Mexico's External Debt Deal', *New York Times*, 24 February 1990.
Claessens, S. and S. van Wijnbergen (1990a). 'Secondary Market Prices under Different Debt
    Reduction Strategies; an Option Pricing Approach with an Application to Mexico', CEPR
    Discussion Paper No. 415.
—— (1990b). 'The Pricing of Contingent Recapture Clauses: an Application to the Mexican and
    Venezuelan Debt Agreements', mimeo, World Bank.
Cohen, D. and T. Verdier (1990). ' "Secret" Buybacks of LDC Debt', CEPR Discussion Paper No.
    462.
Dornbusch, R. (1988). 'Mexico: Stabilization, Debt and Growth', *Economic Policy.*
Éichengreen, B. and R. Portes (1990). 'The Interwar Debt Crisis and its Aftermath', *World Bank
    Research Observer.*
Galan, M. (1990). 'Evaluacion de la Clausula de Recuperacion de Valor', mimeo, Banco de Mexico.
International Monetary Fund (September 1990). *World Economic Outlook*, Washington DC.
Ortiz, G. (1990). 'Mexico beyond the Debt Crisis: Towards Sustainable Growth with Price Stability',
    in M. Bruno (ed.) *Lessons on Economic Stabilization and its Aftermath*, mimeo, Bank of Israel.
Rubinstein, A. (1982). 'Perfect Equilibrium in a Bargaining Model', *Econometrica.*
Sanguines, A. (1989). 'Managing Mexico's External Debt: the Contribution of Debt Reduction
    Schemes', LAC Working Paper Series No. 29, World Bank.
van Wijnbergen, S. (1986). 'Trade Reform, Aggregate Investment and Capital Flight: on Credibility
    and the Value of Information', *Economic Letters.*
—— (1989). 'Growth, Debt and the Real Exchange Rate in Mexico', in A. Wick and D. Brothers
    (eds.) *Towards a New Development Strategy for Mexico*, Westview Press.
—— (1990). 'Growth, Debt Relief and the Real Exchange Rate in Mexico', forthcoming, *World
    Bank Economic Review.*

EMS credibility

Axel Weber

Summary

This article provides a quantitative assessment of the credibility of the European Monetary System during the disinflation period of the 1980s. The results contradict the widely held view that the EMS has operated as a DM-zone. It is shown that, after a brief early phase, the EMS has functioned as a bipolar system with a hard currency option supplied by the German Bundesbank and a soft currency option offered by the Banque de France. Whilst from the onset the Netherlands have chosen the hard currency option, at least in a first stage the remaining smaller economies, Belgium, Denmark and Ireland, adopted the soft currency alternative. At a later stage of the EMS, however, the soft currency block has disintegrated and some countries, most noticeably Ireland and to a lesser extent France, have shifted towards the 'hard currency' standard. It is argued that this increased tightening of the EMS provides a favourable starting condition for the transition to Economic and Monetary Union.

Reputation and Credibility in the European Monetary System

Axel A. Weber
University of Siegen and CEPR

1. Introduction

Has the European Monetary System (EMS) helped member countries to disinflate during the 1980s? Two arguments are usually advanced in support of a positive answer. The *credibility* argument states that the EMS may have reduced the costs of disinflation. The *discipline* argument states that the EMS may have raised the costs of inflation. The main focus here is on the credibility aspects and on a quantified assessment of the presumed 'credibility bonus' provided by EMS membership.

The credibility hypothesis (Giavazzi and Giovannini, 1987, and Giavazzi and Pagano, 1988) views the EMS as an institutional arrangement which has enabled the EMS member countries to borrow the reputation of the Bundesbank by credibly pegging their exchange rates to the German mark. This implies an asymmetric functioning of the EMS: the Bundesbank independently chooses its monetary policy whilst all remaining EMS member countries 'tie their hands' on monetary policy and simply target their exchange rates to the German mark. The EMS is a *de facto* DM-zone.

However, so far no firm evidence has been produced in support of the credibility hypothesis. On the contrary, it has been criticized by De Grauwe (1988), Fratianni and von Hagen (1989, 1990a, b) and Cohen and Wyplosz (1989), among others, mainly on empirical grounds. These

I am indebted to Charles Wyplosz for detailed comments. I furthermore should like to thank the participants at the Panel, in particular Richard Baldwin and Maurice Obstfeld, for useful discussions. Comments from participants at the International Macroeconomic Programme Meeting of the Centre for Economic Policy Research, the Warwick Economics Summer Workshop and seminars at the Center for Economic Research, the Centre for European Policy Studies and the University of Aarhus are also appreciated. This paper is produced as part of the SPES project 'Macroeconomic Policy and Monetary Integration in Europe' [No. SPES-0016-NL (A)]. The financial support of the Commission of the European Communities for this project is gratefully acknowledged.

studies concur in finding a rich structure of cross-country policy interactions: if indeed Germany exerts a significant monetary influence on
many EMS countries, it is itself not immune from influences in the
opposite direction. In addition, some non-German EMS countries, most
noticeably France, are also found to influence monetary policy in other
non-German EMS economies.[1] This evidence is sometimes seen as
providing support to the opposite interpretation, namely that the EMS
in fact functions symmetrically.

The new and different evidence provided in this paper points to a
third view of the EMS. It appears that, after a short early phase, the
EMS has functioned as a bipolar system with a hard currency option
offered by the German Bundesbank and a soft currency option supplied
by the Banque de France. Whilst from the onset the Netherlands have
chosen the hard currency option, at least in a first stage the remaining
smaller economies, Belgium, Denmark and Ireland, adopted the soft
currency alternative. At a later stage, however, this soft currency block
has disintegrated and some countries, most noticeably Ireland and to
a lesser extent France, have shifted towards the hard currency standard,
which itself has somewhat mellowed.

This view is suggested by the evidence shown in Figure 1. Panel (a)
displays the exchange rates of all EMS currencies relative to the German
mark (measured for ease of comparability as indices set at 100 in March
1979). With the exception of some wavering in late 1980, the German
mark has clearly been the hard currency. The figure also identifies
three groupings: first comes the Dutch guilder which has remained
quite stable *vis-a-vis* the mark; second, the Italian lira exhibits a sharp
downward trend throughout the whole EMS period; finally the French
franc, the Belgian franc, the Danish krona and the Irish pound switched,
at various points between late 1982 and early 1987, from a trend of
successive devaluations to stability. Throughout this period, all the
currencies in this last group, with the French franc clearly the weakest,
experienced similar devaluations *vis-a-vis* the mark. The relevance of
this grouping is confirmed in panel (b) of Figure 1 which presents the
exchange rate of EMS currencies *vis-a-vis* the French franc. The implication, to be confirmed below by harder evidence, is that the DM-zone
hypothesis of the EMS is unwarranted: by adopting the soft currency
option of a crawling peg *vis-a-vis* the German mark, Belgium, Denmark
and Ireland have actually shared the inflation 'reputation' of France.

This interpretation is also supported by the evolution of inflation
rates as shown in Figure 2. After the initial adverse impact of the oil

---

[1] See Cohen and Wyplosz (1989) and the survey by Wyplosz (1989).

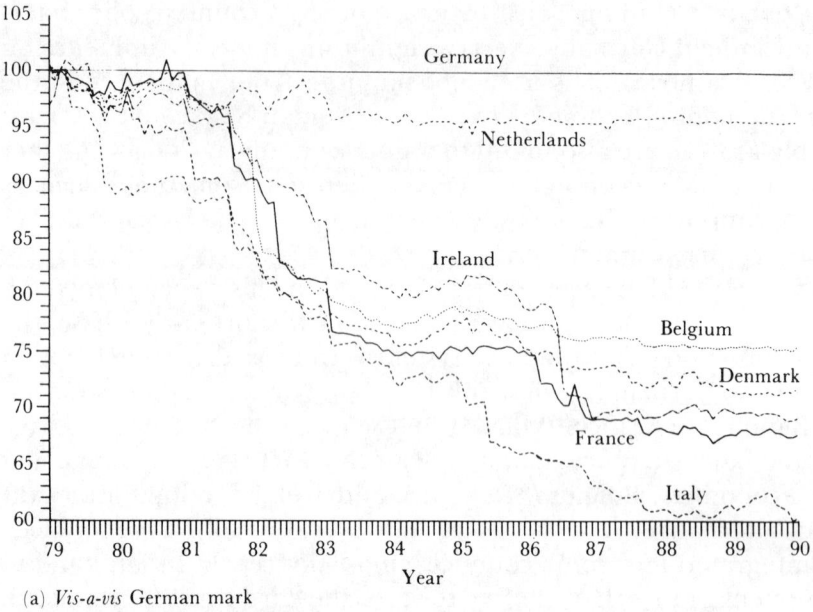

(a) *Vis-a-vis* German mark

Figure 1. Nominal bilateral exchange rates. Index (1979 M3 = 100)

Source: Own calculations from bilateral US dollar spot exchange rates, taken from *IMF International Financial Statistics*, various issues.

price shock in 1979, all EMS countries had considerable success in reducing inflation between early 1982 and late 1986. Yet, convergence to the low German level has been slow and less than complete. Furthermore, the closeness of the German and Dutch inflation rates throughout the entire EMS period depicts a much reduced DM-zone facing a larger French franc-zone, given the apparent similarity of inflation developments in France, Belgium and Denmark during the disinflation period (1982–86).

The existence of the two options in the EMS can also explain the findings by Rogoff (1985b), Ungerer *et al.* (1983, 1986), Collins (1988), Artis (1987) and Weber (1990b) that, as far as disinflation is concerned, the EMS countries have not differed much from the other advanced economies. If anything, disinflation has been slower in the EMS since the exchange rate constraint has prevented its member countries from adopting a 'short sharp shock' treatment (De Grauwe, 1990). Panel (b) of Figure 2 shows that most of the inflation reduction in the UK and the US was achieved relatively quickly in the short period of mid-1980 to mid-1983. In contrast, the German and French disinflations only started in late 1981 and were not completed until late 1986. However,

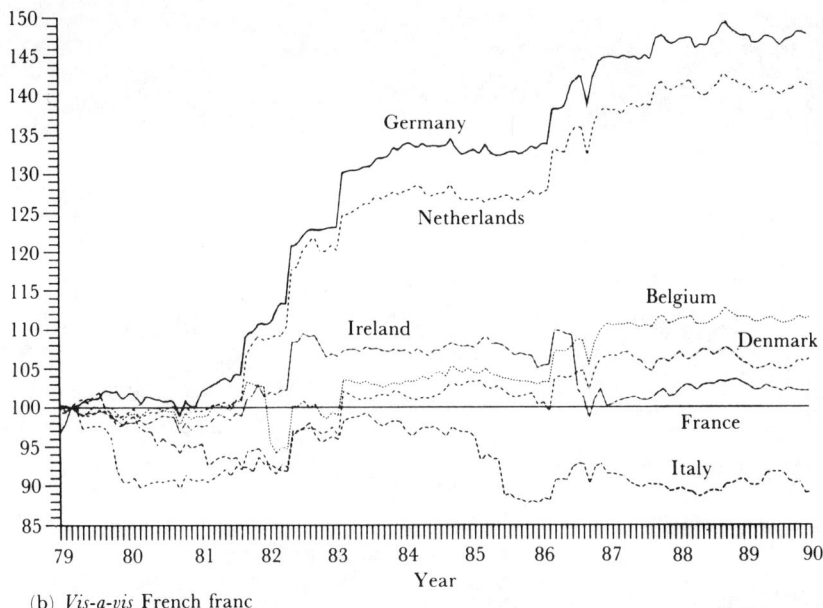

(b) *Vis-a-vis* French franc

Figure 1—continued

while slower, the EMS disinflation has been longer lasting, as exemplified by a strong reflation in the UK and the US after 1987. This fact is interpreted here as the consequence of the recent convergence of the EMS to a hard currency standard which has strengthened the disciplinary effects of the EMS. Germany's anti-inflation policy stance, on the other side, appears to have mellowed slightly, as indicated by the rise in its inflation rate during 1987–90. The DM-zone hypothesis is invalidated by the fact that the hard-currency strategy, pegging to the German mark, has not been a feature of the EMS from its start; it emerged in a later phase and at various points in time as the result of deliberate policy switches in the EMS economies.

The remainder of the paper is organized as follows: Section 2 gives a definition of the concepts of reputation and credibility and discusses their potential role in disinflation. Sections 3, 4, 5 and 6 describe the results of the empirical analysis of counterinflation reputation and of the credibility of money, exchange rate and interest rate targeting, respectively. Section 7 provides a country by country description of the main results, while Section 8 draws some policy implications.

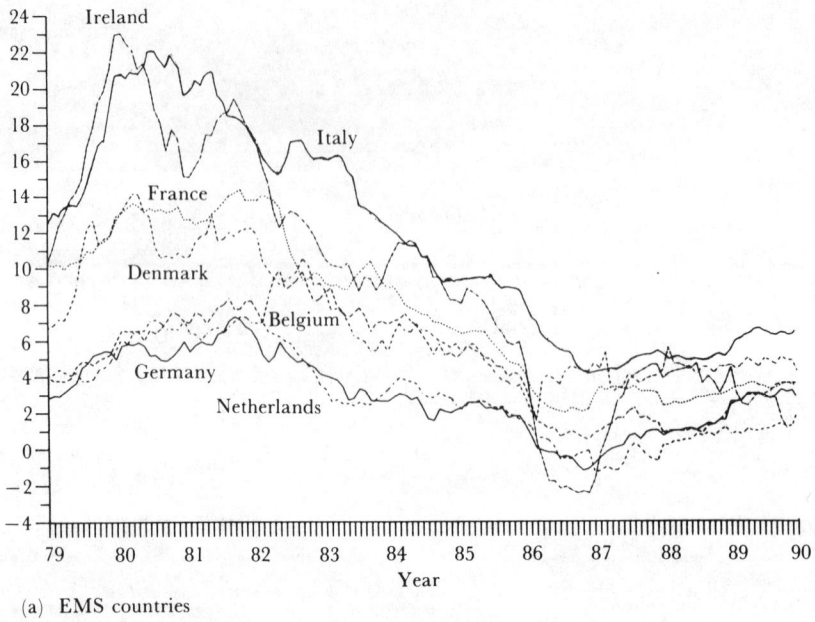

(a) EMS countries

Figure 2. Inflation rates, CPI (% per annum)

Source: Own calculations from *IMF International Financial Statistics*, various issues.
Note: For Ireland monthly wholesale price inflation rates were used.

2. Reputation, credibility and deflation

2.1. The concepts of reputation and credibility

While the terms reputation and credibility are often used interchange-ably,[2] the empirical analysis below proposes a clear distinction between these two concepts. Reputation is defined here in a restrictive sense: it is the probability which the public assigns to the consistent pursuit of a low inflation policy. It is derived by learning over time from the actual behaviour of the monetary authorities. Clearly, a solid counterinflation reputation can only be established by a track record of continuously low inflation. The term credibility is used in a broader context. It is defined as the extent to which beliefs concerning a policy conform to official announcements about this policy. To achieve credibility, the authorities must precommit themselves to a particular policy rule. Such

---

[2] For example in Cukierman's (1986, p.8) discussion of Backus and Driffill (1985). For recent reviews of this policy game literature consult Persson (1988) and Blackburn and Christensen (1989).

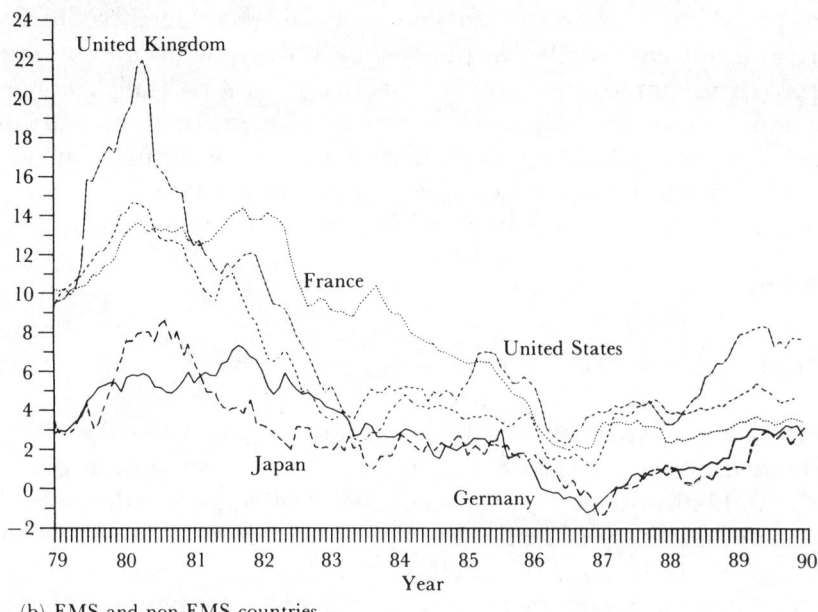

(b) EMS and non-EMS countries

Figure 2—continued

a pre-commitment may or may not be binding. Only the latter case is of interest here since truly binding commitments, such as constitutional laws, by definition imply perfect credibility. Credibility may thus also be viewed as a measure of the degree to which policy-makers tie their hands on future policies by issuing policy announcements (a more formal definition of both concepts is presented in Appendix A). Two measures of credibility are used in this study:

– **average credibility** (AC) measures the extent to which the public expects policy outcomes to deviate from prior policy announcements. The smaller this deviation, the larger is average credibility.

– **marginal credibility** (MC) focuses on the ability of policy announcements to influence the public's expectations; it measures the impact of a change in the announcement on expectations and may be thought of as the weight placed on the announcement when the public forms its expectations. This weight is equal to unity if the policy-maker always makes completely accurate (fully credible) announcements and tends towards zero as the announcements become non-credible.

Undoubtedly, credibility and high reputation are desirable attributes of any kind of public policy. In the case of disinflation, however, they take on special importance and become a crucial advantage. Credibility of a pre-announced disinflation policy may reduce or even eliminate the output or unemployment costs of disinflation if it radically changes expectations at the time when the policy is enacted. In particular, in the case of an unannounced short and sharp shock disinflation, the quicker the policy-maker establishes a counterinflation reputation, the shorter will be the transition period during which expectations adjust.

2.2. Ways of gaining credibility and reputation

Although it is clear that counterinflation reputation may only be established by achieving consistently low inflation, how can central banks establish credibility? One possibility (Rogoff, 1985a) is the adoption of intermediate monetary targets. This widespread feature of the 1970s is viewed as an institutional reform by central banks intent on resolving their credibility problem. In particular, monetary targeting under a central banker unambiguously adverse to inflation, often referred to as 'conservative', can reduce the sustainable rate of inflation. Credibility in a disinflation process speeds up the transition to a low-inflation equilibrium and hence reduces the welfare costs of disinflation (Cukierman and Meltzer, 1986b). An alternative strategy for gaining credibility for a small open economy is to enter a fixed exchange rate system seen as a sort of institutional reform (Giavazzi and Spaventa, 1989). In this case, it is the announcement of an exchange rate target relative to a low-inflation country which reduces the sustainable rate of inflation. Finally, targeting nominal interest rates may be adopted by EMS countries as a short-run operational procedure for targeting the exchange rate within the fluctuation band. Under this strategy, announcing an interest rate target consistent with a fixed exchange rate relatively to a low-inflation country reduces the sustainable rate of inflation.

All three forms of gaining credibility are evaluated in the following sections. Two related questions arise, though. First, we need to know which – if any – of these alternatives has actually been adopted in particular EMS member countries as part of their disinflationary policies. Second, it may well be that monetary policy has not been always driven by just one of these intermediate targets, but may have shifted instead from one target to another. This is why particular attention is devoted to the detection of possible target switches and to the most likely dates of such switches. The identified switches are then related to the timing of major policy events which are summarized in Table 1.

Table 1. EMS realignments and selected policy changes signalling a move towards more deflationary policies in EMS member countries

1979	Mar. 13	**EMS**: exchange rate mechanism (ERM) starts to operate; initial currency weights in ECU currency basket: DM 32.0%, FF 19.0%, UKL 15.0%. LIT 10.2%. Hfl 10.1%, Bf 8.5%, Dkr 2.7%, Dra 1.3%, IRL 1.2%
	Sep. 24	**EMS**: realignment (DM +2%, Dkr −2.9%)
	Nov. 30	**EMS**: realignment (Dkr −4.8%)
		Denmark: short-term price and wage freeze
1981	Mar. 9	**Belgian–Luxembourg Economic Union (BLEU)**: convention for BLEU (fixed parity without bands) renewed for 10 years
	Mar. 22	**EMS**: realignment (LIT −6%)
		Italy: government spending cut plans
	July	**Italy**: Banca d'Italia freed from the obligation to purchase unsold public debt at the Treasury auctions, which gave the government preferential access to monetizing fiscal deficits
	July	**Netherlands**: the Nederlandsche Bank abandons control of domestic liquidity and gears its monetary policy towards the external constraint, in particular the DM exchange rate
	Oct. 5	**EMS**: realignment (DM +5.5%, FF −3%, LIT −3%, Hfl +3.5%)
		France: temporary price and profit freeze
1982	Feb. 22	**EMS**: realignment (Bf −8.5%, Dkr −3%)
		Belgium: general price freeze until end of March, selective freeze thereafter; freeze of wage indexation (until May); also longer-run measures to impede complete wage indexation
	Mar. 25	**Ireland**: tight budget by Fianna Fail government; initiation of an austerity and fiscal consolidation programme
	June 14	**EMS**: realignment (DM +4.25%, FF −5.75%. LIT −2.75%, Hfl +4.25%)
		France: temporary freeze of prices, wages, rents and dividends until October; reduction in 1983 budget deficit plans
	June 23	**Italy**: announcement of budgetary austerity measures
	Oct. 21	**Ireland**: proposal for elimination of budget deficits by 1986
	Oct. 16	**Denmark**: comprehensive stabilization package: automatic wage indexation suspended; wage freeze until March 1983; tight fiscal policy; progressive dismantling of capital controls
	Dec. 30	**Belgium**: selective price freeze extended until end of 1983; wage restraint (flat rate indexation) until the end of 1984
1983	Mar. 21	**EMS**: realignment (DM +5.5%, FF −2.5%, LIT −2–5%, Hfl +3.5%, Bf +1.5%, Dkr +2.5%. IRL −2.5%)
	Mar. 28	**France**: stringent austerity programme aiming at bringing down inflation via monetary restraint, restoring external balance via foreign exchange controls and reducing the public budget deficit by cutting expenditures and raising taxes
	Apr. 12	**Denmark**: government announces further liberalization of capital movements to take place on May 1
	April	**Denmark**: government guidelines for an upper-limit of 2% for the annual wage increase in the new two-year wage agreement
	Dec.	**EEC**: target dates for the expiry of capital restrictions set for France (end of 1986) Italy and Ireland (end of 1987) in order to allow for a gradual relaxation of the controls

Table 1—continued

1984	Sep. 17	**EMS**: revision of currency weights in ECU currency basket (DM 32.0%, FF 19.0%. UKL 15.0%, LIT 10.2%, Nfl 10.1%, Bf 8.5%, Dkr 2.7%, DRA 1.3%, IRL 1.2%)
1985	Jan. 1	**France**: start of a two-year transition of monetary policy operating procedures from quantitative credit controls to a more market-based system of reserve requirements
	Mar. 12	**EMS**: Council of Central Bank Governors decides on a package to strengthen role of the ECU in the EMS
	April	**Denmark**: government enforces a 2% legal upper limit for the annual wage increase in the new two-year wage agreement
	July 22	**EMS**: realignment (DM +2%, FF +2%, LIT −6%, Hfl +2%, BL +2%. Dkr +2%, IRL +2%)
	July	**Italy**: announcement of revenue raising measures to contain the increase in the budget deficit **Italy**: modification of wage indexation mechanism, scala mobile
1986	Feb.	**EEC**: European Single Act sets 31. December 1992 as target date for completion of internal market with free movement of goods, persons, services and capital
	Apr. 7	**EMS**: realignment (DM +3%, FF −3%, Hfl +3%, Bf +1%, Dkr +1%) **France**: steps to slow nominal wage growth; plans to reduce government budget deficit; relaxation of exchange controls
	June	**Denmark**: wage indexation law (suspended 1982) is abolished
	Aug. 4	**EMS**: realignment (IRL −8%) **Ireland**: sharp monetary tightening to offset the destabilizing effects of British pound sterling weakness
1987	Jan. 12	**EMS**: realignment (DM +3%, Hfl +3%, Bf +2%, Dkr +2%)
	Sep. 12	**EMS**: Basle–Nyborg Agreement of the Committee of Central Bank Governors to strengthen the exchange rate mechanism of the EMS; measures include a wider use of fluctuation bands, an extension of the very short-run financing facilities and the use of ECU for inframarginal intervention
1989	Apr. 17	**EMS**: Delors Committee Report proposes a three stage transition to Economic and Monetary Union: stage 1: extension of ERM to all EMS member countries, reduction of fluctuation bands to narrow range, infrequent realignments subject to mutual agreement, full capital mobility; stage 2: creation of new Community institution, increasing co-ordination of national monetary policies; stage 3a: irrevocably fixed exchange rates without bands, new Community institutions (EuroFed) functioning; stage 3b: single currency monetary union at a later date
	June 19	**EMS**: Spain enters the exchange rate mechanism of the EMS with a wide fluctuation margin of ±6%
	June 27	**EMS**: European Council decision to enter the first stage of EMU from the Delors Committee Report on 1 July 1990
	Sep. 21	**EMS**: revision of currency weights in ECU currency basket (DM 30.1%, FF 19.0%, UKL 13.0%, LIT 10.15%, Hfl 9.4%, Bf 7.9%. PES 5 3%, Dkr 2.45%, IRL 1.1%, DRA 0.8%, ESC 0.8%)

Table 1—continued

1990	Jan.	**EMS**: realignment (LIT −3.7%), narrowing of band to ±2.25%
	June	**Belgium**: central bank declares German mark exchange rate as its main official policy target
	July 1	**EMS**: complete removal of all capital controls except for Ireland, Spain, Portugal and Greece (deadline 1992)
	July 1	**Germany**: monetary union between West and East Germany
	Oct. 3	**Germany**: six East German federal states join the Federal Republic of Germany
	Oct. 8	**EMS**: UK enters the exchange rate mechanism of the EMS with a wide fluctuation margin of ±6%

Sources: OECD *Economic Surveys*: *Germany, France, Italy, the Netherlands, Belgium and Luxembourg, Denmark, Ireland,* various issues, Commission of the European Communities *The EMS: Ten Years of Progress in European Monetary Co-operation,* and Ungerer *et al.* (1983, 1986).
Notes: At realignments +(−) indicates a revaluation (devaluation) in % against those currencies whose bilateral parities remained unchanged, except for the two general realignments (March 1983, July 1985), for which the percentages from the official communique are shown.

3. The counterinflation reputation of policy-makers

The first issue is how the EMS has affected the counterinflation orientation of policy-makers. Is the German Bundesbank the central bank with the highest anti-inflation reputation as implied by the borrowing reputation hypothesis? Has German anti-inflation reputation been undermined because of the EMS? As noted above, counterinflation reputation is defined as the probability that policy-makers consistently pursue low-inflation policies. This probability is estimated here over different sub-periods. The adopted (Bayesian) procedure consists in finding out how inflation could be forecasted over each sub-period under various alternative assumptions about the degree to which inflation shocks are allowed by the central bank to become permanent. The relative success of each of these forecasts is then evaluated over time. In particular, the procedure determines the probability that a weighted average of the various forecasts predicts inflation better than each of them separately. The weight attached to the 'low-inflation' forecast yields the desired measure of counterinflation reputation.[3]

The resulting estimates of counterinflation reputation for all EMS economies are presented clockwise along three axes in Figure 3. These

---

[3] The focus is only on period averages of these recursively updated probabilities, which are estimated by applying the Bayesian multi-process Kalman filter, as outlined in detail in Weber (1988) which is updated here. See Appendix B for a further discussion.

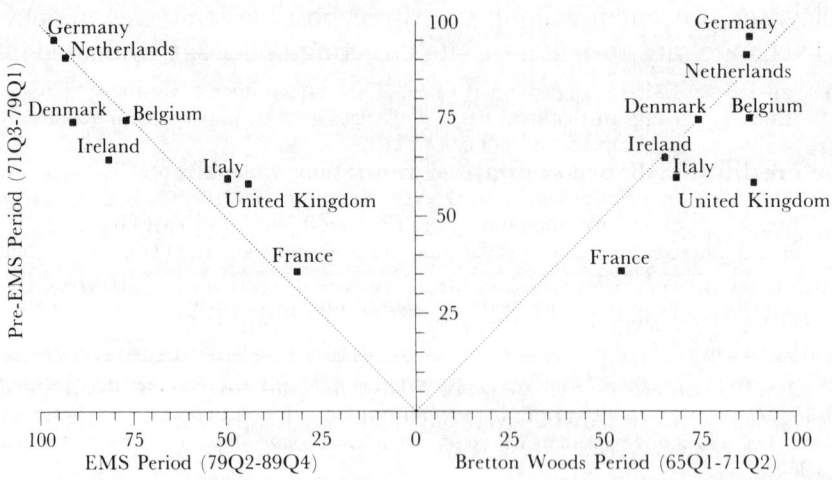

Figure 3. Counterinflation reputation measure. Average prior probability for low-inflation performance (in %)

axes correspond to three periods: the Bretton Woods period (65Q1–71Q2) on the right-most axis, a pre-EMS period (71Q3–79Q1) on the vertical axis, and the EMS period (79Q2–89Q4) on the left-most axis. The 45° line is added to detect most easily how reputation has changed from one period to another. Three main findings emerge. First, Germany, closely followed by the Netherlands, has the highest anti-inflation reputation, prior to and during the EMS period. Second, the smaller EMS economies Belgium, Denmark and Ireland have gained anti-inflation reputation during the EMS period. Finally, France and Italy have the lowest counterinflation reputation, and have not increased their reputation during the EMS period.

These estimates of counterinflation reputation are consistent with the evolution of inflation (Figure 2). Germany and the Netherlands entered the EMS with low inflation rates. The relatively low inflationary impact of the 1979 oil price shock, followed by a smooth disinflation (1982–86) explains the preservation of both countries' reputations. France and Italy, on the other hand, entered the EMS with high inflation, underwent double-digit rates up to 1983, and improved their reputation only quite late in the EMS period. The gains in counterinflation reputation of the smaller EMS economies are consistent with the borrowing reputation argument. In particular, their gains went hand in hand with a reduction and convergence of inflation rates to the low German levels.

The next step is to establish whether there exists a link between the reputation of the monetary authorities and their credibility. Credibility of policy announcements along the three possible strategies, money stock, exchange rate and interest rate targeting policies, is evaluated in the next three sections.[4]

4. The credibility of pre-committed monetary targeting

4.1. Monetary targets

The move to money growth targets may be viewed as an attempt by central banks to resolve a credibility problem. Has this form of signalling policy intentions helped EMS central banks to establish credibility? In answering this question it is important to note that money stock target-ing, which was adopted by Germany, France and Italy in the mid-1970s before the advent of the EMS, has remained part of their practices. However, within the EMS, all monetary authorities cannot indepen-dently target both the exchange rate and the money stock. This may render one of the two policy targets non-credible if they are set incon-sistently with one another.

Under what conditions can money target announcements be expected to command credibility? Andersen and Risager (1988) state that con-tinuity is an important factor. In practice, different money or credit aggregates with differing degrees of controllability have been targeted. All countries have occasionally switched from one aggregate to another in order to improve their control. This is shown in Tables 2 to 5 in the case of Germany, France, Italy and the UK. Such discontinuities rep-resent a serious obstacle to establishing credibility. Furthermore, EMS countries have only had limited success in achieving their money targets. Germany, for example, had some success from 1979 to 1985, but overshot its targets consistently afterwards, and did not improve its record by switching its targets. In France, on the other hand, money targeting has been implemented quite successfully since 1985.

4.2. Credibility measures

In view of the volatile history (see Goodhart, 1989) and limited success of money target announcements in EMS member countries, it is hardly

---

[4] The estimates which follow concern each of the three monetary policy instruments separately. While this allows for an intuitively appealing interpretation of the results, combining the information from these announcements would be a useful next step. It requires formulating a general monetary policy reaction function and relating the relative credibility of each instrument more directly, for example via a demand for money function, to the credibility of the central banks' overall monetary policy stance. Unfortunately, such estimates are difficult to interpret since the relative magnitude of the credibility effects and money supply and demand elasticities cannot be distinguished.

Table 2. German announced money growth targets and realizations, year on year (y.o.y.) and annual average (avg.) of monthly money growth rates (% per annum)

	Target	Target range y.o.y.	avg.	Concretized target	Outcome y.o.y.	avg.
1975	CBM[1]	8.0	—	—	9.9[n]	(7.8)
1976	CBM[2]	—	8.0	—	—	9.3[n]
1977	CBM[2]	—	8.0	—	—	9.0[n]
1978	CBM[2]	—	8.0	—	—	8.5[n]
1979	CBM[2]	6.0–9.0	—	lower limit	6.4[y†]	(8.5)
1980	CBM[3]	5.0–8.0	—	lower limit	4.9[y†]	(4.8)
1981	CBM[3]	4.0–7.0	—	lower half	3.6[y†]	(4.4)
1982	CBM[3]	4.0–7.0	—	upper half	6.1[y†]	(4.9)
1983	CBM[3]	4.0–7.0	—	upper half	7.0[y†]	(7.3)
1984	CBM[3]	4.0–6.0	—	—	4.6[y†]	(4.8)
1985	CBM[3]	3.0–5.0	—	—	4.5[y†]	(4.6)
1986	CBM[3]	3.5–5.5	—	—	7.7[n]	(6.4)
1987	CBM[3]	3.0–6.0	—	—	8.0[n]	(8.1)
1988	M3[3]	3.0–6.0	—	—	8.4[n†]	(6.3)
1989	M3[3]	5.0	—	—	5.5[n]	(9.0)
1990	M3[3]	4.0–6.0	—	—	—	—

Sources: Deutsche Bundesbank, *Geschaeftsbericht*, various issues, OECD *Country Surveys, Germany*, various issues, Neumann (1988) and own calculations using data of OECD *Main Economic Indicators*, various issues.

Notes: CBM is the central bank money stock, comprised of currency in circulation and required reserves on domestic liabilities, calculated at constant reserve ratios (base January 1974). M3 is comprised of cash holdings of non-banks, domestic non-bank sight deposits at banks, time deposits (up to four years) and saving deposits (at statutory notice).

[1] December of preceding year to December of current year.
[2] Annual average.
[3] Fourth quarter of preceding year to fourth quarter of current year.
[y] Actual target achieved (in terms of integer values).
[n] Actual target missed (in terms of integer values).
[†] Annual average of target achieved (in terms of integer values).

surprising that the estimates displayed in Table 6 are relatively low. While France has achieved some gains during the EMS period, credibility has declined for Italy and Germany, drastically in the latter case. Why then did central banks typically fail to establish credibility through money stock target announcements? One possible explanation is 'Goodhart's law', a modification of the Lucas critique. It asserts that the attempt to control the supply of a monetary aggregate destabilizes its demand. This argument has been frequently mentioned as a reason for the Bank of England, the Banque de France and the Bundesbank to switch their money targets. An alternative explanation is that 'central banks prefer to keep some fixed points, even if they overshoot announced targets. The loss of credibility and reputation would be greater in

Table 3. French announced monetary targets and realizations, year on year (y.o.y.) and annual average (avg.) of monthly money growth rates (% per annum)

	Target	Target range	outcome y.o.y	outcome avg.
1977	$M2^1$	12.5	$13.9^{n\dagger}$	(12.3)
1978	$M2^1$	12.0	12.2^y	(13.2)
1979	$M2^1$	11.0	14.4^n	(13.4)
1980	$M2^1$	11.0	$9.8^{n\dagger}$	(11.6)
1981	$M2^1$	10.0–12.0	$11.4^{y\dagger}$	(12.6)
1982	$M2^1$	12.5–13.5	$11.5^{y\dagger}$	(12.3)
1983	$M2^2$	9.0–10.0	$10.2^{y\dagger}$	(10.2)
1984	$M2R^2$	5.5–6.5	7.6^n	(9.9)
1985	$M2R^2$	3.0–5.0	6.9^n	(8.7)
1986	$M3^2$	4.0–6.0	$4.2^{y\dagger}$	(5.3)
1987	$M2^2$	4.0–6.0	4.2^y	(7.3)
	$M3^2$	3.0–5.0	9.9^n	(9.0)
1988	$M2^2$	4.0–6.0	4.0^y	(7.4)
1989	$M2^2$	4.0–6.0	4.3^y	(7.6)
1990	$M2^2$	3.5–5.5	—	—

Sources: OECD *Country Surveys, France,* various issues, Wyplosz (1988), and own calculations using data of OECD *Main Economic Indicators,* various issues
Notes: M2 is currency, demand deposits, savings and all time deposits, certificates of deposits plus short-term non-negotiable financial instruments. M2R is that part of M2 which is held by residents. M3 is total liquidity.
[1] December of preceding year to December current year.
[2] Quarter centred around December of preceding year to the same quarter of current year.
[y] Actual target achieved (in integer values).
[n] Actual target missed (in integer values).
[†] Annual average of target achieved (in integer values).

the case of abolition than it is with overshooting.' (De Boissieu, 1988). The estimates discussed above do not support this view: whilst moderate target overshooting may only reduce credibility, massive target misses result in low and non-significant credibility estimates. Indeed, under these circumstances, monetary target announcements no longer provide the public with useful information and might just as well be abolished.

5. The credibility of precommitted exchange rate targeting

5.1. The EMS compared to previous periods

If money targeting is not particularly credible, how could reputation be improved? The borrowing reputation hypothesis suggests that

Table 4. Italian announced monetary targets and realizations, annual average (avg.) of monthly money growth rates (% per annum)

	Target[1]	Target level[2]	Outcome[3]	Target[1]	Target range	Outcome[3]
1975	TDC	17.9	13.6[n]	—	—	—
1976	TDC	17.5	22.0[y]	—	—	—
1977	TDC	15.1	16.8[y]	—	—	—
1978	TDC	12.9	5.2[y]	—	—	—
1979	TDC	18.4	17.1[y]	—	—	—
1980	TDC	17.4	22.7[n]	—	—	—
1981	TDC	16.0	17.2[n]	—	—	—
1982	TDC	15.2	8.6[y]	—	—	—
1983	TDC	18.3	15.5[y]	—	—	—
1984	TDC	17.5	21.6[n]	M2	11.0	12.3[n]
1985	TDC	16.2	14.1[y]	M2	10.0	14.0[n]
1986	TDC	13.2	9.0[y]	M2	7.0–11.0	8.8[y]
1987	TDC	11.1	12.6[n]	M2	6.0–9.0	10.8[n]
1988	TDC	9.4	12.2[n]	M2	6.0–9.0	7.9[y]
1989	—	—	—	M2	6.0–9.0	9.7[n]
1990	—	—	—	M2	6.0–9.0	—

Sources: OECD *Country Surveys, Italy,* various issues, and own calculations using data of OECD *Main Economic Indicators,* various issues.
Notes: TDC is total domestic credit, announced in terms of a ceiling, and consists of bank and special credit institution loans plus bonds issued by local authorities, public and private companies (net of loans consolidating debt of local authorities) less state sector borrowing requirement. M2 is currency in circulation plus demand and time deposits.
[1] Annual average of growth rate.
[2] Data taken from OECD *Country Surveys, Italy,* various issues.
[3] Calculated as annual average of monthly growth rates from OECD *Main Economic Indicators,* various issues.
[y] Actual target achieved (in terms of integer values).
[n] Actual target missed (in terms of integer values).

credible exchange rate pegging may increase counterinflation reputation. For example, Giavazzi and Spaventa (1989) argue that France and Italy have decided to join the EMS under the belief that exchange rate targets are more credible than monetary targets, maybe because violations are more conspicuous. This clearly motivates the following attempt to measure the credibility of exchange rate targets.

Fixed exchange rates are not a novelty of the EMS. They prevailed during both the Bretton Woods system and, for some countries, during the European currency snake experiment. This is why the credibility measures are calculated over each of these periods. Figure 4 presents the marginal credibility (MC) estimates. The MC measure is best viewed as the proportion (in percentage points) in which exchange rate

Table 5. British announced monetary targets and realizations, year on year (y.o.y.) average of monthly money growth rates (% per annum)

	Target[1]	Target range	Outcome	Target[1]	Target range	Outcome
1976	M3	9.0–13.0	7.3^n	—	—	—
1977	£M3	9.0–13.0	15.4^n	—	—	—
1978	£M3	8.0–12.0	11.4^y	—	—	—
1979	£M3	8.0–12.0	10.3^y	—	—	—
1980	£M3	7.0–11.0	19.4^n	—	—	—
1981	£M3	6.0–10.0	12.8^n	—	—	—
1982	£M3	8.0–12.0	11.2^y	M1	8.0–12.0	12.3^y
1983	£M3	7.0–11.0	9.5^y	M1	7.0–11.0	14.0^n
1984	£M3	6.0–10.0	11.9^n	M0	4.0–8.0	3.1^{n2}
1985	£M3	5.0–9.0	16.5^n	M0	3.0–7.0	4.4^{y2}
1986	£M3	11.0–15.0	18.2^n	M0	2.0–6.0	3.2^{y2}
1987	—	—	—	M0	2.0–6.0	1.8^{y2}
1988	—	—	—	M0	1.0–5.0	5.8^{n2}
1989	—	—	—	M0	1.0–5.0	
1990	—	—	—	M0	1.0–5.0	

Sources: OECD *Country Surveys, United Kingdom,* various issues, Fischer (1988) and own calculations using data of OECD *Main Economic Indicators,* various issues, and IMF *International Financial Statistics,* various issues.

Notes: M3 is currency plus private sector demand and time deposits. £M3 is currency plus private sector sterling demand and time deposits. M1 is currency plus private sector demand deposits. M0 is notes and coins in circulation and in banks, and banks' operational balances with the Bank of England.
[1] Annual average of growth rate during the financial year, that April of preceding year to March of the current year.
[2] Calculated as average of monthly growth rates of the financial year using data of IMF *International Financial Statistics,* various issues.
[y] Actual target achieved (in terms of integer values).
[n] Actual target missed (in terms of integer values).

expectations are influenced by official parity announcements.[5] A natural benchmark for judging credibility is 50%: below that level announcements are dominated by other factors. Two results stand out. First, if exchange rate fixity was mostly credible under both the Bretton Woods system (23 out of 27 MCs exceed 50%) and within the European currency snake (8 cases out of 10), that is not the case under the EMS arrangement (only 7 out of 21 MCs are above 50%). Second, the MC measure reveals that the credibility of the exchange rate commitment

---

[5] Expectations are seen as influenced by official targets or by chartist (backward looking) behaviour. See Appendix B, in particular Equation (B.4), for this feature of the MC estimate.

Table 6. Estimated marginal credibility measure, percentage influence of money growth target announcements on money growth expectations in selected periods[†]

	Germany	France	Italy	UK
75M1–89M12	*9.9*	*12.3*	*17.5*	8.2
	(2.4)	(3.0)	(3.0)	(2.4)
75M1–79M2	*30.7*	19.4	22.5	16.5
	(8.1)	(12.0)	(5.3)	(5.3)
79M3–89M12	*7.5*	*12.7*	*14.1*	*10.1*
	(2.4)	(3.7)	(3.6)	(3.0)
79M3–83M2	*15.6*	*12.3*	*16.6*	*10.0*
	(6.5)	(5.4)	(5.0)	(4.2)
83M3–89M12	5.2	*21.1*	10.9	11.5
	(3.0)	(5.9)	(5.3)	(5.9)

Source: Own calculations using data from OECD *Main Economic Indicators*, various issues and the targets from Tables 2–5.

Notes: The numbers are marginal credibility estimates $\alpha(*100)$ with standard errors (*100 in parenthesis below) from an ordinary least-squares regression equation $(m_t - Em_t|\Omega_{t-1}) = c + \alpha(m_t^a - Em_t|\Omega_{t-1}) + v_t$, $v_t \sim N(0, \sigma^2)$, where m_t and m_t^a are the actual and announced growth rates and $Em_t|\Omega_{t-1}$ is the conditional forecast of actual money growth from a time series model. Estimates are presented for the primarily targeted monetary or credit aggregate only (central bank money stock in Germany, M2 in France, M3 in the UK, total domestic credit in Italy). Numbers in italics highlight a significance at least at the 5% level.

[†] The exact maximum overall sample period for each country is indicated in Tables 2–5.

has declined, in many cases significantly,[6] in the EMS relative to the Bretton Woods or snake systems.

Both results may be explained by the higher degree of exchange rate flexibility in the EMS, as reflected by the wider fluctuation margins of ±2.25% as compared to ±1% under the Bretton Woods system or ±1.125% under the European currency snake system (see Box 1 for a description of the institutional arrangements).[7] The results may also be attributed to the fact that the EMS exhibited both a much higher frequency and size of parity realignments than the Bretton Woods system. In any case, the results indicate that amongst the historical

---

[6] This statement applies when the significance of the decline in credibility is judged on the basis of ±2 standard errors of the MC measure from the Bretton Woods period. These estimates, which are not reported here, are available on request.

[7] The sample period considered here for the European currency snake system covers both the 'snake' and the 'snake in the tunnel' and runs from April 1972 to February 1979 with the exceptions indicated above.

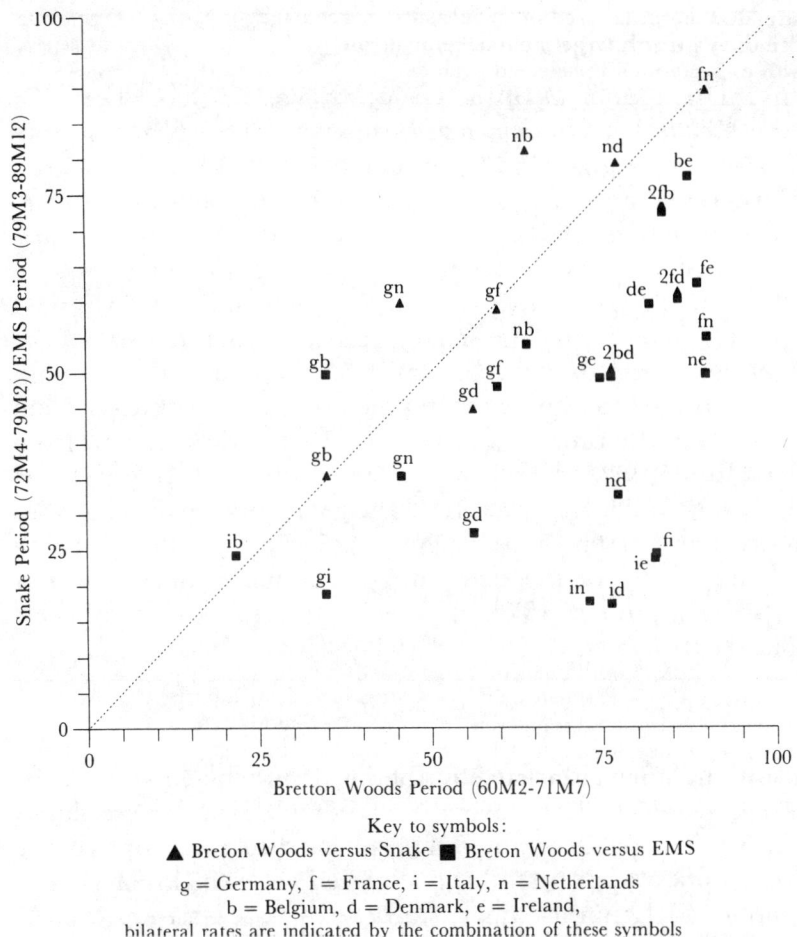

Key to symbols:
▲ Breton Woods versus Snake ■ Breton Woods versus EMS

g = Germany, f = France, i = Italy, n = Netherlands
b = Belgium, d = Denmark, e = Ireland,
bilateral rates are indicated by the combination of these symbols

Figure 4. MC credibility measure for exchange rates. Influence of parity announcements on exchange rate expectations (in %)

post-war systems of fixed but adjustable exchange rates the EMS was the least credible system.

5.2. Hard and soft currency options

Does this imply that the EMS did not provide any disinflation 'credibility bonus'? To answer this question the overall EMS period (79M3–89M12) has been split into three sub-periods (79M3–83M2, 83M2–86M12, 87M1–89M12). The resulting estimates of the MC and AC credibility measures are presented in Figures 5 and 6. The key result from Figure 5 is that the EMS has not functioned as a DM-zone. Instead, the EMS is found to have operated as a bipolar system in which the French franc

Box 1. Pre-EMS exchange rate arrangements

The Smithsonian agreement of the Group of Ten of December 1971 widened the bilateral fluctuation margins against the US dollar from ±1% to ±2.25%. Through the Basle agreement of April 1972 the central banks of Germany, France, Italy, the Netherlands, Belgium and Luxembourg agreed to narrower bilateral fluctuation margins of ±1.125% (±0.75% between the Netherlands and the Belgian–Luxembourg Economic Union, BLUE). In this 'snake in the tunnel' arrangement the narrow bilateral margins (the snake) were set to half the size of the US dollar margins (the tunnel). In May 1972 Denmark, the UK and Ireland joined the snake, but the latter two countries withdrew from both the snake and the tunnel in June 1972. Denmark withdrew from the snake in June 1972, but rejoined in October 1972. Italy left the snake in February 1973. In March 1973 the remaining snake countries decided to let their currencies float jointly against the US dollar, which terminated the period of the snake in the tunnel. France withdrew from the system in January 1974, rejoined in July 1975, and withdrew again in March 1976.

offered a soft currency alternative to the hard currency option of the German mark. With the exception of the Netherlands which were almost from the onset of the EMS committed to the hard currency option, the soft currency option appears to have attracted the remaining smaller EMS economies (Belgium, Denmark and Ireland), at least in the early stages of the EMS. Figure 5 clearly indicates the existence of a soft currency block with France at its centre (box Ia). Exchange rate pegging within this soft currency block of the EMS was credible, as indicated by the high credibility estimates in both pre-1987 periods for the French franc exchange rates of Belgium (fb), Ireland (fe), Denmark (fd) and for the bilateral rates between these economies (be, de). However, the close French franc linkages of Denmark (fd) and Ireland (fe), and to a lesser extent of Belgium (fb), dissolve after 1987 (box Ib). These estimates are strikingly.consistent with the behaviour of exchange rates revealed in Figure 1.

Additional evidence on the existence of a soft currency option in the EMS is provided in Figure 5 by the behaviour of exchange rates within the former currency snake block. The initially relatively credible exchange rate pegs of Belgium and Denmark *vis-a-vis* Germany (gb, gd) and the Netherlands (nb, nd) become non-credible as Belgium and Denmark switch to the soft currency option of the EMS (box III). The

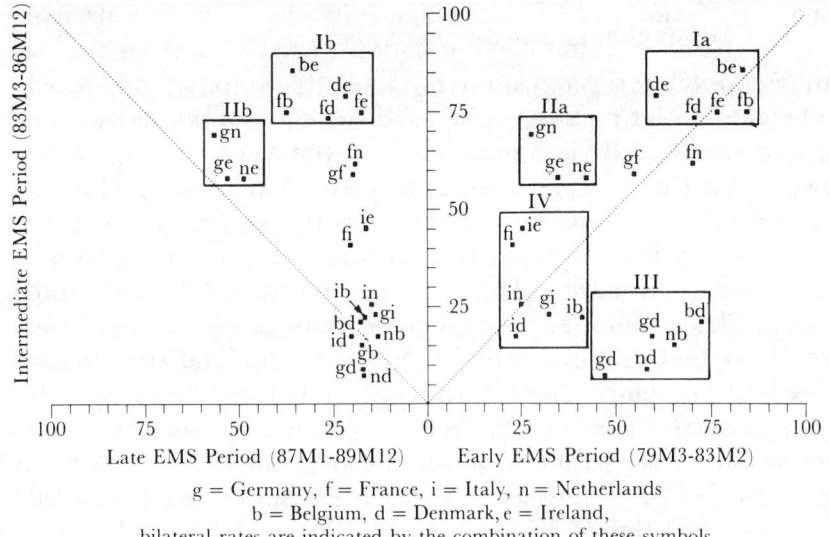

Figure 5. MC credibility measure for exchange rates. Influence of parity announcements on exchange rate expectations (in %)

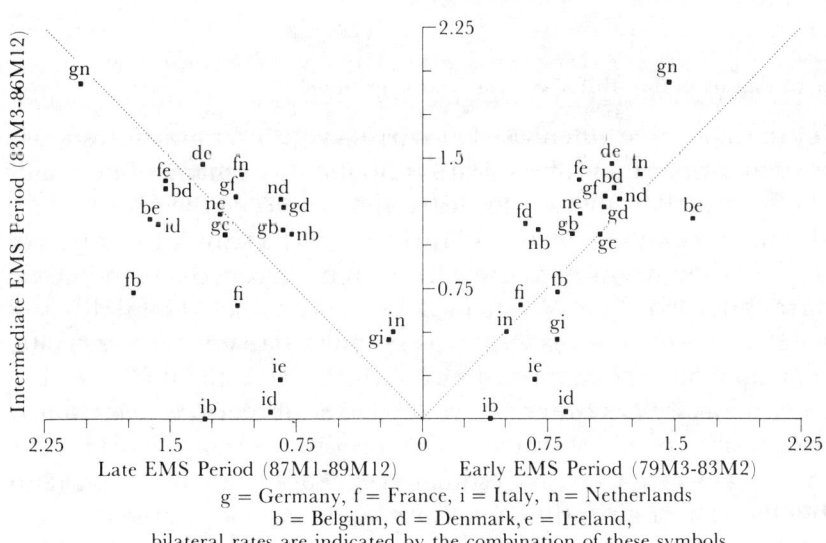

Figure 6. AC credibility measure for exchange rates. Width of the band adjusted for expected deviations of the exchange rate from the official parity (in %)

Note: For Italy a 2.25% band instead of the official 6% band was used in the calculations.

inflationary consequences of this policy shift are most obvious from Figure 2 for Belgium: after 1982 inflation drifts away from the low German and Dutch levels to closely resemble the French (and Danish) rates. The growing attraction of the hard currency option is signalled by the increasingly credible commitments of the Netherlands and Ireland towards the German mark (gn, ge), in particular after 1983 (boxes IIa and IIb). The outstanding credibility of the Dutch–German (gn) exchange rate peg is even more obvious when judged on the basis of the AC credibility measure in Figure 6, nearing the 100% mark in the later period. This would suggest that a *de facto* monetary union is already in place between Germany and the Netherlands. The step toward Economic and Monetary Union with irrevocably fixed exchange rates and hence perfectly credible pegs, as envisaged in stage 3 of the Delors plan (see Table 1), may therefore only involve small credibility gains for the Netherlands. Finally, Figure 5 reveals that the exchange rate commitment of the Banca d'Italia has never been credible (MC below 50%) (box IV). This low credibility is in general also confirmed by the AC measures in Figure 6, but here some evidence of increasingly credible pegs relative to France, Belgium, Denmark and Ireland (fi, ib, id, ie), the former soft currency bloc, is found for the late EMS period. This corresponds to a possible shift in the Italian attitude towards the EMS, as indicated by the adoption of the reduced fluctuation margins for the lira after January 1990.

5.3. The timing of policy shifts and the 'Lucas critique'

In order to determine when the soft currency grouping dissolved, use is made of an implication of the Lucas critique. If exchange rate policy shifts did occur, they should not leave the public's expectations, and therefore the credibility measures, unchanged. To search for the most likely point in time at which such a policy shift occurred, the econometric procedure adopted here (switching regression, see Goldfeld and Quandt, 1973, 1976) postulates some exchange rate (and interest rate, in anticipation of Section 6) processes which are estimated over the overall period as well as over any two separate sub-periods determined by every possible policy shift date. The procedure then identifies the point in time at which the three estimated exchange rate processes (and the three interest rate processes) differ most from one another. Tables 7 (for the exchange rate) and 8 (for the interest rate) report the resulting shift dates.

The EMS has gone through two major periods of change. The first period runs between the realignments of June 1982 and March 1983, when the initially relatively credible pegs among the former snake

Table 7. Percentage effects of parity announcements on exchange rate expectations at the most likely time of policy switch: Long sample period (L), January 1975 to December 1989; Short sample period (S), March 1979 to December 1989

Sample[1]	Exchange rate	Switchpoint		MC (in %)	MC_1 (in %)	MC_2 (in %)
L	Germany–Netherlands	Oct.	1982[†]	*24.7*	*20.2*	*69.3**
L	Germany–Belgium	Mar.	1983[†]	*36.4*	*40.7*	*13.1*
L	Germany–Denmark	June	1982[†]	*28.8*	*37.9*	*8.3*
L	Netherlands–Belgium	Sep.	1982[†]	*49.0*	*61.7**	*13.8*
L	Netherlands–Denmark	Mar.	1983[†]	*39.2*	*55.5**	*9.4*
L	Belgium–Denmark	Mar.	1983[†]	*48.8*	*58.2**	*16.4*
S	Germany–France	Sep.	1987[†]	*48.0*	*57.0**	*66.2**
S	Germany–Italy	July	1985[†]	*18.8*	*23.9*	*9.8*
S	Germany–Netherlands	May	1985[†]	*35.4*	*35.0*	*52.9**
S	Germany–Belgium	Jan.	1983[†]	*49.7*	*59.7**	*15.5*
S	Germany–Denmark	June	1982[†]	*27.4*	*48.2*	*8.3*
S	Germany–Ireland	June	1986[†]	*49.2*	*34.8*	*90.9**
S	France–Italy	Dec.	1986[†]	*24.4*	*26.8*	*25.8*
S	France–Netherlands	Sep.	1987[†]	*55.0**	*66.6**	*68.3**
S	France–Belgium	Dec.	1986[†]	*72.5**	*80.3**	*42.8*
S	France–Denmark	Mar.	1983[†]	*60.3**	*80.0**	*38.2*
S	France–Ireland	Jan.	1987[†]	*62.5**	*74.0**	*17.6*
S	Italy–Netherlands	July	1985	*17.7*	*21.0*	*10.8*
S	Italy–Belgium	July	1985[†]	*24.3*	*30.3*	*10.6*
S	Italy–Denmark	Jan.	1980	*17.4*	*30.7*	*16.3*
S	Italy–Ireland	Sep.	1986[†]	*23.8*	*33.7*	*10.9*
S	Netherlands–Belgium	May	1982[†]	*54.0**	*74.5**	*19.1*
S	Netherlands–Denmark	Feb.	1983	*32.7*	*56.1**	*8.6*
S	Netherlands–Ireland	May	1986	*49.7*	*30.6*	*89.7**
S	Belgium–Denmark	Jan.	1986	*49.4*	*69.7**	*20.6*
S	Belgium–Ireland	Jan.	1987[†]	*77.5**	*80.5**	*35.6*
S	Denmark–Ireland	Jan.	1987[†]	*59.6**	*68.7**	*20.7*

Notes: The marginal credibility measures for the overall period (MC) and the two sub-periods (MC_1, MC_2) are obtained as coefficients estimates (α^*100) from the ordinary least-squares regression $(\varepsilon_t - E\varepsilon_t|\Omega_{t-1}) = c + \alpha(\varepsilon_t^a - E\varepsilon_t|\Omega_{t-1}) + v_t$, $v_t \sim N(0, \sigma^2)$ with ε_t as the actual exchange rate, $E\varepsilon_t|\Omega_{t-1}$ as its conditional forecast from a time series model and ε_t^a as the official exchange rate announcement. Refer to Appendix B for details of the estimates. The numbers in italics indicate significance of the estimates at least at the 5% level, and stars indicate credible announcements. The timing of the most likely policy switch is estimated by switching regression on the basis of the likelihood-ratio test statistic of Quandt (1960). The significance of this structural break is indicated by the superscript '†' if the majority of six parametric stability tests point towards instability. The stability tests performed are the F-test of Chow (1960), the likelihood-ratio test of Quandt (1960), the forward and backward CUSUM[2] test of Brown *et al.* (1975), the test for heteroscedasticity of Goldfeld and Quandt (1965) and a test for heteroscedasticity based on a regression of squared residuals on squared fitted values. For details of these tests see Weber (1990a).

[1] L (S) indicates the long (short) sample period.

participants dissolve, separating out Germany and the Netherlands from Belgium and Denmark. This determines the date when the soft and hard currency blocks were established. The second major period of change lies between the realignment of April 1986 and the Basle–Nyborg Agreement of September 1987. During this period Ireland gives up the soft currency option, and France also commits its currency credibly to the German mark peg.[8] This in turn slightly reduces the credibility of the pegs of the former members of the French franc-zone, particularly Belgium.

The upper part of Table 7 reports the switch dates for the former participants in the European currency snake system. A striking feature of these estimates, which are based on a sample containing observations from both the snake and the EMS period (75M1–89M12),[9] is that all policy shifts occurred between the two realignments of June 1982 (gd, gn, nb) and March 1983 (gb, nd, bd). The formerly credible commitments between the three smaller snake participants, in particular the tight Benelux linkages, decline drastically. Whilst the Belgian and Danish monetary authorities dissolved their DM pegs, the Dutch central bank moved towards an even more credible peg to the German mark after October 1982. This date corresponds nicely to the abandonment, towards the end of 1981, by the Nederlandsche Bank of its money target announcements (the target was the national liquidity ratio i.e. M2/net national product).

The second round of policy shifts, and the new tendency of the EMS to converge to a hard-currency option, are documented in the lower part of Table 7. The shift occurred in Ireland in June 1986, two months ahead of the large unilateral devaluation (-8%) of the Irish pound. It was initiated by the weakness of the Irish pound in the EMS, largely related to a loss of competitiveness following the sharp depreciation of the British pound, the currency of Ireland's main trading partner. The fact that the credibility estimates of the Irish pound relative to both the German mark and the Dutch guilder increased significantly after the shift supports the view of Dornbusch (1989) that the Irish pound has now become one of the hard EMS currencies. For France the break point is September 1987. Yet this shift only slightly improves the credibility of the franc *vis-a-vis* the German mark. The fact that the policy switch occurred the month of the Basle–Nyborg Agreement,

---

[8] The shift of the French franc to a credible German mark commitment is not visible in Figure 5. This is due to the fact that the arbitrarily chosen late EMS period (87M1–89M12) contains, as shown in Table 7, a significant structural break which results in a biased MC estimate.

[9] The more turbulent exchange rate episodes of the snake in the tunnel and of the early snake period are excluded from the sample since they strongly bias the results toward structural breaks in 1973 or early 1974.

which expanded the role of inframarginal interventions and allowed for a wider use of the fluctuation bands (see Table 1), suggests that enhanced French exchange rate credibility may partly be attributed to the existence of better control procedures.

Finally, the credibility of the Italian central bank's commitment to fixed exchange rates relative to Germany, the Netherlands and Belgium decreased significantly after the large unilateral devaluation of the lira in July 1985. However, the credibility of the commitment to the French franc at the time of the most likely switch date, December 1986 just prior to the last general EMS realignment, is the highest of all estimates for Italy, and has remained almost constant. Thus, the recent move of the French franc to becoming a hard currency in the EMS may play a key role in the process of future monetary integration: it provides a drifting anchor for 'weak' currencies in stage 1 of the transition to Economic and Monetary Union (EMU).

6. The credibility of interest rate targeting

At least for the smaller EMS Member States, interest rate targeting is just an operational procedure to control the exchange rate. The combination of foreign interest rate movements and the potential for exchange rate movements within the band translates into a target corridor for the nominal interest rate. However, the co-existence of a hard and a soft currency option implies that there is no automatic link between interest rate targeting and counterinflationary policies.

Panel (a) of Figure 7 documents discount rate targeting. The late 1981 Dutch shift, giving up the national liquidity target in favour of a German mark target, is clearly reflected in the near co-movements of both discount rates, which on many occasions were changed on the same date. The small and relatively constant interest rate differential, which persisted until late 1989, mirrors the less than 100% credibility for the Dutch–German mark exchange rate peg found in the previous section. A second, perhaps more important, stylized fact is the parallel evolution of discount rates in Germany, the Netherlands, Belgium and Ireland after mid-1987, joined by Denmark in late 1989. The average correlation between EMS and German discount rates increases by about 35% (from 0.53 to 0.72) between the intermediate and late EMS period (83M4–86M12 versus 87M1–89M12). These 'Euro-rounds' of discount rate changes, which signal the growing attention paid to a German mark target, support the hypothesis of a convergence of the EMS to a hard currency standard.

Since the discount rate has lost its primacy in many countries, Panel (b) in Figure 7 displays the behaviour of nominal short-term money

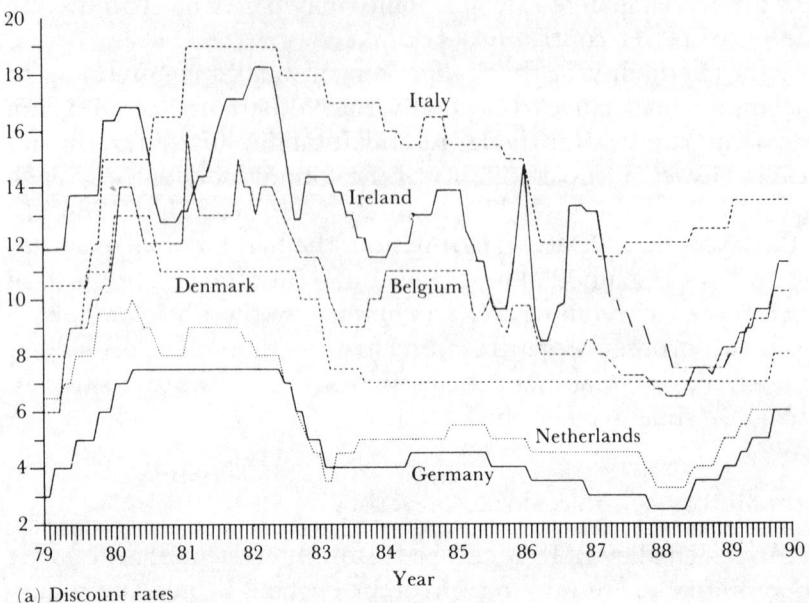

(a) Discount rates

Figure 7. Interest rates (% per annum)

Source: *OECD Main Economic Indicators*, various issues. Money market rates for Germany, France, Italy, the Netherlands, Belgium and Denmark are taken from *IMF International Financial Statistics*, various issues.

market rates. Three sub-periods can be clearly identified. During the early EMS period (1979–83) highly volatile movements at relatively high average levels of interest rates in France, Belgium, Denmark and Ireland corresponded to speculative attacks which resulted in frequent unilateral realignments (see Table 1). Disinflation, capital controls and policy adjustments in the following period (1983–87) reduced this volatility drastically and put a downward trend on the average levels of interest rates. The late EMS period (post-1987) was characterized by relatively parallel movements of interest rates and a marked increase of all rates after 1988. This visual impression of an increasing harmonization of interest rate movements is also reflected in the average correlation between money market interest rates, which first rises slightly from 0.36 (79M3–83M3) to 0.41 (83M4–86M12), but then jumps to 0.63 (87M1–89M12). The data again support the small DM-zone hypothesis. Furthermore, the fact that the Belgian, Danish and Irish interest rates during the disinflation period (1983–87) followed more closely the French rather than the German interest rates lends additional support to the possible existence of a soft currency block in the EMS.

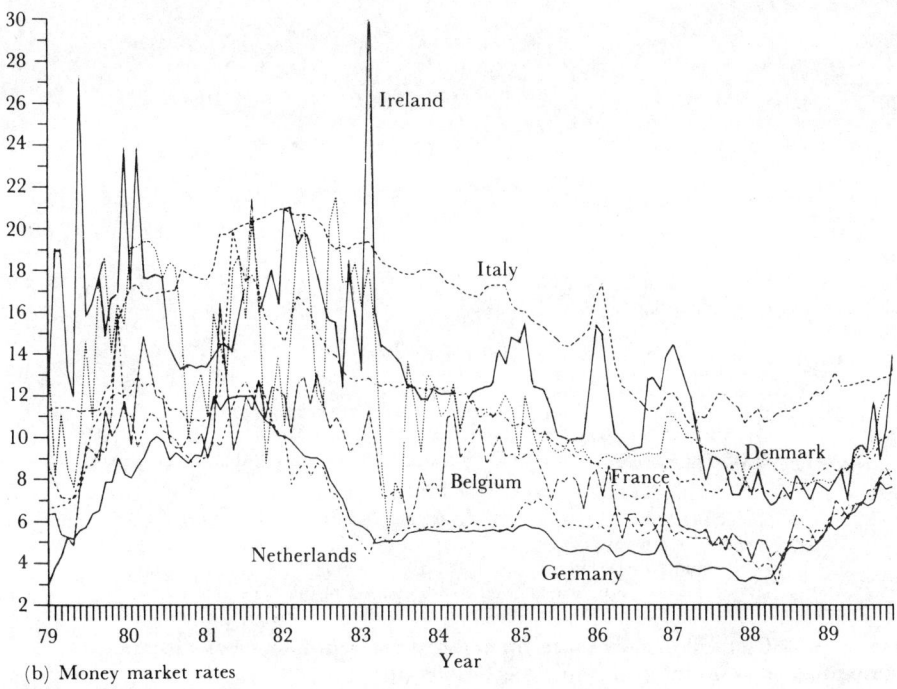

(b) Money market rates

Figure 7—continued

The average and marginal credibility measures of interest rate targets confirm this visual impression. The smaller EMS economies Belgium, the Netherlands, Denmark and Ireland possess short-term credibility but lack long-term credibility: if discount rate changes could effectively be used by the public to forecast movements in short-term money market rates, they had little relevance for predicting the behaviour of long-term government bond rates. This result may be interpreted as evidence of a lack of credibility of anti-inflation policies in the long run (since under zero expected inflation short-term and long-term rates should move closely together and hence be equally responsive to the policy signal). This view is supported by the fact that the highest long-run credibility is found for Germany and the Netherlands, which both had the lowest EMS inflation record.

Figure 8 displays these results graphically. From the onset of the EMS, the short-term interest rate targeting policies of Denmark, Belgium and the Netherlands become credible (MC above 50%) and remain so throughout the EMS period. Credible short-term interest rate targeting is also found for the UK in all three sub-samples and for Ireland

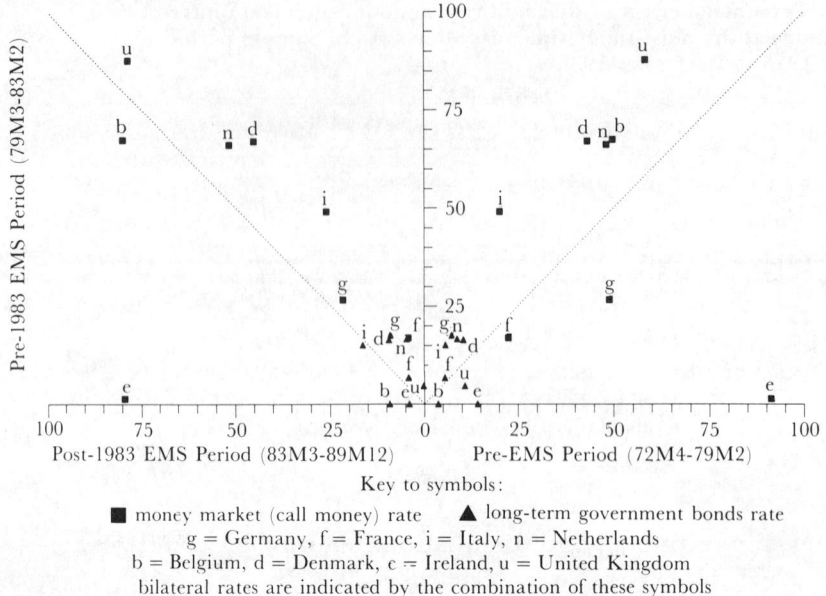

Key to symbols:

■ money market (call money) rate   ▲ long-term government bonds rate
g = Germany, f = France, i = Italy, n = Netherlands
b = Belgium, d = Denmark, e = Ireland, u = United Kingdom
bilateral rates are indicated by the combination of these symbols

Figure 8. MC credibility measure for interest rates. Influence of discount rate announcements on interest rate expectations (in %)

in the pre-EMS (72M4–79M2) and post-1983 EMS period (83M3–89M12). However, this is not true for the Italian, and even less for the German or French monetary authorities, which appear not to have issued credible interest rate signals. This result is not really surprising in the case of France because the discount rate has not been altered since August 1977. The shift from interest rate targeting to money targeting by the Banque de France in early 1977 is a part of the stabilization efforts under the Barre plan. For Germany the sharp decline in the credibility of discount rate announcements for money market rates after 1979 is consistent with the view expressed in Neumann (1988) that the Bundesbank has directly targeted money market interest via short-term treasury bills.

These results indicate that interest rate targeting policies in the EMS have predominantly been oriented towards the stabilization of exchange rates within the band. A confirmation is provided by the estimates of the most likely policy switches for the post-1975 period reported in Table 8: most shifts (five out of seven) occur in the early EMS (79M3–83M2) period, frequently within two months of realignment dates. Another conclusion is that the smaller EMS countries have geared their monetary policies toward pegging the exchange rate through interest rate targeting policies, while the larger EMS countries have had a stronger tendency towards more independent policies.

Table 8. Percentage effect of discount rate announcements on interest rate expectations at the most likely time of policy switch; Sample period January 1975 to December 1989

Country	Switchpoint	MC (in %)	MC_1 (in %)	MC_2 (in %)
Germany	Sep. 1981[†]	*18.8*	13.8	26.0
France	May 1982[†]	*7.5*	*9.5*	3.4
Italy	Oct. 1976[†]	*25.6*	*51.0**	*27.2*
Netherlands	Apr. 1980[†]	*56.3**	*58.7**	41.3
Belgium	June 1981[†]	*58.7**	*59.4**	*81.8**
Denmark	Mar. 1985[†]	*47.7*	*50.4**	*21.8*
Ireland	Mar. 1983[†]	*81.9**	*90.4**	*78.0**
UK	Jan. 1982[†]	*72.1**	*89.0**	*79.6*

Notes: As Table 7, with exchange rates replaced by interest rates.

7. Policy commitments and disinflation: country by country review

The early bipolar nature of the EMS – the joint existence of a hard and a soft currency option – seriously undermines the borrowing reputation hypothesis since the EMS cannot any longer be taken as exhibiting a disinflationary bias. Depending on whether they pegged to a hard or a soft centre country, policy-makers in EMS economies have borrowed a good or a bad counterinflation reputation. The bipolarity hypothesis, furthermore, pretty well accounts for the fact that disinflation has been slower but longer lasting in the EMS. In particular, the recent French commitment towards the hard option, along with a mellowing of the German hard stance, has made the fixed parities more credible and prevented reflation from emerging as strongly as elsewhere.

7.1. Germany

Germany has established and maintained a high counterinflation reputation through a consistently low inflation performance (Figure 2). The inflationary impact of the 1979 oil price shock in Germany was relatively small as inflation rose from about 3% in early 1979 to about 7% in late 1981. By late 1986 inflation had fallen to just below 0%, but between early 1987 and late 1989 it rose to about 3.5%. The German success in controlling and containing inflation cannot be attributed to the use of any particularly credible monetary policy instrument. This may be due to the publicly acknowledged policy stance of the German Bundesbank of not strictly adhering to any particular policy rule, but adopting whatever policy measures appear adequate at the time in order to achieve the prime policy target of a low inflation rate.

7.2. France

French anti-inflation reputation has been relatively low throughout the EMS period. Double-digit inflation rates persisted from 1979 to early 1983, until the stringent austerity programme adopted after the March 1983 realignment (Table 1) brought down inflation to 3% in late 1987. The widespread adoption of foreign exchange controls allowed France to circumvent many of the disciplinary effects of fixed exchange rates, and to effectively pursue an independent monetary policy. Disinflation in France was largely home-made. Finally since 1987 French inflation has remained virtually constant at 3%. The ensuing convergence of inflation rates between Germany and France has been achieved by a rise of German inflation! This implies that the recent convergence of the EMS to a hard currency standard has involved two elements: France has belatedly embraced the hard option, whilst Germany has slightly mellowed its hard stance. The result is a more stable system with less tensions but also less inflation discipline.

7.3. The Netherlands

The Netherlands entered the EMS with inflation only slightly above the German rate. By late 1982, as the German mark exchange rate commitment gained in credibility, the inflation differential had disappeared and has remained that way (Figure 2). If there is one country where the borrowing reputation hypothesis applies, it must be the Netherlands, as confirmed by the measured reputation of the Dutch authorities. In fact the closeness of the timing of discount rate announcements to those of Germany largely enhances the credibility of the exchange rate commitment.

7.4. Belgium

Belgium, which maintained a very close bilateral exchange rate linkage with the Netherlands during the European currency snake period, also entered the EMS with inflation rates only slightly above those of Germany. However, the June 1982 policy shift from credibly pegging to the Dutch guilder (and hence indirectly to the German mark) to adopting the soft currency option of credibly pegging to the French franc resulted in a rise of inflation to French levels. Thereafter, Belgium and France experienced similar inflation performance and macroeconomic policies, dominated by direct price and wage controls and attempts at reducing the inflationary impacts of automatic wage indexation schemes. In spite of the decline in inflation during 1983–86, convergence to the also declining German and Dutch inflation rates was quite limited. The soft currency option helps explain why Belgium despite its gain in counterinflation reputation did not disinflate more quickly. The more recent commitment to pegging to the German mark, confirmed by Belgian participation in the 'Euro-rounds' of discount rate changes, is associated with a gradual convergence of its inflation rate to the German level in the post-1987 period.

7.5. Denmark

Denmark also entered the EMS with inflation rates lower than those in France. Inflation jumped to French levels after the second oil price shock and remained there for some time. During the disinflation period 1982–86 the inflation performances of Denmark and Belgium are almost identical, with an emphasis on wage de-indexation. Thus, the slow Danish disinflation is in accord with its embracing the soft currency option. There is less evidence of any possible recent policy shift towards the hard option. Denmark has only very recently taken part in coordinated discount rate changes, but inflation has remained consistently higher than the French rate since 1987.

7.6. Ireland

The Irish disinflation experience differs. The inflationary impact of the oil price increase was massive. After a slight decline in 1980–81, disinflation started in 1982 with the adoption of an austerity and fiscal consolidation programme. Tight fiscal policies and the foregoing of the two EMS realignments of 1982 helped Ireland to reduce inflation from 19% in late 1981 to French levels of 9% by mid-1983. Between 1983 and early 1986 fiscal consolidation largely eliminated the budget deficit and inflation declined slowly along with the French rate. Throughout this time, credibly pegged exchange rates relative to the soft currency EMS block were maintained. After a period of weakness in mid-1986 and a drastic devaluation (−8%) in August 1986, the Irish pound switched to the hard currency block. Despite the reflationary impact of this devaluation, inflation had declined to the low levels of Germany and the Netherlands by late 1989. The post-1986 move of Ireland to participating in the 'Euro rounds' of discount rate changes, in combination with the high credibility of the Irish discount rate signal, has provided support for the new policy stance of containing inflation.

7.7. Italy

No credible intermediate monetary targeting has been detected in the case of Italy. Whilst the Giavazzi and Spaventa (1989) hypothesis that exchange rate targets have been more credible than money targets is verified, it does not follow that exchange rate targets have been fully credible. In fact, all Italian EMS exchange rate commitments have been non-credible, a finding consistent with the trend movements of most Italian bilateral exchange rates throughout the EMS period. The most credible form of intermediate targeting is interest rate targeting. Yet, even this strategy has not been implemented in a way consistent with fixed exchange rates, as indicated by the still prevailing interest rate and inflation differentials with the remaining EMS countries.

8. Policy implications

What are the benefits and policy options within the new hard EMS which has recently emerged from its bipolar predecessor? An obvious gain is that credible exchange rate pegging to the German mark helps contain inflation. This credibility bonus from EMS membership has presumably strongly influenced Britain's long awaited entry into the ERM in October 1990. The experience of other ERM members, however, suggests that the chosen fluctuation margins for the pound (±6%) may be too wide for establishing credibility. Joining the EMS with a wide band may thus only provide a weak disinflationary bias for the UK, as has been the case for Italy. Second, like the French franc in the early EMS period, Sterling may provide a new soft anchor, which may destabilize the system if some countries were to switch to this new soft option.

The new hard EMS provides favourable starting conditions for the transition to Economic and Monetary Union (EMU) as proposed in the Delors plan. Progress toward the monetary union gives the hard EMS the exchange rate credibility that it still lacks. However, even with perfectly credible exchange rates, the credibility of anti-inflation policies in the monetary union will largely depend on the status and design of the new community institutions. In particular, the new European system of central banks, 'EuroFed', will not necessarily inherit the German Bundesbank's counterinflation reputation; it must establish its reputation independently after having started its operations. This is why inflation control should be a binding policy goal. The constitutional status of the low-inflation objective must be supplemented by institutional rules such that policy-makers will find it desirable to actively adhere to a low inflation objective.

Finally, there is a serious possibility that the hard EMS may be undermined by inflationary developments in Germany as a result of its own unification process which is likely to erode the counterinflation reputation of the Bundesbank. A relatively quick transition to stage three of the Delors plan might be the best way to avoid the inflationary impact of German unification. The EuroFed would have to provide early a credible low-inflation anchor, which would be facilitated by a jump into full monetary union at a time of inflationary pressure in Germany. In addition, this would spare the EuroFed the risk of being unable to establish its own reputation during stage two. Indeed, reputation is tied to the observance of well-understood rules. Yet, stage two means a prolonged period of increased policy coordination with rules to be changed again in stage three. If all ERM member countries agree that inflation control is the prime monetary policy objective, and that the new community institutions will be successful in containing inflation, they should give the EuroFed a vote of confidence by putting the system into operation.

Discussion

Richard Baldwin
Executive Office of the President, Council of Economic Advisers

Axel Weber has written an interesting, relevant and stimulating piece. He takes cutting edge theoretical work and combines it with empirical evidence in an attempt to address an important policy issue, namely the effect that membership in the EMS has on the credibility of the members' monetary policies. The credibility of monetary policy is indeed critical; for instance, it is one of the most important factors which determine how much unemployment must be endured in order to drive down inflation.

The issue of credibility is also of great importance to European policy-makers for at least two reasons. First, the UK has recently joined the ERM partly because she hopes to 'borrow' the credibility of the Bundesbank and thereby minimize the unemployment cost of disinflating. Second, during the move toward Stages Two and Three of EMU, the credibility of national policy-makers' commitment to tighter exchange rates will greatly affect the ease and cost of the transition. If the commitment is perfectly credible, then the transition should be quite smooth and seemingly fixed exchange rates should be observed quite quickly. However, if it is not credible, then the attempts to maintain fixed exchange rates could create no-risk wagers that have in the past led to massive speculation against weak currencies. Of course, the reality will be somewhere between the two extremes. Moreover, evidence about the EMS's past influence on credibility is only suggestive of its credibility in the future.

The author uses some concepts borrowed from game theory, applied to the interaction between workers, firms and the authorities in charge of monetary policy. A universal problem with game theory is that it sounds true and applicable as long as the concepts, like credibility, stay vague. However, when it comes to empirical work, one cannot be vague and compromises on data, methodology and simplifying assumptions have to be made. It is on these compromises that I will focus my comments. I will also limit my discussion to the issue of credibility.

To quantify credibility, the author measures how peoples' expectations are affected by the announcement of a policy. Since data on peoples' expectations before and after the announcement is not available (and would probably be unreliable even if it were collected), the author generates this expectations data from a time series model using a handful of factors, such as lagged values of various macroeconomic indicators, to form a best prediction of the variable in question.

My first criticism is that it is difficult to distinguish between changes in the goodness-of-fit of the time series model generating expectations and changes in the credibility of policy-makers. That is, if we could be sure that the author had an absolutely true model of the economy, then we would know that any change in the relationship between the announcements and the expectations reflected the extent to which people believed the policy-makers' announcements. However, for some of the variables – exchange rates, for instance – we know that economic models just do not fit the data very well. As a result it is hard to be sure that the author has included all other factors. This can be a serious problem if the announcements are correlated with some of the omitted factors.

For example, it is found that the announcements of German monetary authorities match expectations less closely over the recent past than previously. This could be due to a decrease in credibility, or it might be a somewhat spurious decrease in the goodness-of-fit of the time series model generating the expectations, for example because of rising inflation in Germany during the late 1980s. Similarly, the author's statement that EMS initially had a hard option involving countries that borrowed Bundesbank credibility and a soft option offered by the Banque de France should be taken cautiously. It could equally be that some underlying factor, not captured in the time series model, was the driving force behind the movement of the announcements and the expectations. One might argue that strong behaviour of trade unions, and 'weak' governments (which are not in the author's time series model) were the main cause of the exchange rate behaviour and announcements in the soft option countries. In this case the notion that these countries seemed to borrow France's credibility would be largely spurious.

My second criticism is that the policy announcements are not made in a vacuum, so there may be some feedback between the other variables influencing expectations (that are included in the time series model) and the announcements. Again this will tend to distort the estimate of the impact of the announcements on expectations, and thereby alter our judgements concerning credibility. Furthermore, if the degree to which the announcements and other factors are related changes during the sample period, the results will be even more misleading.

As I stated above, theory is easy until one has to make the compromises necessary to take it to the data. The author has done an admirable job of making most sensible compromises. My two criticims were simply meant to indicate that given the author's methodology, alternative interpretations of the results can be put forward.

Maurice Obstfeld
University of California at Berkeley, Harvard University, CEPR and NBER

The objective of Axel Weber's paper is to devise some empirical measures of policy-makers' 'reputation' and 'credibility' and to use those measures to elucidate the evolution of the EMS.

Reputation and credibility are both elusive concepts, which are, however, central to the understanding of the expectational environment in which policy outcomes are determined. In principle, a policy-maker's promises will be credible if it is in her interests to keep those promises, given her preferences and constraints. Since neither the preferences nor the constraints are likely to be public information, the public must infer from past policy actions and announcements what the official payoffs from alternative moves will be. Reputation can be identified loosely with the public's current beliefs about the policy-maker's preferences. Since these beliefs are not directly observable, the econometrician faces a formidable task in the nature of a policy-maker's reputation.

As a first cut at this problem, Weber measures credibility by evaluating the relationship between announced policy targets and the public's expectations of the corresponding policy outcomes. His basic idea is that a policy announcement will receive a heavier weight in private-sector forecasts the greater is the policy-maker's credibility. His empirical estimates of credibility thus inevitably depend on a choice of proxy for the unobservable expectations. But the chosen proxies – essentially least squares predictions on known announced and realized target variables – seem to omit key additional factors that plausibly influence expectations, like competitiveness, employment or the government's debt. The biases in Weber's estimates induced by the resulting errors in variables are difficult to appreciate.

An even more serious problem, I believe, arises from Weber's treatment of policy targets for monetary growth, exchange rates and interest rates, when such targets are expressed in terms of ranges. Weber uses midpoints of target ranges and there are some conceptual problems associated with the translation of ranges to point estimates. For example, when the central bank announces a range of future exchange rates, the impact on the future exchange rate expected by the public necessarily depends on the announced probability distribution of the rate over its range, if indeed any such distribution is announced. This distribution need not be uniform, however, even if the target zone is perfectly credible. For example, in Krugman's (1990) model of a fully credible target zone, the exchange rate's unconditional distribution has relatively more mass concentrated near the zone's edges (see Froot and Obstfeld, 1991). In such a setting, Weber's measure would indicate a serious lack of credibility and these measures probably reveal more about the importance of intra-marginal intervention than about the credibility of the ERM bands. In general, there is indeed no reason to take deviations from the centre, *per se*, as evidence of low credibility. Svensson (1990) has devised an interesting alternative test of target-zone credibility based on international interest differentials, and applied it to recent Swedish data. It would be interesting to see a similar analysis in the EMS context.

An additional and perhaps surprising drawback of Weber's methodology concerns the possibility that even a policy-maker with a credibility problem may be able to announce credible target ranges. In an ingenious application of the concept of 'cheap talk' from game theory, Stein (1989) shows how a policy-maker may be able to communicate truthfully the range in which her target exchange rate lies despite being unable to communicate truthfully a single target rate. In Stein's setting, the public might base its expectations on an announced range even when the policy-maker has incentives to be misleading. But the announcement of a narrower range might not be credible, even if it implies the same expected future exchange rate. Weber's approach might thus lead us to conclude that two policy-makers are 'equally' credible even though one can credibly communicate much more precise information to the public.

Taking Weber's credibility estimates at face value, they still represent some puzzles. For example, Weber suggests at several points that the French commitment to a 'hard' peg against the DM has increased in recent years. Yet, there is no evidence of this in his estimates; according to Figure 5, the marginal credibility of the bilateral exchange rate is quite moderate and has decreased during the late period of the EMS.

At the same time, there is in principle no systematic association between exchange rate commitment and domestic inflation, especially in the short term. On the contrary, allowing the franc to appreciate somewhat in response to favourable export demand developments would have a dampening effect on inflation.

The data seem clearly consistent, however, with Weber's view that disinflation was hampered by a persistent lack of policy credibility on the part of Italy and France. The fact that long-term interest rate differentials have failed to disappear even as capital flows have been liberalized supports this interpretation. So do the high sacrifice ratios that Italy and France have endured during the process of disinflation. In 1989, unemployment rates in France and Italy were respectively 10.9 and 9.6%, up from respectively 8.8 and 8.3% in 1983. In contrast, unemployment rates in Germany and the Netherlands – as well as in the US, UK, Canada and Japan – dropped sharply over this six-year period.

Along with measures of credibility, Weber presents estimates of anti-inflationary 'reputation', defined as the public's subjective probability that inflation follows a stationary stochastic process. The intuitive idea, which is appealing, is that an inflation fighter worthy of his reputation will always bring inflation back down to a low level. But we have to be wary of applying this metric without further thoughts. Consider the position of an infinitely-lived policy-maker setting optimal taxes and inflation rates, as in the analyses of Mankiw (1987), Grilli (1989) and others. Only when the planner can credibly commit herself to future policies will she be able to achieve an optimal plan – which generally involve a non-stationary inflation process. In contrast, a non-credible planner may well end up, in equilibrium, choosing a stationary inflation process, despite a high propensity to resort to inflationary finance on the margin (Obstfeld, 1990).

My concern about this paper's approach reflects a general unease with the use of simple time-series measures of credibility that are not based on a structural model of the European economies. Without knowledge of which policies and institutions have facilitated the credible shifts in patterns of exchange rates, we have indeed no basis to judge the permanence of the apparent move towards a more integrated system of policy choice. Important institutional changes are indeed forthcoming. Following the demise of the Soviet Bloc, German reunification and Britain's entry into the ERM, the early 1990s will provide a rigorous test of both the resolve of European policy-makers and the role of European economic institutions in shaping ultimate policy outcomes.

General discussion

A number of panel members wondered about the appropriate way of measuring credibility. Edmond Malinvaud was concerned that the concept of credibility used by Axel Weber was too narrow. Credibility in his paper is simply a measure of the strength of regressions to central parities (or targets) and Malivaud thought that it could be refined. In particular, he suggested that the environment should be controlled for in assessing credibility. He could, for example, think of a famous French statesman who gained credibility by behaving moderately well in a particularly difficult environment. Similarly, he could think of individuals losing credibility for failing to excel in easy times. Since such insights into the process of building credibility cannot be captured by Weber's methodology, it was suggested that supplementary evidence could be useful; Malinvaud argued in favour of direct methods like a rigorous analysis of opinion surveys and the financial press. Guido Tabellini suggested that the behaviour of interest rate differentials when a currency approaches the lower end of its target could be very informative; a widening of interest rate differentials would naturally be associated with an expected devaluation and hence a lack of credibility for the current target. On the other hand, confidence in the target will fuel expectations of an appreciation and accordingly the interest differential will shrink. Tabellini indicated that some preliminary work had been undertaken along these lines by Luigi Spaventa for Italy. These results suggested that the parity of the lira had gained credibility over time. Sweder van Wijnbergen also warned that the credibility of any particular target could not be assessed independently of policy stances regarding other instruments. He suggested, for example, that the credibility of an exchange rate target was largely dependent on whether fiscal policy was set in such a way that the target could indeed be met. A number of panel members concurred; it was felt that in the context of Weber's methodology, the evaluation of consistency across policy instruments could be addressed by a more refined modelling of expectations. Agents will indeed use relevant information about all instruments in forming their expectations about any particular target. Accordingly, structural equations should be preferred to simple time series models to account for expectations. Weber acknowledged that this was desirable, but somewhat arduous.

David Begg expressed some worry about the exogeneity of the targets themselves. He suggested that policy-makers were setting the targets on the basis of their own expectations of what was achievable. Accordingly, the anticipation of agent expectations is likely to be accounted for by the policy-makers. Targets can therefore not be seen as exogeneous and the mechanism behind the definition of the target could, according to Begg, usefully be modelled.

Some panel members warned that the interpretation of data regarding the behaviour of the various EMS currencies should be cautious; in particular, according to Malinvaud, the statement that there is a French franc zone is somewhat of a caricature. All that is observed is a parallel behaviour on the part of some countries and there is no evidence that the central banks of Denmark or Belgium ever targeted the French franc. While not disputing the argument, Weber retorted that the central banks of Denmark or Belgium had still accepted that their currencies would mimic the French franc rather than the Deutschemark. Even though the members of the 'French franc zone' might not have targeted the franc, they have still accepted a common fate.

On a more general note, Michael Burda wondered whether the announcement of the decision to proceed toward a monetary union in Europe has had a discernable effect on the credibility of the various currencies. Weber indicated that the actual date of announcement was outside his sample but that the recent convergence of all currencies toward the Deutschemark zone could be interpreted as an acknowledgement that monetary union was under way. Georges de Menil echoed Burda's concern for future development by pondering about the effect of German reunification on the credibility of the Deutschemark. Weber indicated that so far no loss of credibility could be detected, but that further study in this area is needed.

Appendix A. Credibility and reputation in models of policy games

The following model, borrowed from Cukierman (1986), assumes that the monetary authority and the public are engaged in a policy game which determines the equilibrium level of output and inflation. Inflation is a monetary phenomenon (A1.1) and output is determined by a Lucas-type supply function (A1.2).[10] As in Barro and Gordon (1983a, b), the central banker's objective function – possibly identical to the social welfare function – assumes that he dislikes inflation π_t and likes economic stimulus, i.e. a level of output y_t above its natural level y^n (A1.3 or A1.4 in terms of m). The public's expectations are of the least-squares error type (A1.6) and are formed rationally on the basis

---

[10] Note that here unexpected inflation rates $\pi_t (\pi_t = p_t - p_{t-1})$, instead of unexpected price levels as in Lucas (1973), explain the deviation of output from its natural level.

Table A1. A stylized model of monetary policy games

$\pi_t = m_t$	Inflation caused by money growth	(A1.1)
$y_t = y^n + \phi(\pi_t - \pi_t^e)$	Output relationship	(A1.2)
$W_t = -\pi_t^2/2 + b(y_t - y^n)$	Policy-makers' objective function	(A1.3)
$W_t = -m_t^2/2 + b\phi(m_t - m_t^e)$	Policy-makers' objective function in m_t	(A1.4)
$m_t = b\phi$	Optimal monetary policy outcome	(A1.5)
$U_t = -(m_t - m_t^e)^2$	Public's objective function	(A1.6)
$m_t^e = Em_t|\Omega_t = b\phi$	Public's rational expectations	(A1.7)

of all available information (A.1.7).[11] The temptation of policy-makers to aim at the unsustainable first-best solution (with $m_t = b\Phi$ and $Em_t|\Omega_{t-1} = 0$) drives the economy away from the second-best, incentive incompatible, solution ($m_t = Em_t|\Omega_{t-1} = 0$), to the inferior but stable third-best Nash solution ($m_t = Em_t|\Omega_{t-1} = b\Phi$). Lower rates of inflation would require that the monetary authority can issue a credible commitment i.e. via a constitutional amendment. Empirically meaningful concepts of credibility and reputation are only derived in policy games with imperfect information.

An example is the sequential equilibrium model of Backus and Driffill (1985) in Table A2. The public is uncertain as to which type of two policy-makers (A2.3a or A2.3b) is in office. This uncertainty, and strategic behaviour (disguise) by the policy-maker, prevents the public from inferring the true state of the central banker preferences from the observable money growth process. Equations (A2.5a) and (A2.5b) state that the observation of zero money growth may be due to a 'hard-nosed' policy-maker who always plays $m_t = 0$, or to a 'wet' policy-maker who disguises as a hard-nosed one with a time-varying probability δ_t. Hence, the public's rational expectation of money growth (A2.7) is the discretionary outcome $b\Phi$ multiplied by the joint probability that the policy-maker is wet $(1 - \psi_t)$ and does not disguise as a hard-nosed one $(1 - \delta_t)$. Reputation in the sense of Backus and Driffill is the subjective probability ψ_t that the central banker is hard-nosed. This probability is updated continuously via Bayesian probability learning.

Cukierman and Meltzer (1986a, b) allow for a combination of incomplete monetary control (A3.5a) and gradually and persistently changing policy objectives b_t (A3.3). Here again the public cannot infer the true state of the central banker's preferences from the actual money growth process. However, central bank watching gradually reveals the degree of monetary noise due to shifting policy objectives. In Cukierman and

---

[11] Since the public cannot observe m_t and there are no contemporary information signals available, $Em_t|\Omega_t$ is identical to $Em_t|\Omega_{t-1}$ in this simple version of the basic game.

Table A2. The Backus and Driffill model

$\pi_t = m_t$	(A2.1)
$y_t = y^n + \phi(\pi_t - \pi_t^e)$	(A2.2)

$$W_t^w = \sum_{t=0}^{\tau} \beta^t[-\pi_t^2/2 + b(y_t - y^n)] \quad \text{(A2.3a)} \qquad W_t^h = \sum_{t=0}^{\tau} \beta^t[-\pi_t^2/2] \quad \text{(A2.3b)}$$

$$W_t^w = \sum_{t=0}^{\tau} \beta^t[-m_t^2/2 + \phi b(m_t - m_t^e)] \quad \text{(A2.4a)} \qquad W_t^h = \sum_{t=0}^{\tau} \beta^t[-m_t^2/2] \quad \text{(A2.4b)}$$

$m_t = (1 - \delta_t)b\phi$	(A2.5a)	$m_t = 0$	(A2.5b)
$U_t = -(m_t - m_t^e)^2$			(A2.6)
$m_t^e = Em_t\|\Omega_t = (1 - \psi_t)(1 - \delta_t)b\phi$			(A2.7)

with Bayesian probability learning about ψ_t and δ_t conditional on $\delta_\tau = 0$.

Table A3. The Cukierman and Meltzer model

$\pi_t = m_t$	(A3.1)
$y_t = y^n + \phi(\pi_t - \pi_t^e)$	(A3.2)

$$W_t = \sum_{t=0}^{\infty} \beta^t[-\pi_t^{p2}/2 + b_t(y_t - y^n)] \tag{A3.3}$$

with $b_t = b + \gamma_t$, $\gamma_t = \rho\gamma_{t-1} + v_t$, $b > 0$, $0 < \rho < 1$, $v_t \sim N(0, \sigma_v^2)$,

$$W_t = \sum_{t=0}^{\infty} \beta^t[-m_t^{p2}/2 + \phi b_t(m_t - m_t^e)] \tag{A3.4}$$

$m_t = m_t^p + \mu_1\zeta_t$, $\zeta_t \sim N(0, \sigma_\zeta^2)$,	(A3.5a)
$m_t^a = m_t^p + \mu_1 u_t$, $u_t \sim N(0, \sigma_u^2)$,	(A3.5b)
$m_t^p = \mu_0\phi b + \mu_1\gamma_t$	(A3.5c)
$U_t = -(m_t - m_t^e)^2$	(A3.6)

$$m_t^e = Em_t|\Omega_t = \frac{(\rho - \lambda)(1 - \theta)}{\lambda + (\rho - \lambda)(1 - \theta)} m_t^a + \frac{\lambda}{\lambda + (\rho - \lambda)(1 - \theta)} Em_t|\Omega_{t-1}$$

$$= \alpha m_t^a + (1 - \alpha)Em_t|\Omega_{t-1} \tag{A3.7}$$

with $\quad \lambda = \frac{1}{2}\left[\frac{1+r}{\rho} + \rho\right] - \sqrt{\frac{1}{4}\left\{\frac{1+r}{\rho} + \rho\right\}^2 - 1}$

$\qquad r = (\sigma_v^2/\sigma_\zeta^2)\{1 + (\sigma_\zeta^2/\sigma_u^2)\}, \qquad \theta = \sigma_u^2/(\sigma_\zeta^2 + \sigma_u^2)$

Meltzer (1986b) the central bank also issues a noisy monetary announce-ment signal (A3.5b), which is treated by the public as one piece of contemporary information used in forming expectations (A3.7).[12] Two

[12] Note that the coefficients μ_0 and μ_1 in the reduced form for the optimal money growth rate (A3.5c) are determined by the requirement of rational expectations in the solution of the public's signal extraction problem (A3.7). See Cukierman and Meltzer (1986b) for the details of these coefficient restrictions.

measures of credibility are proposed: average credibility ($AC = -|m_t^a - Em_t|\Omega_t|$) where m_t^a is the current monetary announcement; marginal credibility (MC) is the extent to which a unit change in the announcement m_t^a affects the public's expectation $Em_t|\Omega_t$ and may be thought of as the weight (α) placed on the announcement in (A3.6). Similar models can be derived for interest or exchange rate targeting.

Appendix B. The empirical implementation of reputation and credibility

Reputation is defined as the probability that policy-makers consistently pursue a low-inflation policy. It is derived here by applying the Bayesian multi-process Kalman filter. In principle this signal extraction algorithm computes inflation forecasts as a probability weighted average of four alternative forecasting models. The first two models assume inflation to be a stationary stochastic process, generated by a combination of transitory and permanent price level shocks, whilst the remaining two models allow inflation rates to exhibit permanent shocks or trend movements. At each point in time each model has a probability which is calculated as a combination of prior information and sample information derived from the forecasting performance of the individual models over the most recent periods. This probability is updated by using Bayes' law, which in Backus and Driffill (1985) is employed to drive the reputation measure. Its empirical counterpart is derived here as the probability that inflation rates follow relatively stationary time-paths. For an exact formalization of this approach and a discussion of the estimating equations, see Weber (1988).

In order to derive an empirical counterpart to the credibility concepts of Appendix A, a modelling of the public's expectations formation process is required. A two-step approach is adopted: first, the optimal time series expectations of the unobservable planned policy targets conditional on past information ($Ex_t^p|\Omega_{t-1}$) are derived by using signal extraction methods. Second, the rational expectations of these policy targets under incomplete contemporary information ($Ex_t^p|\Omega_t$) are derived by incorporating the current announcement into the above time series expectations in a least-squares regression.

The theoretical models in Appendix A imply time series models (see Table B1) for the actual observable policy outcomes ($x_t = \{m_t, i_t, \varepsilon_t\}$) and the policy announcements ($x_t^a = \{m_t^a, i_t^a, \varepsilon_t^a\}$) respectively.[13] By applying

---

[13] Here a slightly modified version of these dynamic linear models has been employed. In particular I assume $\rho = 1$ and let the changes in policy-maker objective b_t follow a non-stationary process by replacing γ_t with $\gamma_t' = \gamma_t + s_t$, where s_t is assumed to be a random walk.

Table B1. Time series model

Time series model for observable policy outcome $x_t = \{m_t, i_t, \varepsilon_t\}$:

$$x_t = x_t^p + \xi_t, \qquad \xi_t \equiv \mu_1 \zeta_t, \qquad E\xi_t | \Omega_{t-1} = 0, \qquad E(\xi_t \xi_t) | \Omega_{t-1} = \sigma_\xi^2 \qquad \text{(B.1a)}$$

$$x_t^p = \rho x_{t-1}^p + \gamma_t, \qquad \gamma_t \equiv v_t / \mu_1, \qquad E\gamma_t | \Omega_{t-1} = 0, \qquad E(\gamma_t \gamma_t) | \Omega_{t-1} = \sigma_\gamma^2 \qquad \text{(B.1b)}$$

Time series model for policy announcement $x_t^3 = \{m_t^a, i_t^a, \varepsilon_t^a\}$:

$$x_t^a = x_t^p + \omega_t, \qquad \omega_t \equiv u_t \mu_1, \qquad E\omega_t | \Omega_{t-1} = 0, \qquad E(\omega_t \omega_t) | \Omega_{t-1} = \sigma_\omega^2 \qquad \text{(B.2a)}$$

$$x_t^p = \rho x_{t-1}^p + \gamma_t, \qquad \gamma_t \equiv v_t / \mu_1, \qquad E\gamma_t | \Omega_{t-1} = 0, \qquad E(\gamma_t \gamma_t) | \Omega_{t-1} = \sigma_\gamma^2 \qquad \text{(B.2b)}$$

Optimal prediction of planned policy under past information Ω_{t-1}:

$$Ex_t^p | \Omega_{t-1} = \theta Ex_t | (x_{t-1}, x_{t-2}, \ldots) + (1 - \theta) Ex_t^a | (x_{t-1}^a, x_{t-2}^a, \ldots) \qquad \text{(B.3)}$$

Optimal prediction of planned policy under contemporary information Ω_t:

$$Ex_t^p | \Omega_t = \alpha x_t^a + (1 - \alpha) Ex_t^p | \Omega_{t-1} \qquad \text{(B.4)}$$

Influence of announcement on expectations under contemporary information:

$$E(x_t^p - Ex_t^p | \Omega_{t-1}) | \Omega_t = \alpha(x_t^a - Ex_t^p | \Omega_{t-1}) \qquad \text{(B.5)}$$

the multi-process Kalman filter, optimal predictions from these time series models are calculated and used as input for the rational expectations equation (B.4). These rational expectations are derived as the fitted value of a least-squares regresssion of the actual observable policy outcome x_t on the policy announcements x_t^a and on the expected policy outcome conditional on past information $(Ex_t | \Omega_{t-1})$, which in principle may be calculated by iterating θ in the weighted average of the two univariate time series expectations (B.3) between zero and one and selecting that value of θ which minimizes the overall sum of squared residuals of the regression equation. Since all three types of announcements are low frequency signals, the information content of past announcements is typically found to be very low and θ is close to one in many cases (Weber, 1990a) so that the restriction $\theta = 1$ was imposed and the influence of the announcement on expectations was estimated directly from Equation (B.5).

Appendix C. Data sources

C1. Quarterly data

Prices: CPI, IMF *International Financial Statistics*, line 64.

C2. Monthly data

Exchange rates: bilateral exchange rates calculated as cross-rates from US dollar rates, from IMF *International Financial Statistics*, line rf. ECU exchange rates: *Eurostatistics*.

Prices: CPI, IMF *International Financial Statistics*, line 64. Exception: for Ireland WPI, line 63.

Interest rates:

call money rates: IMF *International Financial Statistics*, line 60. Exception: for Ireland data from OECD *Main Economic Indicators*.

government bond rates: IMF *International Financial Statistics*, *line* 61.

official discount rates: OECD *Main Economic Indicators*. Exception: for the UK London money market clearing rates.

Money:

central bank money stock: OECD *Main Economic Indicators*.

base money: IMF *International Financial Statistics*, line 14.

narrow money (M1): OECD *Main Economic Indicators*, index (1985 = 100) of seasonally adjusted money.

quasi money (M2, M3): OECD *Main Economic Indicators*, index (1985 = 100) of seasonally adjusted quasi money.

total domestic credit: OECD *Main Economic Indicators*.

Monetary targets:

Data before 1989:

CBM Germany: taken from Neumann (1988).

M2 France: taken from Wyplosz (1988).

TDC Italy: taken from OECD *Country Survey*: *Italy*, various volumes.

M3 UK: taken from Fischer (1988).

Data of 1989 and 1990 are taken for all countries from Federal Reserve Bank of St. Louis *International Economic Conditions*, various issues.

References

Anderson, T. M. and O. Risager (1988). 'Stabilization Policies, Credibility and Interest Rate Determination in a Small Open Economy', *European Economic Review*.

Artis, J. M. (1987). 'The European Monetary System: An Evaluation', *Journal of Policy Modelling*.

Backus, D. and J. Driffill (1985). 'Inflation and Reputation', *American Economic Review*.

Barro, R. J. and D. B. Gordon (1983a). 'A Positive Theory of Monetary Policy in a Natural Rate Model', *Journal of Political Economy*.

—— (1983b). 'Rules, Discretion and Reputation in a Model of Monetary Policy', *Journal of Monetary Economics*.

Blackburn, K. and M. Christensen (1989). 'Monetary Policy and Policy Credibility: Theories and Evidence', *Journal of Economic Literature*.

Brown, R. L., J. Durbin and J. M. Evans (1975). 'Techniques for Testing the Constancy of Regression Relationships over Time', *Journal of the Royal Statistical Society*, Series B.

Chow, G. C. (1960). 'Tests of the Equality Between Two Sets of Coefficients in Two Linear Regressions', *Econometrica*.

Cohen, D. and C. Wyplosz (1989). 'The European Monetary Union: An Agnostic Evaluation', in R. Bryant, J. Frenkel, P. Masson and R. Portes (eds.) *Macroeconomic Policies in an Interdependent World*.

Collins, S. M. (1988). 'Inflation and the EMS', in F. Giavazzi, S. Miccossi and M. Miller (eds.) *The European Monetary System*, Cambridge University Press, Cambridge.

Cukierman, A. (1986). 'Central Bank Behavior and Credibility: Some Recent Theoretical Developments', *Federal Reserve Bank of St. Louis Review*.

Cukierman, A. and A. H. Meltzer (1986a). 'A Theory of Ambiguity, Credibility, and Inflation under Discretion and Asymmetric Information', *Econometrica*.
—— (1986b). 'The Credibility of Monetary Announcements', in M. J. M. Neumann (ed.) *Monetary Policy and Uncertainty*, Nomos Verlag, Baden-Baden.
De Boissieu, C. (1988). 'Financial Liberalization and the Evolution of the EMS', *European Economy*.
De Grauwe, P. (1988). 'Is the European Monetary System a DM-Zone?', Centre for European Policy Studies Working Document No 39.
—— (1990). 'The Cost of Disinflation and the European Monetary System', *Open Economies Review*.
Dornbusch, R. (1989). 'Credibility, Debt and Unemployment: Ireland's failed Stabilization', *Economic Policy*.
Fischer, S. (1988). 'Monetary Policy and Performance in the U.S., Japan and Europe, 1973–1986', *Finanzmarkt und Portfoliomanagement*.
Fratianni, M. and J. von Hagen (1989). 'Asymmetries and Realignments in the EMS', Indiana State University Discussion Paper 429.
—— (1990a). 'German Dominance in the EMS: Evidence from Interest Rates', *Journal of International Money and Finance*.
—— (1990b). 'The European Monetary System: Ten Years After', in Meltzer, A. H. and C. Plosser (eds.) *Carnegie-Rochester Conference Series on Public Policy*.
Froot, K. and M. Obstfeld (1991). 'Exchange-Rate Dynamics under Stochastic Regime Shifts: A Unified Approach', *Journal of International Economics*.
Giavazzi, F. and A. Giovannini (1987). 'The EMS and the Dollar', *Economic Policy*.
Giavazzi, F. and M. Pagano (1988). 'The Advantage of Tying one's Hands: EMS Discipline and Central Bank Credibility', *European Economic Review*.
Giavazzi F. and L. Spaventa (1989). 'Italy: The Real Effects of Inflation and Disinflation', *Economic Policy*.
Goldfeld, S. M. and R. E. Quandt (1965). 'Some Tests for Homoscedasticity', *Journal of the American Statistical Association*.
—— (1973). 'The Estimation of Structural Shifts by Switching Regression', *Annals of Economic and Social Measurement*.
—— (1976). 'Techniques for Estimating Switching Regressions', in S. M. Goldfeld, and R. E. Quandt, *Studies in Nonlinear Estimation*, Cambridge Mass.
Goodhart, C. (1989). 'The Conduct of Monetary Policy', *The Economic Journal*.
Grilli, V. (1989). 'Seigniorage in Europe', in M. de Cecco and A. Giovannini (eds.) *A European Central Bank? Perspectives on Monetary Unification after Ten Years of the EMS*, Cambridge University Press.
Krugman, P. (1990). 'Target Zones and Exchange Rate Dynamics', *Quarterly Journal of Economics*.
Lucas, R. E. (1973). 'Some International Evidence on Output-Inflation Tradeoffs', *American Economic Review*.
—— (1976). 'Economic Policy Evaluation: A Critique', in K. Brunner and A. H. Meltzer (eds.) *Carnegie Rochester Conference Series on Public Policy*.
Mankiw, N. G. (1987). 'The Optimal Collection of Seigniorage: Theory and Evidence', *Journal of Monetary Economics*.
Neumann, M. J. M. (1988). 'Deutsche Geldpolitik: Verfahren und Probleme', *Finanzmarkt und Portfoliomanagement*.
Obstfeld, M. (1990). 'Dynamic Seigniorage Theory: An Exploration', Harvard Institute of Economic Research Disucssion Paper No. 1503, July.
Persson, T. (1988). 'Credibility of Macroeconomic Policy: An Introduction and a Broad Survey', *European Economic Review*.
Quandt, R. E. (1960). 'Test of the Hypothesis That a Linear Regression System Obeys Two Separate Regimes', *Journal of the American Statistical Association*.
Rogoff, K. (1985a). 'The Optimal Degree of Commitment to an Intermediate Monetary Target', *Quarterly Journal of Economics*.
—— (1985b). 'Can Exchange Rate Predictability be Achieved without Monetary Convergence? Evidence from the EMS', *European Economic Review*.
Stein, J. (1989). 'Cheap Talk and the Fed: A Theory of Imprecise Policy Announcements', *American Economic Review*.
Svensson, L. (1990). 'The Simplest Test of Target Zone Credibility', National Bureau of Economic Research Working Paper No. 3394, June.
Ungerer, H., O. Evans and P. Nyberg (1983). 'The European Monetary System: The Experience, 1979–1982', *IMF Occasional Paper* No. 19.
Ungerer, H., O. Evans, T. Mayer and P. Young (1986). 'The European Monetary System: Recent Developments', *IMF Occasional Paper* No. 48.

Weber, A. A. (1988). 'The Credibility of Monetary Policies, Policymakers' Reputation and the EMS-Hypothesis: Empirical Evidence from 13 Countries', Center of Economic Research Discussion Paper No. 8803.
—— (1990a). 'The Credibility of Monetary Target Announcements: An Empirical Evaluation', Center of Economic Research Discussion Paper No. 9031.
—— (1990b). 'European Economic and Monetary Union and Asymmetries and Adjustment Problems in the European Monetary System: Some Empirical Evidence', CEPR Discussion Paper No. 448.
Wyplosz, C. (1988). 'Monetary Policy in France: Monetarism or Darwinism', *Finanzmarkt und Portfoliomanagement.*
—— (1989). 'EMS Puzzles', *Revista Espanola de Economia.*

Aging population

Axel Börsch-Supan

Summary

The expected change in the age structure of the industrialized countries will lead to a dramatically higher proportion of older people. In Germany, for example, 100 employed persons now support about 40 elderly. By 2030, this ratio will rise to 85 elderly people per 100 employed persons. This process will deeply affect labour, financial and housing markets. It will strain the social security systems, change the accumulation of aggregate wealth and skew its intergenerational distribution, while imposing a growing burden on family support by the young generation when the elderly are becoming frail and unable to live independently. This paper investigates the mechanisms at work in labour, financial and housing markets, drawing systematically on comparisons between German and US institutions to determine the role of taxes, subsidies and regulations. The evidence demonstrates that economic policies have powerful effects; some of them are also currently distortionary and interact with existing market imperfections, so that a serious consideration of policy options which may moderate the implications of population aging is called for.

Aging population: problems and policy options in the US and Germany

Axel Börsch-Supan
University of Mannheim and NBER

1. Introduction

The expected change in the age structure of the industrialized countries is dramatic and will lead to a substantially higher proportion of older people. Currently, approximately 13% of the OECD population is aged 65 and above. This is substantially more than the 8.5% prevalent in the 1950s, but is dwarfed by expectations that it will increase to more than 20% over the next 40 years. Figure 1 presents the evidence for Germany where population aging is particularly pronounced.

The implications are wide-ranging; social policy and the economy as a whole are concerned but the labour, financial and housing markets are particularly affected. Some key issues are how social programmes (such as public pension schemes, health insurance, housing subsidies and services for the elderly) have to be restructured, and whether existing distortions will exacerbate the pressure. Some examples indicate that these pressures are dramatic indeed. Consider first public pensions. In Germany, the contributions would have to increase from the current 18.7% of gross income to over 40% in 2030 if the system is to remain unchanged (projections by Prognos, Basel quoted from Schmähl, 1989). Such a contribution would undoubtedly severely affect labour supply by the younger generation. Not only the balance between workers and retirees will change but also the age composition of the work force itself, as the second example shows. It is estimated that the number of workers aged 60 and above will increase by 80% in the US, with substantial effects on the structure of the labour force in terms of work

The American part of the research in this paper was supported by the National Institute on Aging, grant no. 3 PO1 AG05842-01. I am indebted to Anette Reil-Held, Ernst Seiler, Gerald Schehl and Peter Schmidt, who provided valuable research assistance at various stages of this project. I am also grateful to Charles Wyplosz for encouraging advice and editorial help.

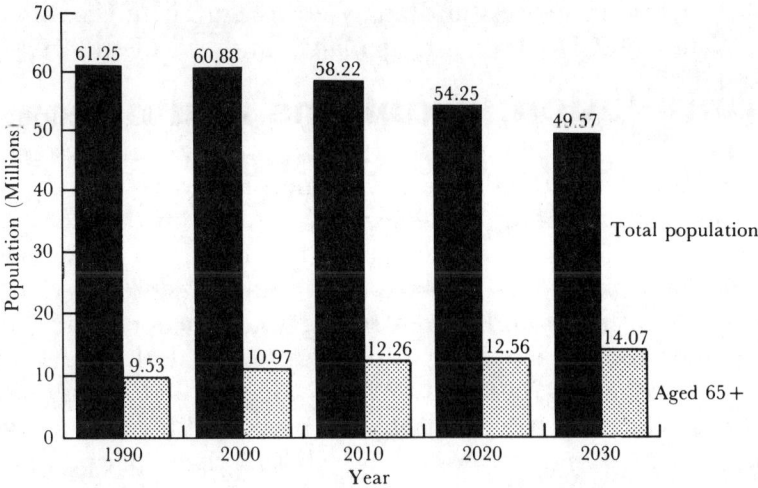

Figure 1. Projected population aging in West Germany

Source: Population forecast of the German census (Model I+D, Version 31.12.86).

experience and labour productivity (Lazear, 1990). The third example concern the financial markets. Auerbach *et al.* (1990) claim that the national saving rate will decrease from 9.1% in 1990 to 5.1% in 2030 in the US, from 19.7 to 13.9% in Germany, and even more dramatically from 21.3 to 3.1% in Japan. If his prediction holds, the capital stock of the industrialized countries could decrease substantially. The fourth and last example is about the housing market. In Germany, increased life expectancy could create an additional demand of about 500,000 dwelling units within the next 10 years, corresponding roughly to a quarter of the capacity of the German construction industry.

What are the policy options? In order to discuss these options, this paper systematically exploits the differences between the US and Germany to shed light on the economic mechanisms underlying retirement, savings and housing choices by the elderly, and how they are affected by public policy, such as institutional arrangements, government regulations and laws. The focus is on three areas: retirement decisions, saving behaviour and housing choices. These three areas are part of the 'Economics of Aging', by now a popular field recently surveyed in the *Journal of Economic Literature* by Clark *et al.* (1978) and by Hurd (1989). Most of the empirical evidence provided here is based on two comparable sets of micro data in West Germany and the US, described in Appendix A. For a more macroeconomic view, the reader is referred to the many comparative studies that describe cross-national differences in the aging process and analyse the aggregate economic implications (e.g. OECD, 1988; Hagemann and Nicoletti, 1989; Auerbach *et al.*, 1990).

The stage is set in Section 2 in which I depict foreseeable demographic changes up until 2030 and wonder whether our social security systems will be able to handle the rapid increase in the proportion of elderly persons. It appears that recent social security reforms in the US and Germany have not fully achieved this goal. In Section 3, I show that there are still some incentives in the public pension systems which encourage early retirement and therefore aggravate the strain on our social security systems. The empirical evidence also reveals that workers have responded strongly to these incentives in the past. Reform is then desirable, and it is likely to achieve its goals. In Section 4, I look at the level of social security payments and wonder whether the public pension system reduces the capital stock by replacing private savings. I conclude that this is only partially the case. Section 5 actually shows that there appears to be an excess of annuity income in old age in West Germany and therefore a surprisingly high level of saving amongst the oldest of the elderly. This raises questions about bequests. Section 6 argues that bequests are largely unintended and can be taxed without distortions.

A third set of policy questions concerns the housing market. Section 7 predicts that the demographic changes will raise the demand for housing, contrary to popular wisdom. In Section 8, I note that distortionary housing subsidies impede mobility, thereby intensifying the strain on housing markets. Moreover, I argue in Section 9 that the elderly are increasingly more likely to live alone than to move in with their adult children, further increasing housing demand and requiring public services. Section 10 pulls together policy conclusions and recommendations.

2. The double aging process in the industrialized countries

Population aging affects all industrialized countries. As Table 1 shows, the proportion of persons aged 65 and more in the OECD area will increase from 13% to more than 20% within the next 40 years. Among the seven large OECD countries, the aging process is most pronounced in Germany, and least pronounced but still dramatic in the UK and in the US. In Germany, the proportion of elderly persons will increase to more than a quarter of the population within the next 40 years. The increase among the oldest old is most pronounced: the absolute number of elderly aged 85 and above will more than double between now and the year 2030. The proportion of households headed by elderly persons

Table 1. Elderly population in seven OECD countries

	Population aged 65 and over (%)				Population aged 80 and over (Millions)	
	1950	1980	1990	2030	1980	2030
Canada	7.7	9.5	11.4	22.4	0.44	1.89
France	11.4	14.0	13.8	21.8	1.53	3.40
Germany	9.4	15.5	15.5	25.8	1.60	2.65
Italy	8.0	13.5	13.8	21.9	1.28	2.56
Japan	5.2	9.1	11.4	20.0	1.63	6.64
UK	10.7	14.9	15.1	19.2	1.48	2.60
US	8.1	11.3	12.2	19.5	5.22	12.43
OECD average	8.5	12.2	13.0	20.5		

Source: OECD (1988).

(aged 60 and above) in the German population is projected to increase from 21% in 1980 to 37% in 2030.[1]

Two distinct processes are causing these startling changes. From 1950–80, life expectancy at birth in the OECD countries has increased by about 7.2% (Table 2). At the same time, fertility has declined in all OECD countries except Ireland and Turkey to a level below that which is required for replacement of the population. The result is the double aging process. It is captured by the old-age dependency ratio in Table 3. This ratio climbs quickly because the numerator (number of elderly) increases due to rising life expectancy while at the same time the denominator (number of non-elderly adults) shrinks due to declining fertility. The numbers for Germany are particularly dramatic. From 1950–80, German life expectancy has increased by almost seven years (from 66.4 to 73.3) while at the same time the fertility rate in West Germany has decreased from 2.1 to 1.4, a rate considerably below the reproduction rate that is necessary for a stable population. These changes imply that eventually almost twice as many elderly aged 65 and above will have to be supported by the same number of persons aged 15 to 64. This ratio will fall again after the year 2030 when the

---

[1] All numbers (source: Statistisches Bundesamt) refer to West Germany. Since East and West Germany have approximately the same age distribution, unification does not significantly affect the conclusions. The only substantive difference is higher fertility in East Germany since 1975, which appears to be caused by the East German child care system that supports both labour force participation and childbearing of young women, in contrast to the severe shortage of child care services in West Germany (Chesnais, 1987). Since the East German child care system is unlikely to be continued, this difference will even out relatively soon.

Table 2. Life expectancy and birth rates for seven OECD countries

	Life expectancy[a]		Fertility rate[b]	
	1950	1980	1950	1980
Canada	68.4	75.0	3.4	1.8
France	66.8	74.3	2.9	1.9
Germany	66.4	73.3	2.1	1.4
Italy	66.1	74.4	2.6	1.7
Japan	59.2	76.4	2.4	1.8
UK	68.9	73.8	3.0	1.8
US	68.4	73.5	2.2	1.8

Source: OECD (1988).
Notes: (a) average life expectancy at birth in years. (b) age-specific fertility rates summed over all ages in child-bearing period.

Table 3. Old-age dependency ratios for seven OECD countries

	1980	2030
Canada	14.1	37.3
France	21.9	35.8
Germany	23.4	43.6
Italy	20.8	35.3
Japan	13.5	31.9
UK	23.2	31.1
US	17.1	31.7
Average of above	19.1	35.2
OECD average	18.9	33.3

Source: OECD (1988).
Note: Number of Persons aged 65 and more per 100 persons aged 15–64.

bulge of the babyboom has worked its way through the age distribution but it is likely to remain at a substantially higher level than now.[2]

3. Social security reform and retirement age

The double aging process will strain our social security systems simply because fewer contributors will have to support more retirees. Without social security reform, the contribution rate necessary to balance the

---

[2] The OECD estimate for the year 2050 is 41.6% for West Germany.

budget of our public pension systems would have to grow proportionally to the ratio of pensioners to workers, roughly in line with the old-age dependency ratio. This is apparent from the budget equation of a pay-as-you-go social security system:

$$\frac{\text{Contribution Rate}}{\text{to Social Security}} = \frac{\text{Pensioners}}{\text{Workers}} \times \frac{\text{Average pension income}}{\text{Average labour income}}$$

$$\times (1 - \text{State subsidy rate})$$

The resulting level of social security taxes will create strong work disincentives. In West Germany, for instance, Schmähl (1989) estimates that contribution rates will exceed 40% of gross labour income. The recent social security reforms in Germany and in the US tried to limit such an increase by raising state subsidies and by effectively lowering the average pension income. Table 4 shows that the problems faced by the social security system may actually be aggravated because the ratio of pensioners to workers could grow substantially faster than the old-age dependency ratio. All major OECD countries have experienced a strong decline in labour supply by the elderly. In West Germany, the average retirement age has fallen well below 60. If this trend goes unchecked, the problems associated with the double aging process will be grossly exacerberated. Until now, the social security reforms in Germany and in the US have only slightly changed the age at which an individual becomes eligible for social security payments. Is it necessary to counter the trend to early retirement more actively?

In principle, as a matter of consumer sovereignty, individuals should be able to decide for themselves when to retire. However, the retirement decision of a generation creates externalities, partly affecting the generation of retirees, but mostly the younger generation. A free-rider problem arises because the older generation could reap higher retirement benefits by retiring earlier. This eventually raises the contribution rate faced by the following generations. The free-rider argument is only valid if social security payments are independent of retirement age, or at least decrease with the retirement age at a pace which is less than is actuarially fair. This is, however, exactly the case in Germany and also, to a lesser extent, in the US. Most of this section investigates whether the trend toward early retirement is actually induced by the current social security system itself, and whether a reduction in the incentives to retire early is likely to result in a reversal of this trend.

There are some other, macroeconomic, effects. If productivity is age-specific, a shift in the average retirement age will change aggregate productivity. If wages are not systematically equal to (marginal) productivity at the individual level, externalities are bound to arise and public policy intervention is warranted. Unfortunately, the evidence on age-earnings profiles, even more so on age-productivity profiles, is scant and contradictory[3] so that the issue is inconclusive. Another macroeconomic effect is the interaction between retirement age and saving behaviour. If earlier retirement implies a quicker accumulation of wealth, the steady-state stock of capital stock could increase, which would raise average aggregate productivity. The size of this effect depends on the extent to which consumption during retirement has to be financed from wealth accumulated while working. Evidence presented in Section 5 shows that the size of this effect is probably quite small.

In order to gauge to which extent retirement policies affect the choice of retirement age – particularly, whether they have contributed to the trend towards early retirement – I use three pieces of evidence. First, I check whether changes in the elderly's labour force participation are linked over time to changes in the ratio of retirement to labour income. Second, I exploit a 1984 survey to see whether the distribution of retirement ages can be explained by institutional differences between Germany and the US. Although both Germany and the US have pay-as-you-go public pension systems which supply in effect a minimum level of retirement income and feature a fairly broad coverage of workers by social security, the two countries differ substantially in the particulars of their pension systems.[4] Finally, I estimate how alternative retirement-age-dependent benefit formulae influence the choice of retirement age. The findings complement earlier research by Kotlikoff and Wise (1987) and Stock and Wise (1990) for the US, and Jacobs *et al.* (1987, 1990) for Germany. They all report that retirement decisions do respond to incentives.

3.1. Changes over time

Although the retirement age in both West Germany and the US has declined, labour force participation of the elderly has reached a substantially lower rate in West Germany (Table 4). The German participation rate is now the lowest in the seven major OECD countries. Only Japan features a very high elderly labour force participation rate. This decline,

---

[3] Lazear (1990) links a rising age-earnings profile to productivity increases. Kotlikoff and Wise (1989) report evidence on hump-shaped age-earnings profiles with productivity falling after age 55 for office workers, and even earlier after age 45 for salesmen. Lehr (1987) stresses the diversity of workers and rejects the validity of universal age-productivity relations. Indirect evidence for quite different age-productivity relations across German industries can be found in Jacobs *et al.* (1990).

[4] In the US, about 95% of all workers are insured by Social Security, including the self-employed, while in West Germany only the self-employed (8.9% of the labour force in 1988) and workers with very small incomes (5.6%) are not covered (Casmir, 1989).

Table 4. Labour force participation rates aged 65 and over for seven OECD countries (%)

	1965	1975	1985
Canada	26.3	18.5	12.3
France	28.3	13.9	5.3
Germany	24.0	10.8	5.2
Italy	18.4	10.4	8.9
Japan	56.3	44.4	37.0
UK	23.7	15.8	7.6
US	26.6	20.7	10.3

Source: OECD (1988).

Table 5. Indices of retirement and wage income

	US		West Germany	
Year	Retirement	Wage income	Retirement	Wage income
1960	100.0	100.0	100.0	100.0
1970	158.8	175.6	218.5	207.4
1980	458.9	374.0	431.2	409.3

Sources: *Statistical Abstracts of the United States, Statistische Jahrbücher für die Bundesrepublik Deutschland.*

and its evolution over time, is in line with the incentives provided by the pension systems. In both the US and Germany retirement income has risen faster than labour income, increasing the attractiveness of retirement (Table 5). In both countries this evolution is due to the indexation of social security benefits. In West Germany, for example, pension benefits have been linked to gross average labour income (the Social Security Reform Act of 1992 has changed this to indexation with respect to net income). Because retirement income is taxed at a much lower rate than labour income, if at all, net retirement income has increased even faster relatively to net labour income. The response of the participation by the elderly to the labour force has been in line. In Germany, the continuing evolution of relative incomes is mirrored by large continuous declines in the participation rate, while in the US the recent slowdown in the decline of the participation rate corresponds to an increase in the ratio of labour to retirement income.

One possible reason for the elderly labour force participation to decline further in Germany than in the US is provided by Table 6. Net replacement ratios (average after-tax retirement income as a percentage

Table 6. Replacement ratios of social security old age pensions

Income (multiple of APW Wages)[a]	New replacement ratio (%)[b]	
	US	Germany
0.5	61	67
0.75	55	66
1	53	71
1.5	45	77
2	41	75
3	30	53

Source: Casmir (1989), p. 508 and 512.
Notes: (a) Wages of an 'Average Production Worker' (OECD definition). (b) Net replacement ratios for a worker with 40 years service. Married couple supplement not included.

of average after-tax labour income) of German public pensions are substantially higher than in the US, particularly so for higher incomes. On average, German social security income (and the associated intangible wealth) is about 33% higher, resulting in an average net replacement ratio of more than 70%, providing German workers with a stronger incentive to retire early.

3.2. Survey of individual behaviour

Other differences between the German and the US pension systems can be used to improve our understanding of the distribution of retirement ages. The first one is mandatory retirement. In West Germany, about a quarter of the labour force is subject to mandatory retirement, including the entire public sector. In most cases, mandatory retirement age is 65. In the US, age discrimination laws prohibit mandatory retirement. Part-time work is also very restricted in West Germany. Next, while social security provisions in both countries offer the opportunity to retire at different ages (the so-called 'window of retirement'), they differ considerably in how benefit levels vary with retirement ages. Table 7 displays these adjustments. They relate the statutory retirement income for retirement at age 65 (normalized to 100%) to the retirement income for earlier or later retirement ages. The first column represents the actuarially fair adjustment that would leave the present discounted value of retirement benefits unchanged for all retirement ages. Neither system is actuarially fair but the US public retirement system offers considerably less incentive for Americans to retire at any particular age during the window of early retirement (and only a small disincentive

Table 7. Adjustment of public pensions by retirement age

| Actual retirement age | Pension as a percentage of the pension that one would obtain if one had retired at age 65 | | | |
	Actuarially fair[a]	US[b]	Germany[c]	
60	59.8	0.0[d]	0.0[d]	87.5[e]
61	65.8	0.0[d]	0.0[d]	90.0[e]
62	72.6	80.0	0.0[d]	92.5[e]
63	80.4	86.7	95.0[f]	
64	89.5	94.4	97.5[f]	
65	100.0	100.0	100.0	
66	112.5	103.0	109.9	
67	127.5	106.0	120.1	
68	145.9	109.0	123.0	
69	168.9	112.0	125.8	
70	198.5	115.0	128.7	

Source: Frerich (1987); Casmir (1989).
Notes: (a) Discount rate = 0.03, life expectancy = 77 years. (b) Social Security (OASDHI) as of 1989. (c) 'Gesetzliche Rentenversicherung' as of 1990. (d) Not yet vested. (e) Right-hand value for women and workers who cannot be appropriately employed due to health or job mismatch reasons. (f) Requires 35 years service.

to retire after 65). The German system tilts retirement heavily towards the earliest possible age.[5]

A third difference concerns the role of private pensions. In the US, private firms provide substantially more retirement income than in West Germany. About half of the American elderly aged 60 and above are covered by private pension plans, and on average, firm pensions contribute to more than 15% of retirement income (Hurd, 1989). In West Germany, private pensions provide only slightly more than 3% of average retirement income (SOEP, 1984). Moreover, firm pension provisions in the US are very diverse across firms even within the same industry (Kotlikoff and Wise, 1987) while pension plans are rather homogeneous in Germany (Jacobs *et al.*, 1987), mainly due to government and union regulations.

All three institutional differences should lead to a more uniform retirement behaviour in Germany than in the US, where there is a host

---

[5] Curiously, the German system provides a large increase in retirement benefits for work at ages 66 and 67 which is ineffective because the inducements to early retirement by far offset this incentive.

Table 8. Male retirement and labour force participation rates

Age	US			West Germany		
	Full-time	Part-time	Retired	Full-time	Part-time	Retired
50–54	76.6	11.0	12.4	91.5	0.6	7.8
55–59	65.9	17.4	16.7	79.1	1.5	19.4
60–64	38.8	16.9	44.3	37.7	1.6	60.8
65–69	12.2	22.3	65.4	4.1	7.5	88.4
70–74	7.2	13.7	79.1	1.7	3.2	95.3
75–79	2.5	12.7	84.8	2.5	1.7	95.7
80+	1.6	4.8	93.5	1.2	0.0	98.8

Source: PSID, 1984, SOEP, 1984, Male heads of household only.
Notes: Full time: More than 35 hours work per week. Part-time: 15–30 hours work per week. Retired: less than 15 hours work per week.

of individual and firm-specific provisions. This is confirmed by Table 8 which presents retirement rates for males in West Germany and the US, based on the survey data described in Appendix A. Since incentives for part-time work are different in the two countries, a distinction is made between full retirement from partial retirement or part-time work and full retirement from full-time work. The range of retirement ages is much larger in the US than in West Germany. While the US feature a smooth transition between work and retirement with a large percentage of part-time work, the German age-retirement profile is characterized by a sudden jump from full-time work to full-time retirement with range 60–64, accompanied by a rather low percentage of part-time occupation. Figure 2 makes this point graphically. With an adjustment of benefits to retirement age close to what is actuarially fair in the US, people retire at all ages in the interior of the window period. In West Germany retirement is concentrated at ages 60, 63 and 65, the earliest retirement ages applicable for three groups of workers in Germany.[6] Only very few people retire at ages in between these dates or after 65.

3.3. The choice of retirement age

In order to capture the economic incentives provided by the pension system (Lazear and Moore, 1988; Stock and Wise, 1990) and thereby to predict the effectiveness of a social security reform, I use the option value of postponing retirement. The option value measures for each retirement age and tradeoff between retiring now (resulting in a stream

---

[6] Women and workers affected by health or mismatch problems may retire at 60. Workers with at least 35 years of service are eligible at age 63, all others at age 65.

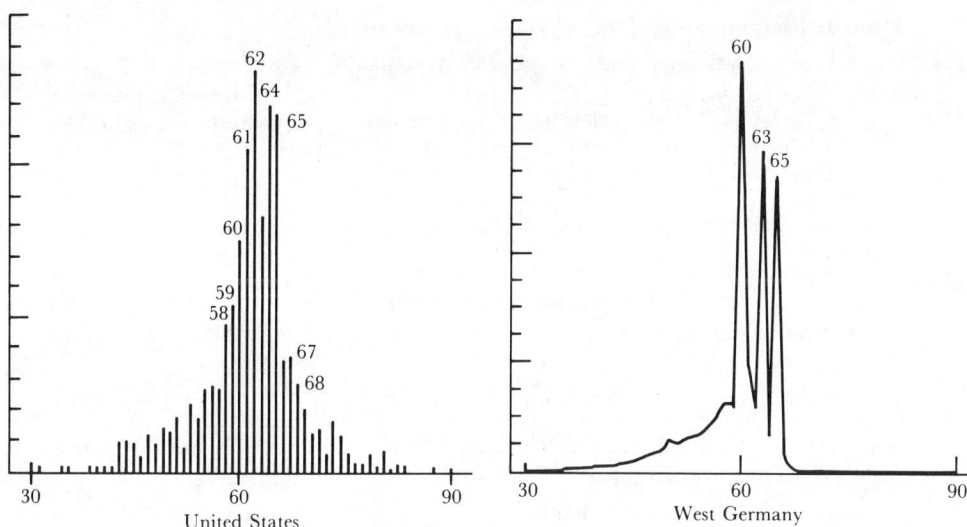

Figure 2. Distribution of retirement ages

Sources: PSID, 1984; 1984 *Rentenzugangs Statistik*.

of retirement benefits that depends on this retirement age) and keeping all options open for some later retirement date (with associated streams of labour and then retirement incomes for all possible later retirement ages). The option value for a specific age is computed as the difference between the maximum attainable consumption (utility) if the worker postpones retirement to some later date minus (the utility of) consumption that the worker can afford if she retired now. Since a worker is likely to retire as soon as the value of the option of postponing retirement becomes smaller than the value of retiring now, retirement probabilities should be negatively related to the option value. Because the attainable consumption depends on the ratio of labour income to retirement income as well as on the adjustment of pensions to retirement age, the option value captures *all* the economic incentives created by the pension system. The construction of the option value is explained in more detail in Appendix B.

The regression equation in Table 9 relates the probability of being retired to the option value, while allowing for other socio-economic characteristics of each individual in the sample. These other characteristics are coded as dummy variables, except for the number of children and housing and non-housing wealth which are defined in Section 4.[7]

---

[7] In order to be conservative and to control for any other age specific effects not captured by socio-demographic and economic variables, e.g. customary retirement dates, a set of dummy variables for each retirement age is included.

Table 9. Determinants of the retirement probability

Variable	US elasticity	*t*-statistic	West Germany elasticity	*t*-statistic
Constant	2.559	5.77	1.237	0.53
Non-white	−0.105	5.02	—	—
Female	−0.681	4.76	0.067	0.26
Married	0.042	0.73	−0.097	0.87
Children	−0.307	3.53	−0.001	0.41
Non-housing assets	1.394	0.85	−0.805	4.39
House value	0.810	1.72	0.200	0.74
Option value to postpone retirement	−0.463	5.32	−0.638	5.61
Age 61	−1.313	3.01	0.605	1.23
Age 62	−0.786	2.62	0.289	0.55
Age 63	−0.395	1.37	1.694	2.55
Age 64	−0.849	2.64	0.575	1.04
Age 65	−0.526	1.69	−0.070	0.11
Age 66	0.048	0.16	1.180	1.73
Age 67	0.160	0.50	1.714	2.97
Age 68 and above	−0.001	0.01	2.080	3.13
Likelihood value	−649.66	(−790.19)	−166.87	(−391.63)
Percent correct	71.3		89.4	
Observations	1,140		565	

Source: PSID, 1984 and SOEP, 1984. Heads of households only.
Notes: Dependent variable is the probability of being retired. The regression equation is $\text{Prob(Retired)} = L(\alpha \text{AGE} + \beta \text{Option value} + \gamma.\text{Worker characteristics})$ where L denotes the logistic transformation. The coefficients β and γ have been converted to elasticities. Age 60 is the reference case for α. Likelihood value is the value of the loglikelihood function at estimated coefficients (at zero in parentheses).

Except for the constant and the age-specific dummy variables, the regression coefficients have been converted to elasticities. They represent the percentage change in the probability of being retired when the respective variable is changed by 1%. The lower fit of the US regression reflects heterogeneity in retirement behaviour and lack of information on the applicable firm-specific private pension plans. The elasticity with respect to the option value is statistically highly significant and quite similar in the two countries. The age-specific coefficients are insignificant except for age 63 and the very late retirees in the German regression. This is a strong finding because it implies that during the main window of retirement, the actual behaviour is well described by the option value. The pattern of the age-specific coefficients helps to assess the predictive power of the option value. If the option value would perfectly predict the distribution of retirement ages, the age-specific coefficients should be insignificant. They are not, partly because

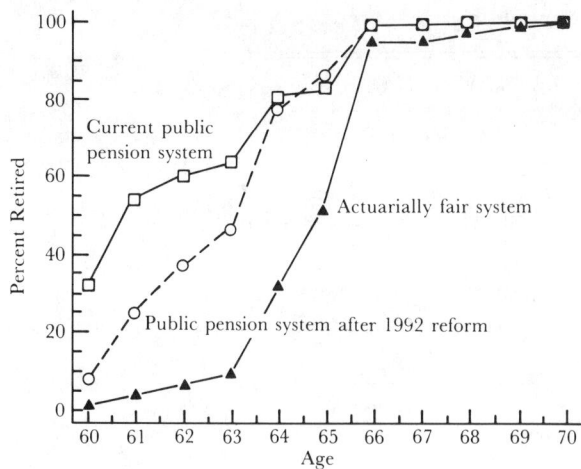

Figure 3. Simulated cumulative retirement probabilities

Source: *West German Retirement Probability Model*, Table 9.

of missing information on the early retirement incentives provided by firm pensions in the US and on eligibility for retirement due to the job mismatch clause in Germany, and partly due to social customs.

The results show that an important part of the trend towards early retirement is induced by the pension systems. Two conclusions follow. First, it is quite ill-advised to use adjustments to the retirement age to balance the budget of the pension system (except for setting eligibility dates for early retirement). Second, existing systems are not actuarially fair. Figure 3 shows that an actuarially fair formula would shift the average retirement age up by about three years in Germany. This simulation uses the retirement probability implied by Table 9 to predict retirement ages under three alternative adjustment formulae: the current German system, the one scheduled for 1992, and the actuarially fair system of Table 7.

4. Does social security wealth replace private wealth?

If social security contributions and private saving were perfect substitutes (the subject of much controversy, see Barro, 1974, and Feldstein, 1974) a fully funded social security system would be preferable to the present pay-as-you-go social security system. Indeed the latter generates a smaller capital stock with lower aggregate productivity, or the need to attract foreign capital. The differences between the German and US social security programmes offer a chance to measure potential substitution effects. The public pension system in Germany provides a

Table 10. Average tangible household wealth

| | Sum of tangible assets ($ 000) | | |
| | US | West Germany | |
Age		Valued at purchasing power	Valued at • exchange rate
50–54	92.1	73.9	46.5
55–59	95.3	73.2	46.1
60–64	86.7	96.4	60.7
65–69	76.6	71.8	45.2
70–74	69.5	68.1	42.9
75–79	75.6	60.1	37.9
80+	67.7	60.8	38.3

Source: PSID, 1984, SOEP, 1988 at 1984 prices.
Notes: Sum of assets reported in Table 13. Average exchange
rate 1984: $1 = DM 2.70. Average purchasing power parity 1984:
$1 = DM 1.70.

substantially more generous replacement of net income across all
income ranges (Table 6). The question arises as to whether the high
replacement ratio in Germany reduces the incentive to save for consumption during retirement more than in the US.

Table 10 displays total tangible wealth by household, stratified by age
categories. Non-housing wealth is defined as the sum of financial wealth
plus real estate, farm and business property, excluding owner-occupied
homes (see Appendix A for details and sources). The roughly 20%
lower private wealth in Germany (valued at purchasing power) corresponds to the 33% higher level of intangible social security wealth
implied by the higher replacement ratio. This shows that there is some
substitution between public and private savings, but by no means a
complete one. The substitution is even less complete when the intangible
wealth provided by the health insurance system is accounted for. In
Germany, virtually all retirees are enrolled in a mandatory health
insurance system which covers all health expenditures, with the only
exception of long-term institutionalized care that is not related to acute
illness. This coverage is far more comprehensive than Medicaid and
Medicare in the US.

One may argue that this evidence is marred by measurement errors
in average household wealth. Table 11 shows, however, that the composition of the elderly's income nicely matches the proportion of private
and public savings. In West Germany, annuity income (almost exclusively social security income) is the most important income source for

Table 11. Sources of income (%)

Age	US			West Germany		
	Wage/salary	Annuities	Assets	Wage/salary	Annuities	Assets
50–54	75.6	18.7	5.6	85.4	7.3	7.3
55–59	66.1	26.0	7.8	76.5	14.4	9.0
60–64	43.2	47.4	9.3	37.0	51.9	11.1
65–69	14.5	70.1	14.8	4.1	87.0	8.9
70–74	6.4	79.9	13.7	2.7	82.0	15.3
75–79	2.6	74.1	23.2	0.6	81.8	17.6
80+	1.8	72.9	25.3	0.7	86.3	12.9

Source: PSID, 1984, SOEP, 1984.
Notes: (a) Wage and salary income includes full- and part-time wages. (b) Annuity income includes social security, pensions and other transfers. (c) Asset income includes interest, dividends, rents and profits.

**Table 12. Aggregate savings rates
(% of personal disposable income)**

Year	US	West Germany
1960	5.8	8.6
1965	7.0	12.2
1970	8.1	13.8
1975	9.2	15.1
1980	7.1	12.8
1985	5.1	11.4

Sources: *Economic Report of the President*, Statistical Appendix. Statistisches Bundesamt, *Volkswirtschaftliche Gesamtrechnung.*

all households aged 60 and above. Asset and labour income play a more important role in the US. For very old Americans (aged 75 and above), income from assets amounts to about a quarter of total income.[8] The incomplete substitution between private and public wealth is also reflected in the higher national saving rate in Germany (Table 12). Although all three pieces of evidence point in the same direction, the findings should be interpreted keeping the pitfalls of any international comparison in mind. One aspect is the historical background. The German elderly have all experienced World War II in a much more frightening

---

[8] These numbers, drawn from the PSID, 1984, are similar to those obtained from the much larger sample of the American Current Population Survey (Hurd, 1989).

Table 13. Assets holdings by age and asset category
(Averages across households, in $ 000)

	US				West Germany			
Age	Savings	Stocks/ bonds	Non- housing	Own housing	Savings	Stocks/ bonds	Non- housing	Own housing
50–54	9.5	7.4	40.2	51.9	9.7	5.3	19.8	54.2
55–59	12.4	13.3	47.1	48.2	10.3	6.1	29.8	43.4
60–64	19.1	10.6	45.1	41.6	10.3	6.6	41.9	54.5
65–69	18.8	4.6	37.8	38.8	9.2	6.6	35.0	36.8
70–74	17.9	6.8	38.0	31.5	9.1	7.6	22.4	45.7
75–79	19.9	8.7	41.3	34.3	9.1	8.0	31.4	28.7
80+	23.8	2.7	37.2	30.5	10.4	8.7	31.0	29.8

Source: PSID, 1984, SOEP, 1988 at 1984 prices, valued at purchasing power parity ($1 = DM 1.70).
Notes: (a) Savings includes pass book savings, MMMFs and dedicated savings (IRA, Keogh, Bausparkassen etc.). (b) Stocks/Bonds. (c) Non-Housing wealth is financial wealth plus real estate (except owner-occupied home), farm and business property. (d) Housing wealth is estimated sales value of owner-occupied home. All value are self-reported.

way than their American contemporaries. Lower customary consumption levels, higher risk-aversion, or public campaigns promoting saving during the so-called economic miracle of the 1950s may also explain the high aggregate saving rates that have emerged in West Germany as soon as a moderate standard of living was achieved in the 1960s.

5. Are the elderly overannuitized?

Table 13 further shows that, at a detailed level, age-wealth profiles are quite different in the two countries. While American elderly's non-housing wealth declines with age after 55, the German age-wealth profile is irregularly shaped with a pronounced peak at ages 60–64, rising again at old ages. This pattern is not specific to the relatively small sample on which Table 13 is based. The same pattern is also evident in a much larger sample (the 1983 Consumer Expenditure Survey, see Börsch-Supan and Stahl, 1990). In the US, the elderly aged 80 and above still hold more than two-thirds of the maximum wealth attained immediately before retirement. Beyond these differences, the age-wealth profiles show that in both countries the elderly have a substantial amount of financial assets even at old age, particularly so in West Germany.

The high saving rate among the very old is puzzling. Even though the age-wealth profiles depicted in Table 13 should be interpreted with care because the cross-sectional data in this table does not allow for a

Table 14. German elderly with expenditures lower than annuity income

| | Percentage of elderly in age group with a ratio of annuity income to consumption expenditures of: | | | |
	<1.0	1.0 to 1.2	1.2 to 1.5	>1.5
50–54	97.7	1.5	0.5	0.3
55–59	92.0	3.9	2.9	1.2
60–64	69.3	13.4	11.4	5.9
65–69	47.3	23.5	18.0	11.2
70–74	42.9	22.7	20.6	13.8
75–79	38.1	19.2	21.6	21.1
80+	30.5	17.3	23.2	29.0

Source: EVS, 1983, based on 18,259 elderly age 50 and above.
Notes: Annuity income include public and private pensions, payments from life insurance and private transfers.

distinction between age and cohort effects, the sheer magnitude of wealth still held in old age (past life expectancy!) contradicts the predictions of the pure life cycle hypothesis. Nor can it be explained by the precautionary saving motive, because the more generous German health insurance system should have generated lower rather than higher private savings in Germany. (Section 6 further argues that bequests are not a powerful saving motive.)

Rather than wondering why the elderly save so much, I ask why they consume so little. Table 14, drawn from Börsch-Supan and Stahl (1990), displays the proportion of elderly households whose consumption is smaller than their annuity income (essentially public pension income in Germany). This proportion increases with age, in line with the age-wealth profiles above. For about a quarter of the elderly aged 75 and more, annuity income is more than 50% above consumption expenditures. The decline in consumption expenditure, much too large to be explained solely by underreporting, can be traced to a drop in food, travel and transportation consumption. These are commodities which we expect to see consumed in lesser amounts as age increases, largely because of poor health. Due to the compulsory health insurance programme in Germany, this decline is not offset by larger health expenditures. Thus, the elderly may actually find themselves saving out of annuity income, and not drawing down their existing wealth as they may have planned to do. Note that even if this decline were anticipated, capital market imperfections and human nature would prevent borrowing against the wealth accumulated in old age.

That the German elderly are 'overannuitized' has implications for social security reform. Notwithstanding the need to prevent poverty among some of the elderly, it may be reasonable to adjust annuity incomes more than the recent social security reforms in Germany and the US did, or at least to tax wealth more heavily. The need to finance social security will require either higher contributions by the young or less benefits to the elderly, possibly including a wealth tax. The efficiency losses from increased contribution rates outweigh the dangers of insufficient savings created by higher wealth taxes since these assets are effectively locked.

6. The taxation of bequests

A prominent motive for holding wealth, even at very old age, is bequests. It is even sometimes asserted that intergenerational transfers contribute more to aggregate wealth accumulation than life cycle savings. Bequests indeed are a major source of wealth. Estimates of the volume of bequests range from about 1.8% of GDP in the US (Kotlikoff and Summers, 1981) to 3% of GDP in France (Kessler, 1990). The taxation of bequests is therefore an important policy issue. Bequests tend to make children of rich people rich themselves and therefore create persistent inequality within generations (Atkinson, 1983). This is a reason to tax heavily bequests and related gifts *inter vivos*. However, bequests may also serve as a mechanism in the economic relationship between generations. They may, for example, serve as an implicit efficient price for family support and care (Kessler, 1990). This is put into an extreme form by Bernheim *et al.* (1985) who claim that bequests are used by the elderly to influence the young's behaviour. If this were the case, taxation of bequests would distort these mechanisms and therefore create inefficiencies, for example, too little family care which must then be supplied, presumably less efficiently, by the state.

This all presumes that bequests are intended. Unintended bequests may arise from precautionary savings to cover health and longevity risks, or from savings due to unanticipated constraints on the ability to enjoy consumption, as noted in the previous section. In that case, the previous equity and efficiency arguments do not apply. To date, there is no sufficient evidence to determine whether bequests are intended or not. The regression in Table 15 shows that wealth is negatively correlated with the number of children. (Although housing wealth is larger for elderly who had children, inclusion of housing wealth does not change the negative sign as long as income is held constant.)

In spite of the differences in saving behaviour and wealth accumulation between Germany and the US, the regression results are quite

Table 15. Regression of non-housing wealth on number of children

Variable	US		West Germany	
	Parameter	t-statistic	Parameter	t-statistic
Constant	−86.24	−2.18	−95.03	−6.01
Net Income	25.58	13.03	32.19	26.52
Age	1.30	2.31	1.12	5.31
Children	−6.64	−1.95	−8.32	−1.84
R-squared	0.13		0.47	
Observations	1,180		805	

Source: PSID, 1984 and SOEP, 1988.
Note: The dependent variable is non-housing wealth as defined in Table 13.

similar for the two countries. The results support the view that bequests are mostly unintended. Two comments on Table 15 are warranted. First, gifts to children while still alive may take the place of bequests. According to survey data, this is not the case, but the data may be subject to severe underreporting. Second, the negative relation between the number of children and wealth may simply reflect the fact that raising children is expensive and may well thwart the accumulation of assets. This argument, however, really suggests that families with many children cannot afford large bequests, so that the taxation of bequests is not likely to create large inefficiencies.

7. Housing market shortages

Even though they have attracted much less attention, the effects of an aging population on future housing markets are no less serious. The housing market concerns almost everyone simply because housing is the single most important household asset as well as the single most important expenditure in the average household budget. Contrary to popular wisdom, the demographic changes in the coming decades are likely to increase, not decrease, housing demand. Population aging, particularly increased life expectancy, implies an increased length of stay in the family home by the older generation. Hence, fewer dwellings are transferred to the younger generation. The intergenerational transfer of housing is an important mechanism of housing supply. The direct transfer alone (the number of homes that are inherited) amounts to 28% of all owned homes in West Germany (SOEP, 1988). The indirect transfer (via moving chains) is much larger: in the US, for instance, about 74% of all recent home buyers purchased existing homes (1983, *Statistical Abstract*).

The magnitude of this effect is substantial enough to create a short-run scarcity of housing. In West Germany, it may correspond to as much as a quarter of the annual number of newly constructed dwellings as can be seen by the following back-of-the-envelope calculation. The 350,000 persons currently aged 80 correspond to approximately 250,000 households. If a one-year increase in life expectancy implies that this cohort will stay one year longer in their current dwellings, housing demand increases by 250,000 units. Since life expectancy has increased by one year in Germany from 1981–86, the demand effect represents some 50,000 units per annum, about 22% of the 225,000 new dwelling units constructed in 1986. The calculation is robust to two criticisms. First, one may argue that the elderly might not be able to spend their increased life span in their own homes, but Section 9 will provide evidence to the contrary. Second, one may wonder whether this effect could not at least partially be offset by the smaller size of young cohorts which enter the housing market. Yet, what determines housing demand is the number of households, not population count; the long-run trend is toward smaller average bousehold size and larger dwellings.

These strains along with market imperfections call for policy intervention. First, the conventional arguments for encouraging housing construction apply *a fortiori* in times of population aging; that supply reacts to demand with long time-lags produces unacceptably large cycles with a corresponding overreaction of housing prices (Mankiw and Weil, 1989). Since housing price cycles are difficult to anticipate, they result in consumption squeezes and intergenerational inequity. This means that housing supply should be encouraged in advance. Second, frictions which inhibit the intergenerational transfer of housing should be alleviated. These frictions include distortionary policy measures that impede mobility (Section 8) and disincentives to household dissolution (Section 9).

8. Mobility distortions

Policy intervention in housing markets is intense both in Germany and in the US. Subsidies and regulations strongly distort the choice of tenure as well as mobility and living arrangement decisions. They are, however, quite different in Germany and the US (Box 1) and make rental housing more attractive in Germany and owned housing more attractive in the US. The German tenants' protection legislation substantially discourages housing mobility. Because mobility in owner-occupied housing is small, subsidies in the US also indirectly reduce mobility.

Box 1. Housing subsidies and regulations in Germany and the US

In the US most subsidies are directed to home ownership, towards rental housing in Germany (Mayo and Barnbrock, 1985). The average home ownership subsidy (deductions from income taxes) is about 2.5 to 3 times higher in the US than in West Germany (Börsch-Supan, 1985). The main reason is that mortgage interest is deductible without upper limit for the purchase of home and land in the US, which induces more consumption in terms of land, dwelling space and housing quality. In Germany, only the depreciation of the dwelling can be deducted up to a limit below the average value of dwelling and land. Rental housing subsidies in the US are directed to low-income families, while the rental allowances in Germany (covering on average 23% of rents) are administered as entitlements, with most older people eligible for housing assistance. These aspects are amplified by differences in rental housing market regulations. Germany has very stringent tenant protection laws, forbidding eviction and severely capping rent increases. On average, a household with a 14-year tenure pays 24% less rent for a comparable dwelling unit than a household which has just moved in (Behring *et al.*, 1988). In the US, only very few cities have rental housing regulations, most notably New York.

Table 16 presents ownership rates and average relative shares of housing and non-housing assets for the elderly. Home ownership among them stands at roughly 70% in the US, while it is below 50% in West Germany. In both countries, ownership rates peak at age 55–59 and decline thereafter. Table 17 presents mobility rates in the two countries, defined as the percentage of all elderly households that have moved within the last 12 months. Mobility rates are much lower in Germany for all age groups, particularly so for those aged 70 and above who move about five times less frequently than their American counterparts. The large number of moves among elderly aged 80 and above in the US are mostly moves to their adult children.

The financial and regulatory incentives which reduce mobility also induce the elderly to live in housing units that are larger (and more expensive) than those which they would choose in an undistorted housing market. If the elderly move, they release larger dwelling units for the younger generation. On average, in both countries recent movers have about one room less than stayers (Table 18). Thus, housing market distortions make it more difficult for younger households to buy larger

Table 16. Ownership rates and shares of housing and non-housing assets (%)

	US			West Germany		
		Asset shares:			Asset shares:	
Age	Ownership rate	Housing	Other	Ownership rate	Housing	Other
50–54	75.8	63.4	36.6	56.3	73.3	26.7
55–59	76.0	61.2	38.8	60.8	59.3	40.7
60–64	73.5	58.4	41.6	53.7	56.5	43.5
65–69	69.2	55.5	44.5	49.2	51.3	48.7
70–74	64.8	50.1	49.9	41.7	67.1	32.9
75–79	68.4	53.1	46.9	46.7	48.3	51.7
80+	62.4	46.2	53.8	40.8	49.0	51.0

Source: PSID, 1984 and SOEP, 1988.
Notes: (a) Housing wealth is estimated sales price of owner-occupied home. See Table 13 for definition of other assets.

Table 17. Mobility rates (%)

Age	US	West Germany
50–54	10.6	2.6
55–59	10.2	2.0
60–64	9.4	2.5
65–69	6.9	2.8
70–74	9.1	1.8
75–79	4.8	1.1
80+	15.4	1.3

Source: PSID, 1984 and SOEP, 1984.
Note: Movers are households who moved within the last 12 months prior to being interviewed. Mobility rate is the percentage of movers among all households.

housing units.[9] Table 18 also shows that mobility-impeding regulations reduce dwelling size adjustments among the aged. Although West Germans have smaller houses than Americans when they are aged

[9] This result is in line with panel data observations (Venti and Wise, 1990; Feinstein and McFadden, 1988). The observed reduction in dwelling size does not, at least on average, imply a reduction in housing quality, thus welfare of the elderly. There is little if any adjustment of housing equity among elderly American homeowners when they move. Other dimensions of housing quality have obviously been exchanged for dwelling size. This observation is important because it implies that there is little 'lock-in', i.e. low income elderly with large housing wealth which they cannot cash in. Elderly homeowners do not, on average, want to exchange it for higher current income. Moreover, almost all elderly with low housing wealth also have low financial wealth (Venti and Wise, 1990).

Table 18. Housing consumption (dwelling size)

Age	US			West Germany		
	Number of rooms			Number of rooms		
	Mover	Non-mover	Per capita	Mover	Non-mover	Per capita
50–54	3.8	5.0	1.9			1.6
55–59	3.2	4.8	2.0			1.7
60–64	2.7	4.5	2.1			2.1
65–69	3.3	4.2	2.2	2.8	3.7	2.3
70–74	3.0	4.1	2.3			2.2
75–79	3.3	3.9	2.3			2.2
80+	2.7	4.0	2.4			2.4

Source: PSID, 1984 and SOEP, 1984.
Notes: Number of rooms excluding kitchen, bathrooms and rooms smaller than six square metres.

50–54, this difference levels out when they become older. In fact, there is little if any reduction of dwelling size among German homeowners as they age. Although movers reduce dwelling size, there are just too few of them to have an impact on average housing consumption. Per capita housing consumption increases in both countries, a natural consequence of the decreasing household size when a spouse deceases. In the US, this increase is partially offset by moves to smaller dwellings, in contrast to West Germany which features a much steeper increase of per capita dwelling size consumption.

9. Living arrangements of the oldest old

Housing and living arrangement choices by the oldest old strongly influence their psychic and economic well-being and have far reaching implications for the welfare of the entire population. Living alone makes coping with illnesses harder and may even induce illnesses because of the feeling of being left alone. Hence, when the elderly choose to stay alone, not only is the scarcity of housing exacerbated, but also the need for social support services, such as district nursing or meals-on-wheels, grows. Elderly who do not choose to stay alone live with others, particularly with family members, or in an institution. However, as the ratio of children to elderly decreases, the capacity of younger families to house their parents will diminish. This scarcity will be amplified by the expected rise of female labour force participation. This will call for an increase in institutional alternatives such as nursing and old-age homes, straining the transfer system because unsubsidized nursing home fees exceed the financial abilities of most of the elderly.[10]

Choices of living arrangements are also distorted by a combination of tax and health insurance provisions in Germany. The German compulsory health insurance includes coverage for unlimited hospital care and for many home care services as a substitute for hospital care, but there is virtually no compensation for in-home care of elderly parents, particularly in the case of a working daughter who gives up her job in order to care for her parent (a tax deduction of just DM 1,800 is awarded in this case). In the US, on the contrary, uncovered hospital and nursing home bills may force the elderly to leave hospital and nursing homes early to stay with their children. In Germany both health care coverage and public subsidies reduce rental housing costs for the elderly. This, along with the generally tighter social safety net for the elderly, produces economic disincentives for family support and shared living arrangements relative to the US.

These disincentives are indeed reflected in cross-national comparisons. In Table 19, an elderly person lives 'independently' if no other person lives in the household, except a spouse or minor children. 'Shared living arrangements' occur if at least one other person lives in the household, most frequently an adult child. Here, I differentiate between 'head' and 'subfamily' status. In the first case, the elderly person is head of the composite household, while in the second case somebody else is the head, most frequently the adult child who has taken her or his parent in. Finally, institutions include nursing homes, old-age homes, etc. The most significant difference in living arrangement choices concerns the percentage of shared living arrangements. In the US almost a third of the very old live with their adult children or others, while this proportion is only one-fifth in West Germany. The percentage living alone is about comparable for the elderly aged 65 and above while the percentage living as couples is substantially lower in the US, due to the much higher divorce rate (22 divorces per 10,000 married women in the US, 8.3 in West Germany in 1986).[11]

---

[10] This is not in contradiction to the results of Section 5. During the entire life cycle, average wealth never even comes close to the level necessary to cover nursing home costs.

[11] The data unfortunately do not produce reliable estimates of institutionalization. The SOEP starts in 1984 with a non-institutionalized sample and therefore underestimates the percentage of elderly living in nursing homes. The PSID attempts to keep track of institutionalized sample persons with less than perfect success. If at all, these panel studies reveal a decreasing proportion of elderly living with adult children and an increasing proportion living alone and in institutions (Börsch-Supan, 1990; Ellwood and Kane, 1990).

Table 19. Living arrangements of the elderly

| | US | | | | West Germany | | | | |
| | Independent | | Shared | | Independent | | Shared | | |
Age	Couple	Alone	Head	Sub-family	Couple	Alone	Head	Sub-family	Institu-tion
50–54	55.3	14.2	17.6	12.2	82.2	7.9	7.3	2.6	0.0
55–59	58.3	16.9	13.8	10.1	82.9	8.5	7.2	1.4	0.0
60–64	51.2	20.1	18.6	9.4	77.2	14.3	5.9	2.4	0.2
65–69	48.7	25.5	14.3	11.2	67.6	22.1	6.4	3.7	0.3
70–74	44.0	33.3	12.0	8.8	56.8	34.2	5.1	3.1	0.8
75–79	38.5	40.3	9.5	11.3	43.9	43.5	3.7	6.5	2.4
80+	18.6	46.6	9.0	23.5	30.1	45.8	4.6	15.3	4.2

Source: PSID, 1984 and SOEP, 1988.
Notes: (a) Independent: No other adult except spouse in household. (b) Shared (Head): Elderly is head of household with another family unit. (c) Shared (Subfamily): Elderly lives in household headed by another person. (d) Institutions: Nursing homes and other health care related facilities. The SOEP started in 1984 with the non-institutionalized population only.

10. Conclusions

Population aging affects future labour, financial and housing markets by creating new problems as well as amplifying the effects of pre-existing distortions. Because retirement decisions, saving behaviour and housing and living arrangement choices are so responsive to incentives such as regulations, taxes and subsidies, economic policy may be very effective in moderating the implications of population aging.

In the labour market, the quickly changing balance between workers and retirees creates labour supply disincentives if social security taxes have to be increased. Rather than delaying retirement to moderate these disincentives, social security regulations in Germany and the US have encouraged early retirement, thus even aggravating the imbalance between the number of workers and pensioners. In Germany, a more age-neutral system is projected to shift the retirement age by about three years. Such a system is also likely to be more efficient because it avoids the bunching of retirement ages that is a current characteristic of German retirement behaviour and that appears to be dictated by existing retirement choices.

Deferring changes in the retirement system will render future reforms more problematic because political power will shift from the working population to the older generation as the dependency ratio surges. In West Germany after 2020 the majority of the voters will be pensioners and workers who will become retired within the next 10 years (Bös and von Weizsäcker, 1989). We then risk facing a typical free-rider situation as the older generation can outvote the younger generation in determining their retirement income as well as the rate of social security taxes the younger generation has to pay.

Private savings substitute only partially for social security wealth. This puts in doubt the call for a replacement of the current pay-as-you-go social security systems by fully funded ones. Other pieces of evidence reinforce the view that financial markets will be less strained than may be expected. The elderly, at least in Germany, have relatively large wealth holdings. In fact the level of annuity income, particularly for the oldest old, is on average considerably larger than their expenditures. As a result, taxing more heavily this emerging wealth is more efficient than further raising social security taxes, since the former can be taxed without large deadweight losses while the latter creates labour supply disincentives. Bequests could also be taxed more heavily without creating much harm because most bequests seem to be largely unintended.

Rapid population aging aggravates the effects of the familiar housing market distortions. Intergenerational transfers are impeded as mobility of the elderly is discouraged. Furthermore, tax incentives in favour of owner-occupied homes create distortions in the direction of too few, too large houses. By lowering the marginal price of land and dwellings, tax deductions in the US channel resources to large houses where the marginal room has little utility, thereby suppressing the supply of a larger number of smaller houses which appears to be more appropriate in times of population aging. In West Germany, the rent adjustment clause, if binding, lowers expected returns for prospective landlords and therefore reduces supply. It is important to stress at this point that tenants' protection *per se* – the prohibition of eviction and a rent increase beyond market rents – is a social achievement particularly important for the elderly who face higher psychic, sometimes also monetary, moving costs. However, the policy dilemma starts when increases in demand raise spot market rents. The rent adjustment provision, once a device against greedy landlords, creates a wedge between spot and long-term rent and suppresses supply at the expense of the newcomers while protecting sitting tenants (and providing windfall gains to them). Population aging aggravates this situation.

There are some economic disincentives for family care and multi-generational living arrangements. The case is strongest in West Germany, where current health insurance policies even create an additional distortion by effectively subsidizing living alone while home care can only be deducted up to a very small amount, not to mention a compensation of lost income when one of the adult children gives up her job in order to take care of a parent. There are several possibilities to create incentives for home care, e.g. a deduction for an elderly person being taken care of just like the deduction for children in the current US and German tax codes, or family splitting in which taxes are based on the number of persons in the household, just like the splitting based on marital status in the current German tax code. It is important to be aware that living alone and living in an institution incur much higher social costs (induced health expenditures, stationary and ambulatory services for the elderly, etc.) than living with others. This supports the case for subsidizing home care of the elderly.

Discussion

Pierre-Andre Chiappori
DELTA

Changes in the age structure of the population will certainly create one of the most serious and delicate problems that western economies will have to face in the coming decades. The analysis presented in this paper is thus particularly welcome and timely.

The approach of the paper stems from the observation that little can be learned about the efficiency of various policy measures from the sole examination of time series data relating to a particular country, because policy changes are too few and hard to disentangle from changes in preferences. As an alternative, the author uses a cross-sectional analysis: for similar countries in terms of social structures and mentalities, cross-country differences in behaviour can presumably be attributed to specific national policies.

I am quite sympathetic to this approach and the paper provides very useful insights and policy advices. One can only regret that the scope of comparison was so limited: it is indeed very difficult to assess whether any two countries are 'sufficiently similar' to warrant a comparison. As a result, it would be desirable to dilute national specificities by considering a larger number of countries. The benefits from broadening the scope could be substantial. Consider, for instance, the level of savings. The higher level of saving observed in Germany is somewhat puzzling, since the incentives for both precautionary and life-cycle savings are much lower in West Germany than in the US (the bequest motive is said to be negligible anyway). The explanation given in the text that in Germany, people over 60 have experienced World War II is quite convincing; yet, the explanation relies upon strong differences in preferences and in this matter, a comparison with other European or non-European countries (such as France, Italy, UK or Japan) would have been of interest.

I would also like to underline the need for a careful welfare analysis, which is sometimes lacking in the paper. As an illustration, consider the incentives to postpone retirement which at a first glance seem reasonable in order to avoid unbearable changes in the public pension scheme. Welfare consequences are still intricate, in particular regarding integenerational equity. It is by no means straightforward that participation rates for those over 65 years should be increased, because the welfare cost for the generation concerned might well appear excessive. In France, for instance, retirement at 60 has been introduced by the left-wing government elected in 1981. During the last decade, the active part of the population (including the author of this comment) has consequently been facing a (comparatively) larger dependency ratio, and as a result has paid larger social security contributions. The introduction of new pensions schemes, providing less favourable conditions for early retirement, would mean that this generation paid the full cost of the 1981 reform without being entitled to any of the benefits. In other words, the final result is a huge transfer from a specific generation – those who, broadly speaking, will be active during the next 20 years – to two other generations – their fathers and sons. Such consequences upon intergenerational equity should be considered from a theoretical viewpoint. It is also doubtful, in any case, that they can be politically accepted.

I have a couple of technical problems with the logit regression of retirement probabilities. First, exogenous variables include the option value to postpone retirement *and* age dummies. Since the age of 63 corresponds, in the German system, to a threshold, the corresponding dummy is likely to capture part of the institutional effect; indeed, it is the only significant dummy (except for the very late retirees). The coefficient of the option value may, because of this, underestimate the total impact of public policy upon retirement. In addition, the option value is computed by implicitly assuming that the last recorded wage is a good indicator of the stream of future wages, should retirement be postponed. This is likely to generate selectivity biases in the regression. Indeed, assume that the distribution of future wages, conditional on present wage, is not uniform: clearly, those for which the stream is relatively lower are more likely to retire. In the population of retirees, then, those agents for which the option value is actually smaller than computed will be overrepresented. The effect of the option value is then likely to be overestimated.

Finally, let me come to the author's conclusion that savings are explained neither by precautionary nor life-cycle nor bequest motives. I am somewhat uncomfortable with the remaining explanation that savings arise from irrational expectations of agents who do not correctly anticipate the sharp decline in needs they will face in old age. Though I am ready to accept that unintended savings may matter, I doubt very much that it is the only possible explanation. There are several problems. First, most conclusions based upon age/assets or age/income profiles are dubious, since the pure life-cycle effects are very difficult to distinguish from cohort effects. Consider, for instance, Table 14, which shows that the proportion of elderly households with 'excess cash' increases with age. This is in contradiction with the life-cycle hypothesis, *but only insofar as preferences of the various age groups can be considered as identical.* On the other hand, it can be noted that the first two rows of the table correspond to people who were less than 10 years old at the beginning of the war, whereas they were more than 36 for the last row. We may think, for instance, that the way in which a traumatic experience affects future behaviour significantly depends on age – in which case a cross-sectional analysis would simply not be relevant for analysing savings behaviour. That is also to say that the author's view can only be fully supported by evidence from *panel* (or at least pseudo-panel) data; cross-sectional results simply cannot provide decisive conclusions.

In the same way, the main argument against the precautionary savings motive is that, should this motive operate, then elderly Germans should hold substantially less liquid assets than elderly Americans. Again, this relies upon the assumption that preferences are identical across the Atlantic. Not only is this assumption particularly strong in this case, but it apparently contradicts the basic observation that Germans, in aggregate, save more than Americans, though they should save less. As I mentioned before, the argument is particularly weak since it relies upon the comparison of only two countries. The role of national specificities cannot be easily eliminated.

A last remark concerns the analysis of bequests. I doubt very much that any convincing conclusion can be reached without explicitly considering in first place a precise, theoretical model of household life-cycle behaviour in the presence of children. In particular, the argument, implicit in the author's discussion, that in the presence of a bequest motive larger families should, other things being equal, leave higher bequests, is far too vague and general. Part of the bequests, for instance, is left in the form of children's human capital, parents having invested in children's training. This effect may well, by itself, turn out to be sufficient to explain the paradox. In addition, one may wonder how should the 'other things being equal' provision should be understood? Certainly it cannot mean 'total income being equal', since, for any given level of income, the standard of living will vary considerably with family size. In the regression of Table 15, some kind of equivalence scale should therefore be introduced in the net income term; again, a theoretical model would probably be needed to do that properly. This issue certainly deserves further investigation.

General discussion

Some panel members wondered whether the public policy debate regarding aging was not slightly misplaced; Henrik Horn emphasized that the problem of aging was first and foremost a problem of fertility. Accordingly, the incentives to have children and the consequences of increased fertility on the female labour supply should be at the centre of the debate. John Black also found it rather odd that Western Europe and the US should worry about a shortage of young workers at a time when excessive immigration is also a major concern. Migration is indeed likely to affect not only the labour market but also aggregate savings and the housing market and should therefore be included in the analysis. Along similar lines, Axel Weber wondered how the reunification of Germany would affect the outlook presented in the paper which excludes the former German Democratic Republic. Axel Börsch-Supan responded to this concern and indicated that the population of the GDR shares many characteristics with that of West Germany, so that the conclusions of the paper should not be unduly affected.

Arie Kapteyn was concerned about the evidence regarding the responsiveness of retirement decisions to economic incentives; for the US, the data refers only to official pension schemes, which account for a limited amount of total pension outlays. At the same time, private pension schemes, by the author's own admission, are quite varied, so that the dispersion of retirement age in the US could very well be associated to the diversity of the pension schemes. More information on the characteristics of private pensions are therefore necessary before a conclusion can be reached. Kapteyn was also worried about the specific assumptions underlying the computation of the option value of retirement. In particular, the assumption of linear utility could be challenged and he recommended that a sensitivity analysis should be performed. Börsch-Supan acknowledged this while insisting that the estimation of option values was by no means a simple exercise, so that an extensive sensitivity analysis was hardly feasible.

Regarding the evidence put forward on the bequest motive, Jean-Charles Rochet proposed an alternative interpretation of data which is consistent with the life cycle hypothesis. He argued that what mattered for households' consumption decisions were the consumption per head in the family and the bequest per child (rather than total consumption and bequest in the household). In the context, the bequest per child becomes a function of accumulated income per head and this relationship is well supported by the data (with an elasticity lower than 1).

Finally, Paul Seabright insisted that the rationale for public policy intervention should be carefully identified; he argued that in the absence of any distortion induced by pension schemes, there was no externality across generations induced by early retirement decisions. To the extent that pension schemes are actuarially fair, early retirement does not involve a shift of the burden to later generations. Policy should therefore be primarily concerned with distortions in pension schemes.

Appendix A. Data Sources

The data is drawn from two rich and comparable micro data sets describing decisions and the economic situation of the elderly: the 1984 American Panel Study of Income Dynamics (abbreviated PSID, 1984) and its German counterpart, the Socio-Economic Panel (abbreviated SOEP, 1984). These data include demographic and economic characteristics of 3,446 (PSID) and 2,796 (SOEP) persons aged 50 and above and are used for labour force participation, income status by source of income, and housing and living arrangements. Table A1 displays sample sizes by age groups.

Data on savings and wealth is harder to obtain. Only the PSID, 1984 and the SOEP, 1988 cross-sections include wealth supplements. German wealth data closer to the year 1984 is obtained from the West German Consumer Expenditure Survey in 1983 ('Einkommens- und Verbrauchstichprobe', abbreviated EVS, 1983), a very large representative cross-section of all West German households with annual gross income below DM 300,000 that also includes 18,259 households with heads aged 50 and above. This survey excludes the very wealthy, approximately the upper 2% tail of the income distribution. In addition to basic demographics, the data contain a detailed account of income by sources, wealth by asset categories and household expenditures, computed from diaries.[12]

Comparing summary statistics of household wealth is not a straightforward task (Wolff, 1990). Wealth distributions are very skewed (average wealth is sensitive to a few very wealthy persons, median wealth is zero for many asset categories). All wealth data is self-reported and thus subject to severe underreporting. The reported values for the US are well in line with data from the American Retirement History Survey

---

[12] Unfortunately, the data lacks important demographic data such as the number of children of an elderly person and his/her health status.

Table A1. Sample sizes in the PSID, 1984 and SOEP cross-sections

Age	US: PSID, 1984				West Germany: SOEP, 1984			
	Male	Female	Total	Percent	Male	Female	Total	Percent
50–54	325	403	728	21.1	333	313	646	23.1
55–59	321	390	711	20.6	249	267	516	18.4
60–64	253	340	593	17.2	238	271	509	18.2
65–69	209	277	486	14.1	163	244	407	14.6
70–74	156	262	418	12.1	108	149	257	9.2
75–79	98	160	258	7.5	93	153	246	8.8
80+	89	163	252	7.3	82	134	216	7.7
Total	1,451	1,995	3,446	100.0	1,266	1,531	2,797	100.0

Source: PSID, 1984, SOEP, 1984.

reported by Hurd (1989, Table I 18) which yields some confidence for both data sets, even though the Retirement History Survey data are subject to the similar measurement problems as the PSID data. The wealth data is roughly comparable between the two countries. Valuation, however, is complicated by the large discrepancy between exchange rate and purchasing power in 1984. The average exchange rate between the Deutsche Mark and the US Dollar was then $1 to DM 2.70, substantially higher than the average purchasing power parity during 1984 ($1 = DM 1.70, according to OECD figures).

Appendix B. Computation of option value to postpone retirement

The option value to postpone retirement at a given age is the maximum attainable expected discounted utility from consumption if the worker would retire at some later age minus the expected discounted utility from consumption if the worker retired now (Lazear and Moore, 1988; Stock and Wise, 1990).

The computation is based on the expected discounted stream of utility from consumption at time t if the worker retires at time R, denoted by $V_t(R)$. It depends on labour earnings YL in periods t through $R-1$ and retirement income $YR(R, YL)$ in periods R through D, the expected time of death. I employ two simplifying assumptions:

(1) The utility function depends on income and is linear.

(2) Labour income will stay constant in periods t through $R-1$.

With these assumptions, the expected present discounted value of income is:

$$V_t(R) = E_t \left[\sum_{s=t}^{R-1} YL_s \beta^{s-t} + \alpha \sum_{s=R}^{D} YR_s(R, YL) \beta^{s-t} \right]$$

Retirement income YR depends on the retirement date R (according to the adjustment formulae displayed in Table 7) and on labour income YL. Since labour income has to be earned by giving up leisure, retirement income is weighted by $\alpha > 1$, where $1/\alpha$ reflects the disutility of work. E_t denotes expectation at time t, and β the discount factor. I use $\alpha = 1.66$ and $\beta = 0.85$, taken from Stock and Wise (1990). α may appear low while the discount rate implicit in β appears high. However, setting $\alpha = 2.5$ and $\beta = 0.95$ does not alter the qualitative regression results in Table 9. The estimation procedure in Table 9 ignores that α and β may be correlated with other parameters in the model (hence should be estimated jointly with them), and a potential feedback of the retirement age on labour income.

Let $R^*(t)$ denote the optimal retirement age if the worker postpones retirement beyond age t, i.e. the $r > t$ that maximizes $V_t(r)$. The option value of postponing retirement at time t is then defined as

$$G(t) = V_t(R^*(t)) - V_t(t)$$

Since a worker is likely to retire as soon as $G(t)$ becomes negative, retirement probabilities should depend negatively on $G(t)$.

In West Germany, the public pension system dominates retirement income. Therefore, the computation of the option value to postpone retirement is based on the age-adjustment rates in Table 7 together with the replacement rates of the public pension system sketched in Table 6. Women and disabled workers are eligible for very early retirement (ages 60–62), represented by the right-hand values in the German panel of Table 7. Male workers who are not disabled are treated as if not vested at ages 60–62.

In the US, private pensions plans may dominate the importance of the public pension system for an individual worker. Since we have no information on the structure of the private pension plan that may be applicable to the individual worker, the American regression in Table 9 can only be suggestive. Specifically, we assume that a private pension supplements the public pension up to a replacement ratio comparable to the West German public system, but without distorting the retirement age-specific incentives created by the old age social security system in the US. This assumption weakens the ability to predict individual retirement behaviour, but appears plausible on average.

References

Atkinson, A. B. (1983). *The Economics of Inequality*, 2nd ed., Oxford University Press, Oxford, England.

Auerbach, A. J., L. J. Kotlikoff, R. P. Hagemann and G. Nicoletti (1990). 'The Economic Dynamics of an Aging Population: The Case of Four OECD Countries', OECD Economic Studies No. 14.

Barro, R. J. (1974). 'Are Government Bonds Net Wealth?', *Journal of Political Economy*.

Behring, K., A. Börsch-Supan and G. Goldrian (1988). *Analyse und Prognose der Nachfrage nach Miet- und Eigentümerwohnungen in der Bundesrepublik Deutschland*, Duncker und Humblot, Berlin.

Bernheim, B. D., A. Shleifer and L. H. Summers (1985). 'The Manipulative Bequest Motive', *Journal of Political Economy*.

Börsch-Supan, A. (1985). 'Tenure Choice and Housing Demand', in K. Stahl and R. Struyk (ed.) *U.S. and West German Housing Markets*, The Urban Institute Press, Washington, D.C.

—— (1990). 'Elderly Americans: A Dynamic Analysis of Household Dissolution and Living Arrangement Transitions', in D. Wise (ed.) *Issues in the Economics of Aging*, University of Chicago Press, Chicago.

Börsch-Supan, A. and K. Stahl (1990). 'Life Cycle Savings and Consumption Constraints', Paper prepared for the ISPE-Conference on Fiscal Implications of an Ageing Population', mimeo, University of Mannheim.

Bös, D. and R. K. von Weizsäcker (1989). 'Economic Consequences of an Aging Population', *European Economic Review*.

Casmir, B. (1989). *Staatliche Rentenversicherungssysteme im internationalen Vergleich*, Lang, Frankfurt.

Chesnais, J. C. (1987). 'Quand un peuple en devient deux: une Allemagne et l'autre', *Population et Societes*.

Clark, R. L., J. Kreps and J. J. Spengler (1978). 'Economics of Aging: A Survey', *Journal of Economic Literature*.

Ellwood, D. and T. Kane (1990). 'An American Way of Aging', in D. Wise (ed.) *Issues in the Economics of Aging*, University of Chicago Press, Chicago.

Feinstein, J. and McFadden (1988). 'The Dynamics of Housing Demand by the Elderly', in D. Wise (ed.) *The Economics of Aging*, University of Chicago Press, Chicago.

Feldstein, M. (1974). 'Social Security, Induced Retirement, and Aggregate Capital Accumulation', *Journal of Political Economy*.

Frerich, J. (1987). *Sozialpolitik*, Oldenbourg, München.

Hagemann, R. P. and G. Nicoletti (1989). 'Population Ageing: Economic Effects and Some Policy Implications for Financing Public Pensions', OECD Economic Studies No. 12.

Hurd, M. D. (1989). 'Issues and Results from Research on the Elderly: Economic Status, Retirement, and Savings', NBER Working Paper No. 3018, Cambridge, Massachusetts, prepared for *Journal of Economic Literature*.

Jacobs, K., M. Kohli and M. Rein (1987). 'Testing the Industry-Mix Hypothesis of Early Exit', Discussion Paper Wissenschaftszentrum, Berlin.

—— (1990). 'Germany: the Diversity of Pathways', in M. Kohli, M. Rein, A.-M. Guillemard and H. van Gunsteren (eds.) *Time for Retirement: Comparative Studies of Early Exit from the Labor Force*, Cambridge University Press, Cambridge, New York.

Kessler, D. (1990). 'Presidential Address at the Fourth Annual Meeting of the European Society of Population Economics', Istanbul (forthcoming in *Journal of Population Economics*).

Kotlikoff, L. J. and L. Summers (1981). 'The Role of Intergenerational Transfers in Aggregate Capital Accumulation', *Journal of Political Economy*.

Kotlikoff, L. J. and D. A. Wise (1987). 'Incentive Effects of Private Pension Plans', in Z. Bodie, J. Shoven and D. Wise (eds.) *Issues in Pension Economics*, University of Chicago Press, Chicago.

—— (1989). 'Employee Retirement and a Firm's Pension Plan', in D. Wise (ed.) *The Economics of Aging*, Chicago University Press, Chicago.

Lazear, E. P. (1990). 'Adjusting to an Aging Labor Force', in D. Wise (ed.) *Issues in the Economics of Aging*, University of Chicago Press, Chicago.

Lazear, E. P. and R. L. Moore (1988). 'Pensions and Turnover', in Z. Bodie, J. Shoven and D. Wise (eds.) *Pensions in the U.S. Economy*, University of Chicago Press, Chicago.

Lehr, U. (1987). *Psychologie des Alterns*, 7th ed., Quelle und Meyer, Heidelberg, Wiesbaden.

Mankiw, G. and D. Weil (1989). 'The Baby Boom, the Baby Bust, and the Housing Market', *Regional Science and Urban Economics*.

Mayo, S. K. and J. Barnbrock (1985). 'Rental Housing Subsidy Programs in West Germany and the United States', in K. Stahl and R. Struyk (eds.) *U.S. and West German Housing Markets*, The Urban Institute Press, Washington, D.C.

OECD (1988). *Ageing Populations: The Social Policy Implications*, Paris.

Schmähl, W. (1989). 'Labour Force Participation and Social Pension Systems', in P. Johnson, C. Conrad and D. Thomson (eds.) *Workers versus Pensioners: Intergenerational Justice in an Ageing World*, Manchester University Press, Manchester, New York.

Stock, J. H. and D. A. Wise (1990). 'Pensions, The Option Value of Work, and Retirement', *Econometrica*.

Venti, S. F. and D. A. Wise (1990). 'But They Don't Want to Reduce Equity', in D. Wise (ed.) *Issues in the Economics of Aging*, University of Chicago Press, Chicago.

Wolff, E. N. (1990). 'Methodological Issues in the Estimation of the Size Distribution of Household Wealth', *Journal of Econometrics*.

Economic Policy   April 1991   Printed in Great Britain

Economic reform in China

Athar Hussain and Nicholas Stern

Summary

This paper examines some problems of transition from a command to a market economy through an analysis of the most important example to date – the reforms in the Chinese economy since the late 1970s. Our focus is on the links between enterprise reforms, effective demand and public finance. The reforms have created a curious and problematic hybrid of market and command economies with serious problems of coordination. They have concentrated almost exclusively on the delegation of decision-making to enterprises from the higher to lower tiers of the government without taking into account its implications for investment, consumption and public finance. An understanding of future policy and lessons for other countries requires a careful examination of the effects of these past policies.

Granting discretion to enterprises over investment and wages has resulted in both an investment and consumption boom but, paradoxically, a fall in profits. There are strong reasons to suppose that the investment ratio has been too high in recent years, fuelling inflation and slowing additions to supply by prolonging the gestation period of investment. There has been a large increase in liquid assets in the hands of households, which makes their expectations increasingly important for macroeconomic policy. There is need for concerted financial innovation to diversify household wealth away from liquid assets. Finally, the changes in the composition of government revenue and expenditure are disturbing. There is an urgent need for a flexible and broad-based tax system and for reducing price subsidies and subsidies to loss-making enterprises.

Effective demand, enterprise reforms and public finance in China

Athar Hussain and Nicholas Stern
London School of Economics

1. Introduction

To design economic policy we must understand the effects of government actions. This task can be difficult, and becomes formidable when structural change lies at the heart of policy. We examine some of the problems of economic transition by analysing the most important modern example of decentralization – Chinese economic reform since the late 1970s. Reform of agriculture began in 1978, but it is the subsequent reforms of industrial enterprises in the mid-1980s on which we concentrate.

Our analysis of the enterprise reforms must go beyond a narrow microeconomic focus. We highlight the links between three elements: the behaviour and decisions of enterprises; those of the government; and the implications for the economy as a whole. Understanding these linkages is crucial to the formation of sensible policies and the success of new departures. The Chinese experience carries important analytical and practical lessons for other countries that have embarked more recently on reforms.

We emphasize that reforms have important implications for effective demand and public finance. The decentralization of decisions to enterprises implies their demands can no longer be 'coordinated' through the plan. What are the implications of abandoning coordination

We have received helpful comments from David Begg, John Black, Michael Burda, David Newbery, Paul Seabright, David Winter and Shahid Yusuf, and financial support from the Bradley Foundation, the Ford Foundation and the UK Overseas Development Administration, to all of whom we are very grateful. This paper arises from the China Research Programme at the Suntory–Toyota International Centre for Economics and Related Disciplines at the London School of Economics and thanks are due to STICERD for its support and to our Chinese collaborators, in particular Wang Huijiong and Li Poxi of the Development Research Centre of the State Council in that programme.

without the complementary apparatus of a smoothly functioning market economy together with government fiscal and monetary mechanisms?

We shall argue that in China, notwithstanding a most impressive supply performance, the cumulation of effective demand generated the inflation of the late 1980s. Our purpose is not to write down a formal macro model of the Chinese economy, nor a detailed study of inflation *per se*. We are concerned with the logically prior, and deeper, question of relating the emergence of effective demand to the new economic structures and particularly the enterprise reforms. We shall show that the relaxation of planning controls and decentralization of decisions to firms, without effective aggregate control through credit markets or otherwise, and without recognition of the need for a government tax and revenue system to replace the profits from public enterprises, together led to excess demand. We also examine the components of demand and their relation to institutional and economic structure and to policy. Our analysis carries basic lessons for the economic modelling of economies in transition; for the consequences of decentralization in such circumstances; and for future policy design both in China and elsewhere.

We first provide a brief introduction to the Chinese reforms and then an overall picture of macroeconomic developments in China. Our emphasis is on the demand side. The impressive rise in Chinese output in the 1980s will be discussed only briefly in this paper (see, e.g. Perkins, 1988, and Lin, 1989) and is not our main topic here. We then discuss the enterprise reforms and demand arising from Chinese enterprises via both investment and wages. The institutional structure of the Chinese enterprise is critical, particularly the somewhat entangled three-way relationship between government, managers and workers. Next we examine public finance. In both cases, we shall see that while the simple models of standard economic theory carry important lessons, they must be adapted, reinterpreted and reconstructed to understand the economic effects of the structural changes. At the same time we shall point to basic difficulties arising from current policies and structures which future reforms must overcome.

The main reforms of the last 10 years comprise: a shift from collective farming to household farming; financial autonomy and operational autonomy for state-owned enterprises; a decentralization of government, delegating control from the higher to lower government tiers; encouraging private and foreign enterprises; and an open-door policy towards foreign trade and investment.

Broadly, during the first period of reforms, 1978–84, rural activities occupied the centre of the stage and enterprise reforms did not go beyond administrative decentralization, allowing enterprises a measure of operational autonomy and giving them disposal of a portion of their gross profits. From 1984 the focus of the reforms shifted from the countryside to enterprises and the urban economy in general. Only in the second phase were market transactions allowed to coexist with 'administered transactions' and influence the pattern of enterprise output. Since 1987, attention has been focused on the links between enterprise management and the government.

A common thread running through various reforms has been the decentralization of decision-making, from higher government tiers to lower tiers and from the government to enterprises. Markets in goods and services have grown rapidly, but they are awkwardly segmented and multiple prices are pervasive. Capital and labour markets still remain fairly primitive. The price structure involving 'plan prices' and 'non-plan prices' is heavily distorted. The reforms have created a curious and problematic hybrid of market and command economies. Problems of coordination are particularly serious for two reasons. First, the assortment of administrative and market constraints which economic agents face do not cohere, leaving gaps and loopholes to be exploited for private profit. Second, administrative and market constraints are often 'incentive incompatible'. For example, the coexistence of the plan with a market where goods fetch higher prices generates a permanent incentive not to fulfil plan quotas. Similarly, the absence of bankruptcy provides an incentive to enterprises to disregard the financial constraints implied by prices.

The reform period since 1978 has been characterized by a Chinese version of a stop–go cycle, alternating between loosening administrative controls and bold economic reforms in the 'go' phase, and reimposition of controls and a cautious attitude towards further reforms in the 'stop' phase (Komiya, 1989). The economy has been in a 'stop' phase since the autumn of 1988, and a further round of reforms is not expected to begin until the end of 1991. The sharp acceleration in the inflation rate in 1988, which forced the Chinese leadership to embark on a policy of macroeconomic stabilization, suggests that some basic policy measures or structural elements were missing from the strategy of the reforms pursued from 1984–88.

This paper focuses on the implications of three central aspects of the enterprise reforms: the delegation of decision-making on investment and its financing to enterprises; the introduction of performance-linked wages and bonuses and the delegation of decisions concerning wages to enterprises; and the separation of enterprise budgets from the government budget.

Table 1. Real growth and inflation (% per annum)

	Growth rates			
	Net national income	Agriculture	Other	Inflation
1971–77	4.6	1.6	5.8	0.4
1978–83	8.1	6.7	8.8	2.4
1984–88	11.3	4.9	14.5	8.6
1978	12.3	3.9	16.4	0.7
1979	7.0	6.4	7.3	2.0
1980	6.4	−1.8	11.0	6.0
1981	4.9	7.1	2.2	2.4
1982	8.3	11.7	6.0	1.9
1983	9.8	8.5	10.7	1.5
1984	13.5	13.0	13.8	2.8
1985	13.1	1.7	19.4	8.8
1986	8.0	3.7	10.3	6.0
1987	10.5	4.5	13.6	7.3
1988	11.5	2.2	16.0	18.5
1989	3.7	NA	NA	17.8

Source: Growth rates from SSB (1990a): 25. Inflation rates refer to the retail index and are from SSB (1990a): 589. The 1989 figure is from SSB (1990b).
Note: Chinese statistical sources provide net national income figures.

2. Recent macroeconomic developments in China

We provide in this section a picture of the Chinese macroeconomy over the last two decades. Our analysis looks first at the overall rate of change of real national income and of prices. We then examine domestic components of demand, distinguishing between consumption arising through institutions and through households. We discuss the role of liquidity in determining household consumption demands. Finally, we look at the foreign sector.

We have divided the post-1978 period into two sub-periods 'up to 1983' and 'since 1984' corresponding to the two phases described in the preceding section. The pre-1978 economy is described in terms of annual averages for the period 1971–77. We start with 1971 because that marks the beginning of the relatively settled phase of the Cultural Revolution following the turmoil of 1966–71. (See Table 1.)

Over the reform period (1978–89), the Chinese population grew by 1.2% per annum, which gives an annual growth rate of per capita income around 8%. The contribution of agriculture to growth in the different periods is closely linked to the phasing of the reforms. During 1978–83 almost half of the acceleration in the GNP growth rate was due to faster agricultural growth, which may reasonably be attributed to the rural reforms. In the second period, the higher growth rate of the non-agricultural sector, of which industry is by far the largest component, more than offset the deceleration in agriculture. But the higher aggregate growth rate in the second sub-period was accompanied by rising inflation and, as we shall see, a comparatively large balance-of-payments deficit.

One must interpret official growth rates with some circumspection since there are significant measurement problems (see, e.g. Summers and Heston, 1988). Nevertheless, the output growth in particular sectors and the visible increase in consumption levels suggest real and impressive advances.

The reforms turned sour in 1988, when inflation leapt from 7% to around 19%. In cities, inflation was over 21%, and food prices rose by over 25% (SSB 1990: 691). This provoked a panic run on banks and forced the leadership to embark on a stabilization policy with stringent credit and investment controls, due to last until the end of 1991 (see *Beijing Review* 1990: No. 7). In 1989 growth dropped to 3.7%, though inflation fell only marginally. Eventually inflation also came down; the figure for 1990 is likely to be well under 10%.

In terms of the growth of national and per-capita incomes, the Chinese reforms appear to be an outstanding success. Why have the Chinese reforms been more successful than those in Eastern Europe? The answer may lie in structural differences in the pre-reform economies.

First, central planning had a comparatively limited remit in China and the economy was highly decentralized with a great deal of discretion to provinces and the lower government tiers. There was substantial flexibility built into the economy. Second, an overwhelming proportion of the labour force (around 75%) was in rural areas and organized at the household level, even if the overall deployment of labour was determined by collective institutions. This meant that agriculture, a comparatively high proportion of national income and efficient by the standards of developing economies, could be decollectivized very easily, yielding spectacular results quickly and launching the industrial reforms on a sound footing (see Nolan, 1988). Providing some rights of households to the usufruct of the land cultivated through the contract-responsibility system produced sharp increases in output without involving the full property rights of private ownership. Incentives to effort brought forth a very large response (see McMillan *et al.*, 1989). Third, China's abundance of labour has eased the problems of redeployment. Fourth, China had no foreign debts on the eve of the reforms and could borrow abroad. Being a low-income developing country enabled some access to loans at preferential rates from the International Development Association (IDA) of the World Bank Group.

Inflation in the Chinese economy raises a number of measurement and conceptual problems (see, e.g. Naughton, 1990a), chiefly because of multiple prices (for the same goods) and widespread rationing, involving both principal industrial inputs and daily consumer goods. A commodity may have several plan or government-controlled prices and 'negotiated' prices (at which, for example, outputs above 'plan agreements' can be sold). Plan prices have almost invariably been lower than negotiated prices and involve rationing. We sometimes refer to negotiated prices as 'white' market prices in contrast to the many 'black' markets which also exist. These multiple prices raise the problem of the choice of weights in price indices. The weights used in the official price indices are not published. Illegal or semi-legal arbitrage, purchasing at lower plan prices for resale at higher prices, imply that official price indices underestimate the prices actually paid by users of commodities. Reports in the Chinese press suggest that such transactions were widespread until the crackdown on corruption following the protest movement of May and June 1989.

The underestimation of the extent of transactions at higher negotiated prices suggests that the official inflation rate figures may be biased downwards when the fraction of transactions at the higher prices is increasing. This underestimation may be especially severe during the period 1984–88 when inflation was accelerating: negotiated prices, being more susceptible to excess demand pressure, rise faster than controlled prices when the official figures show accelerating inflation.

Ceteris paribus, the relaxation of quantitative restrictions on purchases involved in a shift from a planned economy towards a market economy will show up as an acceleration in the inflation rate as the fraction of transactions at the plan or ration prices decreases. Arguably, inflation arising from the relaxation of price controls is a once-and-for-all adjustment of prices which should be distinguished from continuing inflation. Nevertheless, the changing extent of rationing and price control does seem to have played a role in determining inflation in China which goes deeper than this simple 'adjustment' interpretation. The government has tended to respond to a rise in inflation by extending price controls, as it did in 1989–90. Changes in the range of price controls have to be seen in part, therefore, as a tool of macroeconomic policy.

However, price controls are not independent of the principal determinant of underlying inflation, the pressure of demand. In a transitional economy, the range of price controls which can be enforced depends on demand pressure: higher demand increases the frequency of price-control violations, forcing the government to reduce the range of price controls. Similarly, an extension of price controls is contingent on measures to reduce aggregate demand. This is exactly what has happened in China in 1989–90. Once economic reforms have granted a degree of discretion to economic agents, the enforcement of administrative controls depends not just on coercion but also on economic incentives, giving rise to a two-way causation between controls and the macroeconomic environment.

We turn now to a description of movements in the composition of aggregate demand, as shown in Table 2. Chinese national income statistics present the components of demand in terms of household consumption (HC), social consumption (SC: non-investment expenditure by institutions) and investment (I). We discuss foreign trade later. Column 4 gives the ratio of net changes in household bank deposits, both current and fixed-term, to national income (HD/NI), which in the absence of figures for personal incomes may be taken as a proxy for the ratio of household savings to national income. The last column gives the estimated share of household incomes to national income (HI/NI) as the sum of Columns 1 and 4.

Over the reform period, there has been a significant shift away from household consumption towards investment and social consumption. *Per se*, such shifts on the expenditure side do not tell us anything about excess-demand pressure in the economy. But, given widespread quantity constraints on consumers, it is difficult to argue that the shift towards investment and social consumption would have been accommodated entirely by an increase in 'voluntary savings': while the share of consumption fell, the share of household income in national income rose. Column 4 shows a steady rise in the ratio of changes in household bank deposits to national income over the whole of the reform period except for 1988. The dip in 1988 is interesting because it coincides with a sharp acceleration in the inflation rate (see Table 1). Arguably, the rise in the savings rate is in part due to an increase in 'involuntary' savings, which suggests willingness on the part of households to pay higher prices. In addition to the pressure of demand in consumer goods markets, the increase in the investment ratio in the second sub-period, which we discuss in Section 3, has been accompanied with increasing reports of widespread shortages of industrial inputs such as coal, cement and steel.

'Involuntary savings' arising from unsatisfied demand for consumer goods increase the volume of liquid assets in possession of households: the so-called 'monetary overhang'. Quantity constraints on household purchases, analogously to liquidity constraints on households in market economies, may have implications for labour supply and the rate of substitution of future for current consumption (see Portes, 1989). In

Table 2. Composition of aggregate demand and changes in household bank deposits (%)

	HC/NI	SC/NI	I/NI	δHD/NI	HI/NI
1971–77	60.5	6.9	32.6	0.6	61.1
1978–83	60.2	8.2	31.6	2.9	63.1
1984–88	57.4	8.5	33.9	6.6	64.1
1978	56.3	7.2	36.5	1.0	57.3
1979	56.9	8.5	34.6	2.1	59.0
1980	60.2	10.5	31.5	3.2	63.4
1981	63.4	8.3	28.3	3.2	66.6
1982	62.7	8.5	28.8	3.5	66.2
1983	61.8	8.5	29.7	4.5	66.3
1984	59.6	8.9	31.5	5.6	65.2
1985	56.6	8.2	35.0	5.8	62.4
1986	56.6	8.6	34.7	7.2	63.8
1987	56.9	8.4	34.2	8.7	65.6
1988	57.5	8.4	34.1	6.0	63.5
1989	NA	NA	30.8	10.3	NA

Definitions: HC/NI: household consumption to national income; SC/NI: social consumption to national income; I/NI: investment ratio; $δHD/NI$: Changes in household bank deposits to national income; HI/NI: Household income to national income, $HI = HC + δHD$.
Note: All ratios are ratios with respect to magnitudes at current prices.
Source: SSB (1990a): 28 and 624. The 1989 figures are preliminary and from SSB (1990b): 3 and 44.

economies in transition, looser (or more loosely enforced) price controls on transactions, which in China take the form of white (or black) parallel markets, provide a mechanism for a partial translation of cumulated involuntary savings into higher prices. Looser controls also provide Chinese households with an option, albeit still not an easy one, of holding their wealth in other forms such as stocks of goods or foreign currency.

The changes in household bank deposits to national income, as shown by Column 4 in Table 2, have a wider significance for macroeconomic policy in China. The fall in the household bank-deposits ratio in 1988 corroborates the stories of a panic run on banks in the autumn of 1988. The spectacular rise in the ratio in 1989 is based on the preliminary figures, but fits with the 8% drop in retail sales in real terms (see *Beijing Review* 1990, No. 9: 'Documents'). The steady rise in the ratio poses a puzzle. A part of the rise may simply be due to a gradual spread of the 'banking habit' among households. But, a substantial part of the increase may be due to a rise in personal wealth which in large part, given the relative absence of other assets, is held in money. For a discussion of the demand for money see Portes and Santomero (1988).

With the large increase in liquid assets in the hands of households, the expectations of households assume an increasing importance for macroeconomic policy. Before 1978 the government could disregard any effect of expectations on household demands, given the limited scope they had for altering their consumption and saving pattern. But now with the large volume of liquid assets in the hands of households and a significant shift towards a market economy, expectations begin to matter. In particular, changes in expectations concerning future inflation could have a large impact on the current inflation rate: given that the ratio of household bank deposits to national income is currently around 40%, a decision by households to reduce their bank deposits by one percentage point would immediately add around 0.4% to aggregate demand.

The success of an anti-inflationary policy in the present-day Chinese economy depends crucially on its credibility and on providing households with financial and physical assets carrying some insurance against inflation. Currently, Chinese households, urban ones in particular, have precious few possibilities of holding their wealth in tangible or non-liquid assets. Almost all housing in urban areas is publicly owned. The increasing importance of household bank deposits also suggests that the control of inflation through a re-imposition of price controls and rationing, as in 1989–90, may lower the inflation rate, but at the cost of storing up a problem for the future. A re-acceleration of inflation may prompt households to decrease their bank deposits thus further accelerating inflation.

The components of effective demand concern foreign trade and are set out in Table 3. Two features stand out: the massive expansion in foreign trade relative to national income and the trade deficit as a regular feature of the Chinese economy.

The Chinese economy is now as open as any large developing economy, and this has a number of important implications for links between domestic and international price levels and resource allocation. Trade flows are still heavily controlled by the government via Foreign Trade Corporations (FTCs), which in the pre-reform period formed a tight 'air-lock' between the domestic economy and the world market. The 'air-lock' remains but is punctured by two reforms in the 1980s: the decentralization of foreign trade and the opening of parallel markets at negotiated prices. Provincial branches of the previously centralized FTCs were transformed into separate units, and the provincial and municipal authorities given the power to create their own FTCs, a power which they used enthusiastically (see, e.g. Vogel, 1989, and World Bank, 1988). At the end of 1989 there were 6,000 FTCs, in contrast to around a dozen in 1978. In addition, some large enterprises were permitted

**Table 3. Foreign trade and the balance of trade
(% of national income)**

	Foreign trade ratio*	BOT surplus
1971–77	5.0	0.3
1978–83	8.0	−0.2
1984–88	14.5	−3.1
1978	6.0	−0.7
1979	6.8	−0.9
1980	7.6	−0.5
1981	9.4	0.0
1982	9.0	1.3
1983	9.0	0.3
1984	10.5	−0.7
1985	14.5	−6.0
1986	15.7	−5.0
1987	16.2	−1.5
1988	15.6	−2.4

* Weighted average of exports and imports to national
income.
Source: SSB (1990a): 28 and 546.

to conduct foreign trade. The competition between exporters arising
out of the large-scale decentralization and the opening of the parallel
markets in goods have considerably reduced the percentage of goods
for exports procured at plan prices, which in the pre-reform period
used to be 100. This has opened up a channel for the domestic inflation
to spill over into the prices of exported goods as the FTCs bid up prices
in the knowledge that the foreign exchange that they will gain from
their sale will yield a premium (either in white or black markets).

A similar story holds for imports. In the past imported goods were
sold at the plan prices for their domestic substitutes, if they existed, or
otherwise at cost (converted at official exchange rates) plus import duties
and handling costs. Such a pricing policy for imports implies a reduction
in their profits, or bigger losses, compared with open market pricing.
This has confronted the government with the uncomfortable option of
either absorbing the losses of FTCs or allowing them to sell imported
goods at negotiated prices. Further, the decentralization of foreign
trade has made it increasingly difficult to enforce the pricing policy for
imports. As in other fields, the government has followed a mixed policy:
absorbing the losses of FTCs, allowing some imports to be sold at higher
negotiated prices and devaluing the exchange rate (to reduce the black
or white market premium). The general point is that with an increasing
trade ratio and a partial decontrol of domestic prices, the maintenance

of an 'air-lock' has a heavy cost for public finance and eventually something has to give.

The decentralization of foreign trade has gone together with a decentralization of foreign exchange holdings. Units engaging in foreign trade are allowed to retain a part of their foreign exchange earnings and since 1988 also to sell them at negotiated prices through Foreign Exchange Adjustment Centres (FEACs). In 1989, around 15% of export earnings were transacted through FEACs (World Bank, 1990b). Their establishment has considerably reduced the importance of the black markets in foreign currency and amounted to a partial introduction of floating exchange rates and put pressure on the authorities to devalue so as to contain the divergence between the open-market rates and the official rate. The official exchange rate has been devalued a number of times in recent years, in 1986, then by 21% in November 1989 and by a further 9% in November 1990 (*Beijing Review*, No. 49: 6). Given the high inflation rate in 1988, which continued into 1989, the 1989 devaluation was too late and perhaps not enough fully to reverse the appreciation in the real exchange rate. Generally it seems that unlike many developing economies, the Chinese authorities seem quick to adjust the nominal exchange rate. This may be attributed to two factors: first, the very strong desire to sustain the high rate of growth of exports and, second, to reduce the dependence on foreign borrowing.

The recurrence of trade deficits since 1978 is not a sign of a chronic problem but of a radical change in the attitude of the Chinese leadership towards foreign borrowing. In the early 1950s, China borrowed from the USSR and East European economies to finance its industrialization. With the deterioration in relations with the USSR in 1959, the Chinese government eschewed all foreign borrowing. In the 19 years between 1959–77, the balance of trade was in deficit only three times, and the sum of surpluses far exceed the sum of deficits. In fact, over the period China was a net lender to selected African and Asian economies.

Since 1978, the reformist leadership, discarding the previous policy of 'self-reliance' has come to rely on foreign borrowing and welcome foreign investment. Foreign borrowing, which has been mainly from international organizations and governments, would appear to have contributed to the combination of a significantly higher growth than in the pre-reform period and an unprecedented increase in household consumption. China's total foreign debt at the end of 1989 was around $42 bn. Given that exports in 1989 were around $52 bn., by international standards the Chinese economy does not face a significant debt servicing problem (SSB 1990: 97) and could service a higher level of foreign debts without undue discomfort.

Should the Chinese economy borrow more (for some discussion see World Bank, 1990a, b)? In response, one should ask, for what purpose? Neither the growth rate nor the investment ratio has been low by international standards. The case for foreign borrowing to boost a low growth rate or investment ratio would seem to be weak in the Chinese case. Extra foreign borrowing to finance the import of goods in short supply will ease the inflationary pressure in certain areas, but will not serve, at least in the short run, to increase the supply of non-tradeables, which still account for an overwhelming proportion of total expenditure. International experience shows that borrowing abroad to address a problem created by internal imbalance simply postpones it and may make it worse. There is justification for China borrowing abroad to finance projects with an expected rate of return exceeding the expected cost. But this is not an argument which can be accepted without discrimination at the macro level on the general presumption that rates of return in China are high.

To summarize the salient macroeconomic features of the Chinese economy, the growth rates of national income and of exports since 1978 have been extremely impressive, and do not look out of place among the growth records of East Asian economies. Rapid growth has brought in its train a variety of problems, in particular inflation. The current macroeconomic problems of the Chinese economy look increasingly similar to those in other economies. What is, however, missing from our account is the problem of unemployment. The 'measured' unemployment rate is exceptionally low in China. China faces a huge problem of unemployment but most of it is 'disguised' because of life-time employment in industry and stringent restrictions on migration from rural to urban areas (even if these are partially evaded). The macroeconomic problems of the Chinese economy have some very special features because of the hybrid of a command and a market economy. In particular, while the reforms have either removed administrative control on economic decisions or weakened the remaining ones, they have not succeeded in creating an environment where prices and budgets act as clear constraints on economic decisions. Moreover, the expectations of economic agents, enterprises as well as households, and their response to government policy have assumed an importance which they did not have before.

Inflation in the Chinese economy does not look that high (again by international comparisons), especially when considered together with the growth rate. But the problem of inflation may be more serious than is conveyed by the figures. First, there are reasons to suspect that the actual inflation has been higher than indicated by the official figures. Second, the efficiency costs of inflation in the Chinese economy may be particularly high, since anti-inflationary policies rely heavily on an extension of price controls. This has a strong bearing on relative prices since the proportion of sales at government controlled prices varies widely across commodities. There is a two-way relation between the enterprise reforms and inflation. As we shall see in Sections 3 and 4, the enterprise reforms have been amongst the main factors responsible for inflation. As inflation accelerated in 1988, the government resorted to direct controls on investment and wages, partially reversing the enterprise reforms. In addition, inflation has an adverse effect on public finance: tax revenue is inelastic with respect to inflation, but government expenditure, especially subsidies on prices and to loss-making enterprises, rises sharply with inflation. Finally, the emergence of sharp inequalities in a previously rather more equal society may be socially disruptive – China has not had any effective apparatus for relating incomes to inflation and some groups have been hit by inflation at the same time as others have benefited greatly from the new economic opportunities.

3. Investment and wages

The primary purpose of this section is to analyse the behaviour of investment and wages and their links with the enterprise reforms. We begin by providing a brief description of China's industrial structure and of the reforms.

3.1. Industrial structure and enterprise reforms

China has a peculiar industrial structure (for a discussion see Komiya, 1987). There are 421,000 'independent' industrial enterprises (*duli hesuan gongye*), including rural township enterprises (*xiangban gongye*) but not village enterprises (*cunban gongye*). Were the latter to be included the total would be a massive 1.2 million. The focus of the enterprise reforms has mainly been on 'independent' enterprises, which in 1988 accounted for around 84% of total industrial output. These enterprises are not only numerous but also diverse in terms of ownership and size. State-owned and collectively-owned are the main categories, both of which are heterogeneous, covering a wide range of ownership and organizational arrangements. The ownership status of an enterprise determines the constraints and incentives it faces, and has an important influence on its access to inputs and investment funds. Collective enterprises are, in principle, like employee cooperatives in market economies, and, unlike state-owned enterprises (SOEs), they are relatively free of detailed government control and output planning. They are predominantly small in size.

There are around 72,500 SOEs widely dispersed across different branches of industry, but dominant in metallurgy, heavy capital goods, and in energy. Around 11,000 (15%) SOEs are classified as large and medium size on the basis of the value of their fixed assets, and the rest are small. Unlike collective enterprises, SOEs, especially those of large and medium size, are subject to output planning: they have to sell a proportion of their output at lower plan prices, and correspondingly receive a proportion of their inputs at plan prices. The share of SOEs in industrial output has fallen from about 78% in 1978 to 57% in 1988 because of the faster growth of collective enterprises. Given their special importance to the Chinese economy, we shall concentrate on SOEs (for a detailed discussion of industrial structure see Hussain, 1990).

A schematic chronology of the reforms bearing on SOEs is as follows (see also Granick, 1990, and Tidrick and Chen Jiyuan, 1987).

Main features of SOE reforms

1978–83 Letting enterprises produce outside the plan, retain depreciation allowances and a portion of profits; shift in the financing of working capital and investment from the government budget to internal funds and bank loans; discretion over labour recruitment and the introduction of performance-linked wage bonuses.

1984–86 Letting enterprises sell above-plan output at negotiated prices to other economic agents directly and plan their output accordingly; the replacement of profit remittances to the government with profit taxes; the emergence of commercial banking.

1987–90 Formalization of the role of enterprise directors, their methods of appointment and criteria for the evaluation of their performance; the introduction of multi-year contracts for the payment of taxes, as part of the 'Contract Management Responsibility System' (CMR).

Following the change in leadership in June 1989, enterprise reforms stopped altogether and were even reversed in certain respects. The power of enterprise party committees has been increased and the scope of quantitative planning and price controls extended. But China seems likely to embark on another round of enterprise reforms from 1991.

The central aspects of the reforms on which we now focus are: (i) the delegation of decision-making on investment to enterprises, its financial liberalization, and the implications for investment (Section 3.2); (ii) allowing enterprises discretion over money wages and benefits

Table 4. Share of government investment in total and sources of investment funds in SOEs (%)

| | GI/TI[1] | Sources of investment funds in SOEs | | | | |
		Govt. budget	Bank loans	Foreign investment	Own funds	Other[2]
1981	36.0	44	14	—	42	
1982	29.9	39	16	—	45	
1983	25.0	41	14	2	43	
1984	26.9	39	15	2	39	4
1985	27.2	26	23	3	40	7
1986	22.2	24	23	5	38	10
1987	23.0	21	25	7	38	9
1988	18.5	15	24	9	40	12

[1] GI: government financed investment; TI: total investment in the economy.
[2] Other includes government funds not included in the budget and investment funds provided by other enterpises.
Note: The figures are rounded and may not add to 100.
Sources: The SOE figures for 1981–82 are from SSB (1987b): 14, which does not provide the figures for foreign investment. The rest are from SSB (1986): 417; SSB (1987a): 371; SSB (1988): 405; SSB (1989): 565; SSB (1990a): 411.

in kind and the introduction performance-related bonuses, and their implications for wages (Section 3.3); and (iii) the separation of enterprise budgets from the government budget, multi-period tax contracts, and their implications for public finance (Section 4).

3.2. Financial liberalization and investment

As intended by the reforms, there has been a massive decrease in the percentage of government-financed investment (GI) in total investment (TI), and a substantial change in the sources of investment funds in SOEs, as shown by Table 4. Government-financed includes both public investment and government-funded investment in SOEs.

Two features stand out in Table 4. First, the percentage of government-financed investment in both total investment and investment in SOEs fell in seven years to around half of the figure in 1981. In SOEs, the fall was especially pronounced in 1984–85, following the introduction of the enterprise reform package in the autumn of 1984. Second, the percentage of loan-financed investment nearly doubled. The share of own-financed investment shows no upward trend since 1984, by which date the first set of reforms had already transferred the disposal of gross profits to enterprises. The share of own-financed investment probably increased substantially during 1977–84. The main effect of

Table 5. Annual interest rates on deposits and loans (weighted averages) and the growth rate of bank loans to enterprises (%)

	Deposit rate	Loan rate[1]	Inflation	Real loan rate	Growth rate of loans
1978	2.1	5.0	0.7	4.3	5.1
1979	2.4	4.9	2.0	2.9	3.3
1980	2.8	4.8	6.0	1.2	17.7
1981	2.9	4.9	2.4	2.5	11.7
1982	3.2	6.9	1.9	5.0	7.3
1983	3.3	6.8	1.5	5.3	11.3
1984	3.5	6.7	2.8	3.9	38.3
1985	4.0	7.3	8.8	-1.5	24.9
1986	4.3	7.6	6.0	1.6	43.9
1987	4.4	7.6	7.3	0.3	20.4
1988	4.8	7.8	18.5	-10.7	22.2
1989	8.0	10.9	17.8	-6.9	NA

[1] Includes the rates for budgetary loans.
Source: WB (1991): inflation rates are the same as in Table 1.

enterprise reforms since 1984 has been an increase in investment financed by loans, mostly from banks.

The introduction of loans instead of grants and a positive interest charge for investment funds have been an important feature of the enterprise reforms. Bank loans carry a positive nominal interest rate, own-funds have an opportunity cost and investment funds to enterprises from the government budget take the form of loans. However, the government has considerably weakened the impact of the reform by keeping nominal interest rates low (see Table 5) and, more important, allowing enterprises to deduct the principal as well as the interest from taxable profit, which can reduce the effective interest rate to zero or below. Thus, the tax system provides an incentive to enterprises to substitute bank loans for own-funds for financing investment.

The shift in the sources of investment funds raises two related questions. First, given the government ownership and control of the banking system, what is the significance of the shift? Second, what are its macroeconomic implications? Part of the shift is no more than a change in label: the government, rather than borrowing to provide funds to enterprises, short-circuits the process, instructing banks to lend to enterprises. Nevertheless, the shift represents a real change and its significance lies in the relaxation of rationing on investment funds. The banking system, although government owned, is not closely integrated into government planning machinery. Since 1984, like enterprises, banks have had operational autonomy, and until the tightening of credit in 1989, central control on local branches was weak. Table 5 shows that

Table 6. **Investment as a percentage of value-added**

	State-owned enterprises	Whole economy
1971–77	55.4	32.6
1978–83	55.8	31.6
1984–88	83.4	33.9
1978	57.9	36.5
1979	54.7	34.6
1980	54.4	31.5
1981	48.5	28.3
1982	58.3	28.8
1983	60.8	29.7
1984	68.2	31.5
1985	81.9	35.0
1986	88.9	34.7
1987	90.3	34.2
1988	87.9	34.1

Note: Value added for the state-owned enterprises is estimated by multiplying the value added in the industrial sector
by the share of SOEs in gross industrial output.
Source: SSB (1990a): 24, 225 and 410.

1984 seems to have been a watershed. The real interest rate on loans
dropped, then stayed exceptionally low and negative, by a wide margin,
in 1988 and 1989. The growth rate of bank lending to industrial
enterprises shot up and stayed high, and both money and real wages
increased sharply. The inflation rate accelerated, ending at around
18–19% in 1988–89. The 'real effective' rate of interest was considerably
lower than the 'real loan' rate, given the tax deductibility of principal
repayments.

The massive growth in bank lending to enterprises went together
with a steep rise in the investment rate in SOEs and in the economy in
general, as shown by Table 6. In the five years since 1984, the economy-
wide investment ratio has averaged around 34%. This is exceptionally
high by international standards and is higher than during the pre-
reform period (1971–77), when investment was mostly financed by
budgetary grants, or the first phase of the reforms (1978–83).

The investment ratio in SOEs shows a steady upward trend since
1982. It rose dramatically by 14 percentage points during 1984–85,
immediately following the promulgation of the law on the reform of
SOEs in Autumn 1984.

High investment ratios, especially since 1985, seem due to the lifting
of restraints on enterprises to invest and on banks to lend. The pattern
since 1984 conforms to the familiar multiplier-accelerator interaction:
an increase in investment raised the growth rate, which in turn, via an

increase in demand and resulting shortages, stimulated a further increase in investment. Accelerating inflation since 1985 could be attributed to the economy coming up against supply constraints due to rapid growth. The introduction of the market track in 1984 provided the mechanism which translated shortages into inflation. Given the double-digit output growth since 1984, it seems surprising that inflation climbed to double figures as late as 1988. The main explanation lies in the trade deficits of 5–6% of national income between 1985–86 (see Table 3), which were large by previous standards. The situation changed after 1987: growth remained high, but the government succeeded in reducing the trade deficit to only 1.5% of national income: the result was an accelerating inflation rate.

Given performance since 1984–85, one might argue that with present economic structures the Chinese economy cannot sustain investment ratios of 34–35% without encountering a large balance of trade deficit or a runaway inflation (for further discussion see Naughton, 1990b, c). There is nothing magical about these figures. In principle, such rates of investment could be sustained by controlling household incomes, increasing public-sector savings or by foreign borrowing. As we argued earlier, foreign borrowing would not entirely solve the problem of inflation given the importance of non-tradeables in total expenditure. Nor does the Chinese government want to add significantly to its foreign debt in order to sustain a high level of investment. The implication is that the burden of macroeconomic adjustment has to come via the control of investment or consumption. Economic instruments for controlling consumption have become less strong. As we shall see, government control of wages and salaries has weakened, and personal incomes are largely untaxed. As we saw earlier, households have a large volume of wealth in the form of liquid assets. Higher indirect taxes on consumption goods may appear as a feasible option, but is severely constrained by the aim of keeping inflation low. In sum, there are political and social constraints on controlling consumption in order to accommodate a high investment ratio. A major part of the control of aggregate demand must be through curtailing enterprise investment and bank credit to enterprises. Since Autumn 1988, stringent quantitative controls on enterprise investment and bank credit to enterprises have succeeded in bringing down inflation substantially. Officially, such controls will remain in force until the end of 1992 (see *Beijing Review* 1990, No 9: 'Documents').

In the remaining part of this section we concentrate on three issues: the control of enterprise investment, the case for quantitative controls on investments and credit and the microeconomic effects of high investment ratios. Taking the first issue, the case for increasing the 'real effective' cost of credit, by increasing the nominal interest rate and abolishing the tax deductibility of principal repayments, seems to be strong.

But the problem of constraining enterprise borrowings goes beyond raising the interest rate. The massive expansion of bank lending to enterprises, especially since 1984, was not justified on economic grounds (i.e. the returns on the investment relative to cost of funds) and would not have taken place had banks not been subject to political pressure, especially by lower tiers of the government. Although political pressure was important in credit expansion, the problem does not solely reside there. There would have been an excessive credit creation even with a banking system such as those in market economies. To elaborate, we turn to the capital account of enterprises. Financial autonomy granted to SOEs includes *inter alia* freedom to borrow and to dispose of physical assets within certain limits. Chinese SOEs, and other enterprises, have a capital balance sheet with special features. As many of their assets still date from the period when investment was financed by government grants, they inherited few financial liabilities but comparatively large assets.

The economic reforms introduced the principle that the use of capital should carry a charge, but applied the principle only to new investment, not to the assets inherited from the pre-reform era. The 'adjustment tax' on net-of-tax profits is meant to take into account that inheritance, but its impact is considerably weakened since it is not based on a systematic valuation of assets. The general point is that with a very large volume of physical assets relative to financial liabilities, Chinese SOEs would have a high credit rating in a market economy even if they were running at a loss. The policy suggestion is that if enterprises are allowed to borrow and banks to lend, then the reforms need to concern themselves with the capital account as well as the current account of enterprises, which they have not done thus far.

One way of constraining SOEs in their borrowing would be to create loan liabilities to the government to match the value of inherited assets. This would be equivalent to a 'leveraged buy-out' by the enterprise of the inherited assets and involves a valuation of assets which is necessary not only for financial transactions but also for any radical change in the ownership of SOEs. The raising of interest rates on its own does not address the issue raised here, because it does not discriminate between enterprises according to the volume of inherited assets.

Quantitative controls on investment and credit, although in principle incompatible with a free-market economy, have not been rare in market economies. Even in well-functioning market economies there may be a good theoretical case for encouraging or restricting the use of commodities where the social opportunity cost diverges from the prices faced by users (Guesnerie and Roberts, 1984). The need for stabilization points to some serious weaknesses in the enterprise reforms thus far. When prices are heavily distorted and enterprises are not subject to the types of constraints to which firms in a market economy are subject, the delegation of economic decision-making to enterprises is not invariably a desirable development.

The strong case for raising the 'real effective' interest rate does not preclude quantitative controls on credit and investment in the short run. There are economic arguments for quantitative controls as a supplement to desirable price adjustments. First, it is usually infeasible to remove all major price distortions at one stroke. Second, estimating the exact change in quantity in response to a change in price, which is what one needs for policy, may be subject to a wide margin of error, and deviation from the intended target may have a high cost (Weitzman, 1974). Under the present set up in China, it is far from clear what level of 'real effective' interest rate would achieve a level of investment compatible with particular targets for the inflation and the trade deficit. It would seem prudent to retain some direct control on the quantity and allocation of investment and gradually relax that control as markets function better and prices give less distorted signals.

We turn now to the microeconomic effect of a high investment ratio. The total value of investment started but yet to be completed in 1988 was 1,300 bn. yuan, which is over three times the rate of investment and exceeded national income during the year. Between 1987 and 1988, the ratio of investment in gestation to new investment rose by 12 percentage points, even though the investment ratio remained constant (see Table 6). This may indicate an excessively high investment ratio. Given the general shortages of inputs such as steel and cement, the start of a major investment project is likely to prolong the gestation period of already started investment projects, but this cost is not taken into account by enterprises when they embark upon new investment because it is not relevant to them. This congestion externality is analogous to taking a car on a congested road in a regime where charges for the use of a road are low or non-existent.

Chinese enterprises do not face serious risks of bankruptcy or take-over. With distorted prices and free insurance against downside risks, an investment project may appear profitable to enterprises but be highly unprofitable from the social point of view. Similar problems arise in the utilization of the existing capital stock, which may be hampered by a serious shortage of electricity and fuel. Quantitative controls on investment projects may improve the utilization of existing capital. Alternatively, sharp increases in the prices of goods in short supply would be appropriate but this, via inflation, may be politically difficult.

For macroeconomic control it is total investment that matters; for efficiency and the allocation of resources, the sectoral allocation of investment is critical. Indeed macroeconomic excess demand can appear through supply-side inefficiencies and misallocations. China has had relatively low investment in infrastructure, transportation and energy, a failure of investment planning. Ideally the macroeconomic control of investment should be complemented with improvements in investment planning. The Chinese economy will remain a planned economy over the medium term, but the reform of the planning system has been neglected. Planning in China should move away from output planning, the control of trade in commodities, towards investment planning, which remains necessary while market prices are severely distorted. This strategy, properly executed, should overcome some of the distortions so that more can be left to the market, and government actions can be concentrated on infrastructure.

3.3. Wages

In the pre-1978 period, labour earnings in SOEs, and also in collective enterprises, were controlled by the government and independent of the unit of employment. Wages conformed to a national wage scale and enterprises had little discretion over the assignment of workers to wage grades. The wage bonus linked to enterprise performance, introduced in the 1950s, was suppressed during the Cultural Revolution's move from material to moral incentives.

There has been a radical change in the composition of industrial earnings, as shown by Table 7. In particular, there has been a marked shift away from time wages and, as with the change in investment financing, the net effect has been to loosen the government's control on industrial earnings. A national wage scale still governs time wages in state-owned enterprises, though not in collective enterprises. Piece wages are largely decided by enterprises, because what constitutes a piece of work varies from enterprise to enterprise. The shift towards piece wages forms part of the attempt to increase labour productivity by providing incentives. Wage bonuses linked to enterprise perform-ance, reintroduced in 1983, are not under direct government control. Besides, enterprise managers now have greater power to promote or demote workers than they did before the reforms. Subsidies are mainly compensation for inflation, and have gone up with the increase in inflation, reflecting the onset of a wage-price spiral familiar in market economies. As yet there is no formal nation-wide indexation.

Table 7. Composition of nominal wages in the state sector (%)

	Time wages	Piece wages	Bonuses	Subsidies	Other
1978	85.0	0.8	2.3	6.5	5.4
1980	69.8	3.2	9.1	14.1	3.8
1983	63.5	8.5	11.1	14.1	2.8
1984	58.5	9.5	14.4	14.5	3.1
1985	57.2	9.5	12.4	18.5	2.4
1986	56.3	8.7	12.8	18.8	3.4
1987	54.3	9.2	14.7	18.9	2.9
1988	49.0	9.4	17.2	21.4	3.0

Note: The figures refer to all state sector employees. Subsidies refer to cost-of living payments.
Source: SSB (1989): 182; SSB (1990a): 102.

In addition to cash income, employees receive a sizeable income in kind, notably, heavily subsidized housing. Around three-quarters of housing in urban areas is owned by organizations (or work units), which can increase the income of employees by investing in housing. This increased sharply with the industrial reforms: the share of housing in total investment rose from 12% during the fifth five-year plan (1976–80) to over 21% during the sixth five-year plan (1981–85), then fell to 16% during 1986–87 (SSB 1989: 567). The increase may have seemed 'necessary' given its previously low level, but it also implied a substantial increase in the real incomes of employees – house rents in China are often too low to cover even the maintenance cost of dwellings. The fact that a substantial proportion of personal earnings accrue in kind is of considerable significance. First, government control over personal earnings is much looser than is indicated by control over wages and salaries in cash. Second, enterprises can evade profit tax by using operational profit to provide benefits in kind to their employees, which are not taxable under the personal income tax (which plays a negligible role in China). Third, as benefits in kind for employees vary considerably among work units, inequality among the labour force of the state sector is greater than inequality in cash income.

Government control over personal earnings, although still formidable, is a lot weaker than it was before the reforms. The shift in the composition of earnings indicated by Table 7 has gone together with a rapid increase in labour earnings, as shown by Table 8. While the high rates of increase in real wages between 1979 and 1980 might be regarded as a 'correction' for low wages in the pre-reform period, the sharp acceleration in nominal and real wages between 1984–86 seems to be due, first, to the enterprise reforms, which gave enterprises a

Table 8. Annual increase in nominal and real labour earnings in SOEs (%)

	Nominal wages	Cost of living[1]	Real wages
1979	9.0	1.9	7.6
1980	13.5	7.5	6.0
1981	0.6	2.5	−1.9
1982	1.6	2.0	−0.4
1983	2.1	2.0	0.1
1984	20.7	2.7	18.0
1985	17.1	11.9	5.2
1986	15.4	7.0	8.4
1987	10.7	8.8	1.9
1988	20.4	20.7	−0.3

[1] The cost of living index for 'workers and staff', which is not the same as the retail price index for the whole economy given in Table 1.
Source: SSB (1989): 194. The 1988 figure is from SSB (1990a): 110.

greater discretion over the wages of their employees, and, second, to the acceleration in the inflation rate. Real wages fell slightly in 1988, which fits in with the widespread disenchantment with the economic reforms in 1988.

The acceleration in wages coincides fairly closely with the increase in the investment ratio. The reforms simultaneously loosened control over enterprise investment and wages, thereby engineering both a consumption and an investment boom. The conjunction of the two, together with the extension of the market determination of prices, eventually led to a rapid inflation. Again, one can make a case for control of personal earnings. In the pre-reform period, with tight direct control over wages, and there was no need for personal taxation to control disposable income. Now those direct controls have been considerably weakened, there is a need for additional policy instruments such as taxes on personal incomes. As with investment, we have an interesting problem of sequencing. The goal is to free markets and if all were operating smoothly there would be little argument for quantitative controls in any of them. However, freeing just one set of decisions may create serious difficulties.

The argument usually advanced for wage controls in market economies holds also for the Chinese economy, but with a greater force. Employees care not only about how many yuan per month they get but also how many yuan per month other employees get. Arguably, sensitivity to relative wages is greater in China than in market economies because until recently a national wage scale covered all employees of the state sector. Wage differences between occupations and industries were very small. Interestingly, after enquiry about one's age, marital status and work units one of the first questions one gets asked in China is 'how much do you earn?'.

The rise in wages since 1984 has been coupled with significant changes in relative wages. A common refrain in China is that a hotel waiter gets more than professor and a barber more than a surgeon (Liu Guoguang, 1989). The upheaval in the structure of relative wages is widely regarded as unjust and has been one of the major causes of disenchantment with the reforms. There is a pattern to these changes. Whilst the incomes of the self-employed and of those engaged in the production of marketed goods and services have raced ahead, those of groups engaged in providing non-marketed services such as education, health and in the government have fallen behind. Some changes in relative wages may have been conducive to furthering labour efficiency, especially within an enterprise; others have created disenchantment.

Finally, we turn to an issue implicit in the discussions of wage increases. Liu Guoguang (1989) has remarked that enterprises have used their autonomy to grant wage increases unrelated to increases in productivity. There is also anecdotal evidence that in many cases enterprise managers, rather than resisting, have exploited gaps and loopholes in the regulations to meet the demands of their labour force for wage increases. The general suggestion is that in many cases enterprise managers collude with their labour force. Rather than pursuing profit they seek to increase the income of their labour force. There are three parties to the enterprise reforms: the government, enterprise managers and the enterprise labour force. The presence of the third party means that enterprise reforms should take into account the relation between the enterprise management and the labour force, and the possibility of collusion between them against the government. This implies that a mere transfer of decision-making to enterprise managers may not be sufficient to induce profit seeking. Enterprise reforms must also introduce incentive schemes and constraints to prevent collusion between enterprise management and the labour force to the detriment of the economy at large.

4. Public finance

A central feature of the enterprise reforms has been the disengagement of enterprise budgets from the government budget. This implies a reduction in government revenue and expenditure relative to national income (see Blejer and Szapary, 1989). We are concerned with the magnitude of this reduction; the impact of the enterprise reforms on the composition of government revenue and expenditure; and the size of budget deficits in the reform period, and their role in the acceleration of inflation. We shall argue that the deficit was not of sufficient magnitude to play a major role in accounting for the inflation. We do, however, stress disturbing trends on both the expenditure and revenue sides. The reforms have led to very large subsidies as price incentives to producers are offered at the same time as attempting to hold prices to the consumers. And the provision of revenues to finance future government expenditures is likely to require the building of a tax system appropriate for a more decentralized economy to replace the public profits on which the earlier system was based.

In the pre-reform period, gross profits of state-owned enterprises (SOEs) with some exceptions accrued to the government. In effect, SOEs were subject to a 100% tax on their operational profit. In turn, the government provided SOEs with working capital and investment funds as grants. Following the 1984 enterprise reforms, most SOEs have become financially independent, retaining their depreciation allowances and profits net of taxes, which can be used for investment or wage bonuses. Financially independent SOEs are expected to finance their working capital and their investment from own-funds or bank loans. Funds for enterprises still provided from the government budget now carry an interest charge, though, as we indicated in Section 3 it loses much of its impact because of the tax policy.

The enterprise reforms have had an effect on the government budget which is asymmetric between profits and losses. The government has decreased its share in positive profits from 100% to 55% or less (under the profit tax), but still has to bear 100% of losses. As in other socialist economies undergoing market-oriented reforms, making enterprises responsible for their own profit and loss means many enterprises are not financially viable. This confronts the Chinese government with an especially difficult dilemma: given the extensive social welfare and other obligations of enterprises to their employees and pensioners, it is wary of letting loss-making enterprises go bankrupt; conversely, sustaining loss-making enterprises through budget subsidies goes against the 'incentive' spirit of the reforms and creates a substantial public finance problem.

The enterprise reforms did not, it seems, fully take into account their consequences for public finance. The decline in government revenue relative to national income appears to have been much greater than expected, a point of substantial importance to all economies attempting decentralization. If incomes or profits are left in the hands of individuals or enterprises to provide incentives, government activities must be financed in some other way. Decentralization requires a new tax system. We turn now to the impact of the enterprise reforms on government revenue, expenditure and budget deficit.

Table 9. The composition of government revenue

	Govt. revenue/ National income (%)	% of government revenue			% of national income		
		Enterprise taxes			Enterprise taxes		
		Direct	Indirect	Other	Direct	Indirect	Other
1978	41.4	60.0	32.0	8.0	24.9	13.3	3.3
1979	37.6	60.0	33.7	6.3	22.6	12.7	2.4
1980	35.6	59.3	34.5	6.2	21.1	12.3	2.2
1981	35.5	57.2	35.4	7.4	20.3	12.6	2.6
1982	32.9	52.5	38.7	8.8	17.3	12.8	2.9
1983	33.4	47.2	35.1	17.7	15.8	11.7	5.9
1984	32.3	44.0	36.5	19.5	14.2	11.7	6.3
1985	29.7	33.2	41.7	25.1	9.9	12.7	7.2
1986	28.8	33.6	42.6	22.2	9.6	12.2	6.9
1987	26.5	31.9	42.5	22.2	8.9	11.3	6.4
1988	23.7	24.9	43.6	33.0	5.9	10.3	7.8
1989	23.2	17.9	46.3	37.4	4.1	10.5	8.5

Source: SSB (1990a): 24 and World Bank (1990a).

4.1. Government revenue

The massive decline in the ratio of government revenue to national income is shown by Table 9. Over the 12 years from 1978–89, the government revenue ratio has fallen by over 18 percentage points, eight percentage points during the first phase of the enterprise reforms, then another 10 percentage points in just six years spanning the second phase 1984–89. Thus, the shift of focus from rural to the enterprise reforms in 1984 sharply accelerated the decline. This may be due to the 'Contract Management Responsibility System' (CMR), which began to be introduced on a large scale at that time (see Section 3).

It is also helpful to look at changes in the components of government revenue, which we divide into three parts: taxes on enterprise profits, indirect taxes, which are nominally paid by enterprises, and the rest. The rest covers *inter alia* agricultural taxes, customs duties, non-tax revenue and personal taxes (for a discussion of the tax system see Easson and Li Jiyan, 1987).

Table 9 brings out a number of significant points. The decrease in the revenue ratio between 1978–89 is almost entirely accounted for by the decrease in the ratio of direct taxes from the enterprise sector to national income. *Prima facie*, this decrease could arise as a result of two factors: first, a reduction in the proportion of profits taken by taxes; and second, a reduction in the share of profits in national income. The latter if true would be somewhat paradoxical, given that the general thrust of the reforms is to encourage profit seeking. But, as we saw in the preceding section, there is some indirect evidence that this may have happened.

As one would expect given the fall in direct enterprise taxes, the share of indirect taxes in government revenue has risen. But, significantly, the ratio of indirect taxes to national income also seems to have fallen, especially since 1985. The fall is a little puzzling because it would be difficult to attribute this to the enterprise reforms as such. This may be due partly to the problems of tax collection created by the reform and partly the 'Contract Management Responsibility System'. A large part of the increase in the 'other' is due to the increase in customs revenue arising from the substantial of the expansion of foreign trade.

Direct taxes in Table 9 include remittances to the government from enterprises and the profit tax. Until 1983, government revenue from enterprises largely accrued in the form of 'remittances', which were enterprise-specific and decided through bilateral bargaining. Since then, for 'financially independent' SOEs, a profit tax has replaced remittances. The profit tax in China has two peculiar features: first, tax rates vary with the size (defined in terms of the value of assets) and also the ownership status of enterprises, which makes the yield from the profit tax dependent on the distribution of output across ownership categories. Second, not only interest on loans but also the repayment of principal by SOEs is tax-deductible. This must be responsible for a significant erosion of the tax base, given the expansion in the borrowings by SOEs (see Table 4). Large- and medium-size SOEs are subject to a tax rate of 55%, and they may also be subject to an enterprise-specific 'income adjustment tax', which is meant to take account of the differential endowment of assets inherited from the pre-reform era free of charge. Small SOEs and collective enterprises are subject to a non-linear tax schedule with a maximum marginal rate of 55%. Collective enterprises, which are mostly small, are more lightly taxed than their state-owned counterparts. This has an adverse long-term implication for government revenue in that the share of collective enterprises in industrial has been increasing.

Indirect taxes paid by enterprises include Product Tax, Value Added Tax and the Business Tax. Product Tax applies to a wide range of products, is similar to a sales tax, and is levied at widely different rates on the purchaser price, (rather than the producer price). It cannot be shifted to purchasers when the product is sold at government-fixed prices. Value Added Tax is gradually replacing Product Tax, and it too is levied on the purchaser price. As output and prices are, in many cases, regulated, indirect taxes often act like direct taxes.

Another central feature of the Chinese tax system is that direct and indirect taxes paid by enterprises may depart considerably from formal rates. This is due to the CMR, which is intended to reduce government interference in enterprise management, and since 1986 has covered around 70% of SOEs (for a discussion of the CMR see Koo, 1990). Under the system an enterprise pre-commits itself to handing over to the government fixed amounts of not merely direct but also indirect taxes every year over the period of contract, which ranges over two to five years. The contracted sum is usually equal to the tax bill for the year preceding the start of the contract, and may rise at a pre-set rate over the contract period. These contracts, which are arrived at by bargaining between the supervising agency and the enterprise, vary widely. The contracted sum of taxes is fixed in nominal terms. Where an enterprise is 'unable' to meet the contract, it can appeal to the government for a revision of the contract on the ground of circumstances beyond its control. In 1988, around 9% of enterprises covered by the CMR failed to meet their tax target; the figure for 1989 is expected to be considerably higher.

The CMR has a number of important consequences for government revenue. First, the tax rate on above-target profit is zero. Similarly, pre-set quotas for indirect taxes imply that output in excess of some level is free of taxes. Both reduce the income elasticity of government revenue. The quotas for indirect taxes may account for the fall in the ratio of indirect taxes to national income mentioned above. Second, government tax revenue bears (in real terms) the consequences of an unforeseen increase in the inflation rate and variations in enterprise profits. If profit exceeds the government estimate implicit in the contract then the whole of the unforeseen profit accrues to the enterprise. Where profit is below expectation, the enterprise is expected to meet the contract from its reserves. However, if the enterprise is simply unable to meet the contract then the government has no option but to revise the contracted sum downwards, as inability to meet financial obligations is still not regarded as a sufficient reason for bankruptcy. The implications of the CMR for government revenue are clearly of significance because between 1986–88, direct and indirect taxes on enterprises accounted for around three-quarters of government revenue.

From the point of view of public finance there is little to be said in favour of the CMR other than that it simplifies some aspects of tax collection. The effect of the system on economic incentives is not clear either. The regime is not one of lump-sum taxes, since in addition to the tax quotas of the CMR, enterprises are subject to various forms of *ad hoc* levies and forced contributions by the local government, and these depend on the financial position of the enterprise. These are

illegal but appear to be widespread, given that they were singled out
for criticism in the Central Committee communique at the end of the
important November 1989 plenum (see *Beijing Review* 1990: No. 7).
Besides, the period of CMR contracts is only two to five years. Expectations concerning the terms of the next contract are likely to have a
strong bearing on current enterprise behaviour. Generally speaking,
enterprises would expect that the target rate of profit and thus tax
quotas in the next contract would depend on the difference between
the target and the actual rate of profit during the current contract
period. This would give rise to the 'ratchet effect' common under the
traditional output planning in socialist economies. The current
performance acts like a notched gear wheel in fixing the target for the
following contract period (for a discussion see Weitzman, 1980).
Moreover, multi-year fiscal contracts are like a built-in macroeconomic
destabilizer, in that they make the disposable enterprise profit high
when the growth rate and the inflation rate are higher than the trend
rates and conversely when the growth and inflation are low.

4.2. Government expenditure

Government expenditure has also fallen substantially, the fall being
roughly similar in magnitude to the fall in the revenue ratio, though
somewhat smaller. The patterns of decline in the two are not the same.
As a result, as we point out later, there has usually been a budget deficit
in the post-1978 period. For the present purposes what is particularly
notable is the change in the composition of government expenditure,
as shown by Table 10.

Two features stand out: a substantial shift from capital to current
expenditure, and a large increase in price subsidies and subsidies to
loss-making enterprises. Both are direct consequences of the economic
reforms. Together they may have pre-empted investment in infrastructure needed to maintain the growth in the economy. The decline in
capital expenditure is implied by the transfer of the financing of investment from the government to enterprises. However, there are limits
to the displacement of government investment by enterprise investment,
as there are items of investment which cannot be so shifted. These
include not only investment in infrastructure but also investment in
those industries which are forced to sell a significant proportion of their
output at low 'plan prices'. These industries include the coal, electricity,
oil and steel industries. Electricity and coal have been in short supply
throughout the reform period.

The increase in price subsidies has been due mainly to large increases
in the procurement prices of agricultural commodities (in particular

Table 10. Composition of government expenditure (%)

	Govt. expenditure/ National income	Current expenditure			Capital expenditure
		Total	Price subsidies	Enterprise losses	
1978	41.2	56.5	6.4	2.9	43.5
1979	43.8	58.7	10.9	2.4	41.3
1980	39.6	67.7	16.4	2.3	32.3
1981	37.0	74.2	22.7	2.9	25.8
1982	34.6	76.3	21.6	3.5	23.7
1983	35.5	74.8	18.9	6.2	25.2
1984	34.0	71.2	16.7	4.4	28.8
1985	31.0	72.3	14.1	7.7	27.7
1986	30.9	71.3	9.2	12.3	28.7
1987	27.1	73.3	10.4	13.3	26.7
1988	26.6	74.6	9.8	13.9	25.4
1989	25.5	77.7	11.8	15.1	22.3

Note: Price subsidies largely consist of those on grain, cooking oil and fertilizers.
Source: World Bank (1990a).

grain), by way of economic incentives, which were not fully passed on to urban consumers. The share of price subsidies in total government expenditure fell substantially after 1982, but began to rise from 1987 with the acceleration in the inflation rate. The deceleration in the inflation rate between autumn 1989 and autumn 1990 has relied heavily on the control of purchaser prices for consumer goods. Unlike in the pre-reform period, the government can no longer exercise complete control over procurement prices and rely entirely on commands to meet its procurement targets. It has to provide sufficient economic incentives to producers. The parallel markets in agriculture produce, together with the discretion of households over the deployment of their labour, set a lower bound on procurement prices and mean that low consumer ration prices cannot be offset by low procurement prices.

The share of expenditure on subsidies to loss-making enterprises has risen fairly steadily since 1980; and the 1984 enterprise reforms, which included the introduction of the two-track system, seem to have accelerated the upward trend. Comparing Tables 9 and 10, the yield of direct enterprise taxes in relative terms has fallen substantially, but the share of government expenditure on subsidies to loss-making enterprises has risen sharply. The effect of this two-way squeeze on the public finances may be illustrated by looking at the net yield from the profit tax: the revenue from profit tax less the subsidies to loss-making enterprises (see Table 11).

**Table 11. Net yield from
profit tax as a percentage
of national income**

1978	23.7
1979	21.6
1980	20.2
1981	19.3
1982	16.1
1983	13.6
1984	12.7
1985	7.5
1986	5.4
1987	5.3
1988	2.2
1989	0.2

Source: Net yield is equal to
profit tax minus subsidies to
loss-making enterprises and is
derived from Tables 9 and 10.

Notwithstanding the decrease in the percentage of enterprise profit accruing to the government, it would seem that enterprise profitability has fallen significantly, especially since 1985. The decrease in the net yield from the profit tax since 1985 coincides fairly closely with the massive increase in borrowing by SOEs (see Table 4) and a sharp acceleration in the wage rate increases in SOEs (see Table 8). The first lowers taxable profits significantly, as both interest and principal repayments are tax-deductible, and the second reduces operational profits.

4.3. Budget deficits

The ratio of the (measured) budget deficit to national income over the 12 years is provided in Table 12. Since 1978 when the budget was roughly in balance, the expenditure ratio has more or less tracked the revenue ratio but with a lag. As a result, the Chinese government has run a deficit every year since 1978. By international standards the ratios of deficits to national income are comparatively small. There are two points to be made about the pattern of the financing of deficits over the reform period. First, there has been a noticeable shift from borrowing from the central bank (The People's Bank), which amounts to the printing of money, to the other two sources. Second, the importance of foreign borrowing has increased in later years. The growing importance of bond financing is connected with the development of the financial market, which did not exist at the outset of the reforms.

Table 12. Budget deficits relative to national income and their financing (%)

	Deficit/NI[1]	Source of deficit financing as % of deficit[2]		
		Money Creation[3]	Bonds[4]	Foreign borrowing
1978	−0.20	125.0	0.0	−25.0
1979	6.10	82.5	0.0	17.5
1980	4.00	84.9	0.0	15.1
1981	1.50	−39.7	84.5	55.2
1982	1.70	40.8	62.0	−2.8
1983	2.00	44.8	43.8	11.4
1984	1.80	42.9	40.0	17.1
1985	1.30	−51.2	148.8	2.4
1986	2.10	39.7	30.7	29.6
1987	0.60	26.0	46.0	28.0
1988	2.90	22.6	44.5	32.9
1989	2.30	NA	NA	NA

Source:
[1] Derived from Tables 9 and 10.
[2] From World Bank (1990a).
[3] Denotes borrowing from the central bank.
[4] Includes borrowing from banks, enterprises and individuals.

In assessing what level of domestically financed deficits (seigniorage plus bonds) may be sustainable in the Chinese economy, one must keep in mind the fact that the financial market is still in its infancy in China. Even with what appear to be relatively low levels of bond holdings, the government has had to force enterprises and wage and salary earners to purchase government bonds (for details of the method of sale of bonds see World Bank, 1991). The government cannot assume that an unforeseen increase in expenditure can always be financed by an increase in the budget deficit.

Estimating budget deficits and analysing their impact in an economy undergoing transition from a command economy to a market economy raises some fundamental issues. The distinction between the government and the non-government sector, in particular the enterprise sector, is not clear cut. Visible subsidies to loss-making enterprises are included in the budget. But bank lending to enterprises, at the behest of the government, which is not justified by commercial criteria, constitutes a potential financial liability for the government but is not included in the budget. As the volume of such lending appears to be substantial, measured budget deficits may underestimate actual budget deficits by a significant margin.

Accurate measurement of budget deficits is important for the planning of public finance, but we must recognize the size of the budget

deficit is unlikely to be the main problem with public finance in China
(see also Blejer and Szapary, 1989 and Takahashi, 1989). The government with its control of the banking system and coercive power over
enterprise can finance its expenditure. Rather, we would suggest,
the main problems lie with the tax system and the composition of
expenditure.

5. Concluding comments

Our primary purpose in this paper has been an examination of the
implications of the reforms in China since 1978 for effective demand
and public finance. We have linked the reforms to the development of
the central components of demand, of revenue and of expenditure.
We have seen that the standard macroeconomic framework with one
good, and with consumers, firms and government as separate agents,
is inadequate to understand developments in China during this period.
There are a number of reasons for this. First, the agricultural sector
has been treated differently from industry and in ways which have had
an important bearing on supplies, demands and public finance. Second,
managers, workers and government interact in the determination of
outputs, investments, incomes, consumption and taxes in a manner
which the standard division into consumers, firms and government fails
to capture. Third, while the expansion of foreign trade has been of
substantial importance, the rest of the economy has been partially
insulated from it. Fourth, the labour market responds to demand
increases and decreases predominantly by changing labour allocations
within firms rather than by open unemployment. Fifth, consumption
decisions are taken in large part through enterprises rather than entirely
through households and the distinction between consumption and
investment can be blurred. As a result the detail of the workings of the
institutions and of the reforms matters a great deal to the understanding
of both their micro and macro implications. In these circumstances a
crude application of simple standard macroeconomic models is likely
to obscure some central questions in the understanding of the determinants of effective demand and of the public finances.

The three central sections of this paper traced the recent macroeconomic developments, the behaviour of investment and wages and
the changes in the public finances. We concentrated primarily on
the analysis of the effects of government policy. We shall highlight our
main conclusions following the order described, emphasizing those
implications which have lessons for other countries and which require
close attention in the subsequent development of policy.

The reform period in China has been characterized by very rapid growth both by historical and international standards. In the period 1978–83, when the reforms were concentrated on agriculture, the growth of agriculture was particularly rapid (almost as fast as industry) but subsequently, during the period of the industrial enterprise reforms, growth in industry outstripped that of agriculture. There is little doubt that the rewarding of, or sharing in, productivity increases has produced a massive supply response. It is much less easy to judge how far allocative efficiency has improved. There are still many price distortions and the hybrid between a command and a market economy, for example the two-track pricing system, seems to lead to substantial effort being devoted to arbitraging and manipulating a highly distorted system (where post-arbitrage allocations and prices may be no less distorted than pre-arbitrage). Further, the scope for reallocations between firms is still highly restricted by the inflexibilities in factor markets.

Inflation rose dramatically at the end of the 1980s causing great concern and leading to a severe reaction. The stop phase consisted in large part of a control in demand through the reimposition of controls. There was also an attempt to impose greater tightness through credit markets but it seems that the older methods had the more substantial effect. In the Chinese economy there is a two-way relationship between inflation and excess demand on the one hand and controls on the other. Controls are harder to enforce with higher demand, yet their relaxation leads to an increase in measured inflation to which the government reacts by a cut in demand and a reimposition of controls.

The decentralization of economic decisions and the rising importance of individual behaviour has not been confined to production. The government has now to take much more careful account of household choices and expectations. This is exemplified by our brief discussion of the dramatic rise in household bank deposits relative to national income. With the rise in household bank deposits, which we have treated as a proxy for household wealth, and the shift towards a market economy, the expectations of households have assumed an increasing importance for the conduct of macroeconomic policy. One can approach the problem posed by household bank deposit either in terms of reducing real balances (via inflation or taxes) or providing households (especially urban ones) with a wider menu of assets to hold. The former seems politically unattractive, but the consideration of the latter points to an important lacuna in the Chinese economic reforms.

The reforms have taken into account households as consumers, producers (as in the case of rural households or the self-employed in cities) or as suppliers of wage labour. But, as yet, they have neglected the forms in which households hold assets and their implications. In spite of a dramatic increase in household income and wealth, the assets available to urban households are not significantly different from those in the pre-reform period. There is a strong argument in favour of concerted financial innovation to diversify household wealth away from liquid assets. Such innovations could include the sale of equity in state-owned enterprises and urban housing to individuals and an increase in the coverage of contributory old-age pensions; pensions for the most part are still non-contributory.

Our discussion of the determination of investment and wages was set out in Section 3. We argued that the relaxing of controls on investment, the encouragement to take profitable opportunities, the transfer of control over assets without corresponding liabilities, the granting of effective insurance against losses while lowering taxes on profits, and the weakness of the banking and credit systems, all combined to produce a strong investment boom. At the same time the loosening of control over wages, the provision of wage incentives, and the expansion of opportunities for perks and social- or enterprise-based consumption led to strong wage and consumption pressure and, paradoxically, the decline of profitability at the moment when the seeking of profits was being encouraged and facilitated.

There are now serious problems concerning investment in the Chinese economy. The investment ratio has been too high in recent years, creating problems both for demand and supply. It has not only fuelled aggregate demand, it has also slowed addition to supply, by prolonging the gestation period of investment projects, and reducing the rate of utilization of existing capital stock. Severe congestion difficulties imply that the problem lies not merely with high investment but, equally important, also with the composition of investment. The decentralization of investment decisions without appropriate price signals, charges for investment funds and attention to the capital account of enterprises may have reduced the efficiency of capital use.

The solution to these problems with investment should lie eventually with a reform of the price system to give better incentives, a tax system which does not excessively distort, a genuine possibility of bankruptcy to punish errors, labour market flexibility to allow for adjustment and a social security system that protects against its most severe costs. It is naive in the extreme to expect that all these things can appear overnight. In the interim China has to control its investment and try to improve its allocation. One cannot in the short run automatically assume that direct controls should be eschewed both for the aggregate and its distribution across sectors and projects. A possibility for the improved use of such controls would be a more extensive application of systems of project appraisal.

The effects of the enterprise reforms on government revenue and expenditure were not adequately assessed in advance. The steep fall in the revenue ratio should have been anticipated, but, perhaps more important, the massive rise in government expenditure on price subsidies and subsidies to loss-making enterprises has also been a direct consequence of the reforms. This has a number of implications for public policy. First, there is an urgent need for a systematic evaluation of the effects of the enterprise reforms on public finance. Second, since the tenor of the enterprise reforms is to decrease the importance of the enterprise sector as the source of government revenue, a diversification of the sources of government revenue is required. In particular, there is a strong argument for the introduction of a more wide-ranging tax on personal incomes, covering both incomes in cash and kind. Such a tax should *prima facie* be easier to introduce in China than in many other developing economies, as almost all of the formally employed labour force (25% of the total labour force) is either in the state or the collective sector, both of which are under close government control. Such taxation would have a role not only in raising revenue but also in regulating demand.

The change in the composition of government expenditure reflects major problems. Although the enterprise reforms imply a decrease in the percentage of government expenditure devoted to investment, limitations on government investment are creating problems in sustaining growth. There are widespread shortages of goods and services which depend crucially in their production and distribution on infrastructure such as electricity and transport. Further, a high proportion of government expenditure on both price subsidies and subsidies to loss-making enterprises suggests a careful re-examination of their social and economic benefits. As long as enterprise bankruptcies remain rare, and the government feels constrained to rely almost exclusively on price subsidies to attain social welfare objectives, subsidies will remain largely beyond government control.

It is the composition of revenue and expenditure that causes most concern for the future. Given the strong controls available to the government, deficits can be controlled and there does not seem to be strong evidence that they were the prime source of recent inflation. Future government responsibilities for infrastructure, together with an expansion of responsibilities for education, health and social security (given the likelihood of a declining role for the enterprise in these areas) will require a strong revenue base and this must now be reconstructed. At the same time a major contribution both to finance and efficiency can come from redirecting expenditure away from subsidies and towards productive investment.

Generally we see that the problems of public finance both on the revenue and expenditure sides are very different in a decentralized market economy from a command economy. For revenue the government could rely primarily on profits of enterprise. If these are to be increasingly left with enterprises, other sources of revenue are necessary. Decentralization inevitably requires new forms of taxation and this basic lesson was not appreciated at the outset. Similarly the pattern of expenditures must change. Old responsibilities, such as those for investment, can be shed but new ones must be accepted. In particular if enterprises are to be allowed to react flexibility, shed labour where necessary and even go bankrupt, the government must play an increased role in the provision of health, education, social security and, in part, housing. Economic policy in transition must recognize that what is at issue is not simply a matter of reducing government: a clear understanding of the requirements of a radical change in their composition is essential.

China's record of growth under the reforms has been most impressive. The problems we have indicated may, however, seriously impede building on that success and may devalue the reforms in the eyes of those who might otherwise be ready to go further. The problems that China has already faced and the achievements it has secured have strong lessons for those countries embarking on their transition more recently. These countries have a great deal to learn from the study of China's experience.

Discussion

Michael Burda
INSEAD

This paper gives an excellent analysis of economic reform in China since 1984. In these comments I shall play the devil's advocate and claim that China is, from a macroeconomic perspective, not fundamentally different from other developing countries, and that developments in China are readily understood with simple macroeconomic models. Thus, most of what I have to say will under-emphasize the role of institutions, except for the importance of bankruptcy, an institution that is lacking in China as in most East European economies in transition. Overall, the lesson is simply that liberalized economies function poorly with soft budget constraints, a lesson not restricted to China in the 1980s.

Intermediation, Investment and Growth

I would characterize the Chinese experience in the latter half of the 1980s as a remarkable investment boom, led by state-owned enterprises (SOEs) and funded with massive intermediation by a liberalized banking system and the blessing of the central bank. Real interest rates were remarkably low in this period, and made even lower through the curious tax deductability of amortized principal payments. This was no doubt aggravated by the sensitivity of after-tax real interest rates when nominal interest is deductable and inflation is rising. Given the lack of financial assets around, might not fixed business investment also represent a vehicle for protection against inflation? Irrespective of causation, high rates of investment are associated with high growth rates, and China is no exception. The authors raise a valid concern about the supply-side effects of this investment boom, with strong concentration by SOEs. But China is still moving from an agrarian to an industrial phase of development, in which the SOEs are of prime importance, so it is hard to tell whether their concern is justified. Congestion externalities of heavy investment are present in all developing countries, and little hard evidence is adduced here that resources are being wasted. Similarly, a more detailed discussion of the supply-side implications of low investment in infrastructure, transport and energy would have made this case more convincing.

Perhaps wishing to encourage intermediation for efficiency and welfare reasons, the central bank accommodated the explosion of credit which ultimately led to inflation in 1988–89. Was all this intermediation really efficient? The authors suggest that it was mainly a reflection of opportunistic behaviour of SOE managers and workers, who are simply levering up their companies on the back of the government. In this view, what has happened in China is a transfer to SOEs and their workers (via investment and wages) financed by debt which is ultimately the liability of the government. The authors advocate quantitative restrictions on credit allocation to enterprises and control of investment projects, rather than raising real interest rates to positive levels, or removing tax-based distortions at the source. Their justification is that without quantitative restrictions, companies with high physical capital endowments will then get all the credit, since they are the best collateralized. More importantly, leverage does not discipline managers in China the way it does in Western economies.

In my opinion, this phenomenon rather clearly underscores the need for bankruptcy as a disciplining device in decentralizing socialist economies. If firms faced bankruptcy risk and if managers were accountable, subjective valuation of the assets would represent a sufficient constraint on firm borrowing. Wage increases that threatened enterprise viability would be resisted. Lacking a bankruptcy threat, however, SOEs will continue to behave as if they faced a soft budget constraint: they will continue to spend and borrow until controls are imposed. Domestic credit has risen from 61% of GNP in 1983 to 85% of GNP in 1989, nearly all of which was enterprise debt. As long as enterprise debt is indistinguishable from government debt, the consolidated budget deficit of public, SOE, and other accounts is the ultimate engine of inflation. A concrete quantification of the aggregate budget constraints of public, SOE, and other accounts was sorely missing in this paper.

I would have liked to see far more emphasis in this paper on the exchange rate in the inflation transmission mechanism. Devaluations mentioned only in passing by the authors have increased the yuan price of the dollar by 138.4% between 1983 and 1989 (the earnings index reported by the IMF rose by 136.0% over the same period, while the less reliable consumer price index increased by 87.8%). This is no coincidence. The authors also neglect to remark that the reason for the devaluations appears to be the reserve position of the Chinese central bank, which fell by more than 45% from 1984–86. The availability and ownership of foreign exchange is probably more pervasive than suspected: a nation of 1.1 bn. people is likely to own considerable foreign currency stashed away in mattresses, and now it appears that decentralized export/import companies have converted this black market for foreign assets into a white one.

Lessons for Eastern Europe

While the Chinese experience predated that of Eastern Europe, it is still too early to judge which has been more successful. The common themes in the two sets of experiences are more remarkable than their differences. The behaviour of Chinese 'super-creditworthy' enterprises could have been predicted by observing that of East German managers before monetary union – who faced exactly the opposite situation of being saddled with 'hard' DM debt which many tried desperately to prepay. Similarly, in the months following unification, firm managers granted wage increases largely unlinked to productivity, knowing they would be financed via the soft budget constraint by West Germany. Similar problems exist in Poland and Czechoslovakia. Disciplining such 'agents without principals' will require the contingency of bankruptcy or some form of corporate accountability. The public finance aspects of decentralization and liberalization of enterprises on the budget have been just as evident in the USSR and what was once the German Democratic Republic as they are in the People's Republic of China.

David Newbery
DAE, Cambridge

The Chinese economic reforms are of central importance, not only as they affect one-fifth of the world's population, but because they provide a rare example of the transformation of a planned economy towards a more market oriented economy. As Eastern Europe, and even more, the USSR, contemplate such a move, they look anxiously for relevant precedents to guide their reform programme. What lessons does the Chinese example hold for them, and, conversely, how might China have managed matters better?

The argument of the Hussain–Stern paper is that decentralization without an associated fiscal reform and careful demand management can, and in China's case, did lead to excess demand, budget and trade deficits. The key point in China's case is that decentralization of enterprise finance meant that enterprise profits were no longer subject to an effective 100% tax rate, nor were they dependent on central allocation for investment funds. They paid lower taxes, retained more profits and were able to borrow. Not surprisingly, they have increased investment. They also appear to have raised real wages sharply – in short, not surprisingly, given the opportunity they have pursued goals more in the interest of the enterprise than the government. This would not have had adverse macroeconomic consequences if the central government had increased other taxes to replace the fall in profits tax, or had cut expenditures in line with income. Figures A.1 and A.2 show that the fall in profits tax and the rise in transfers (price subsidies and

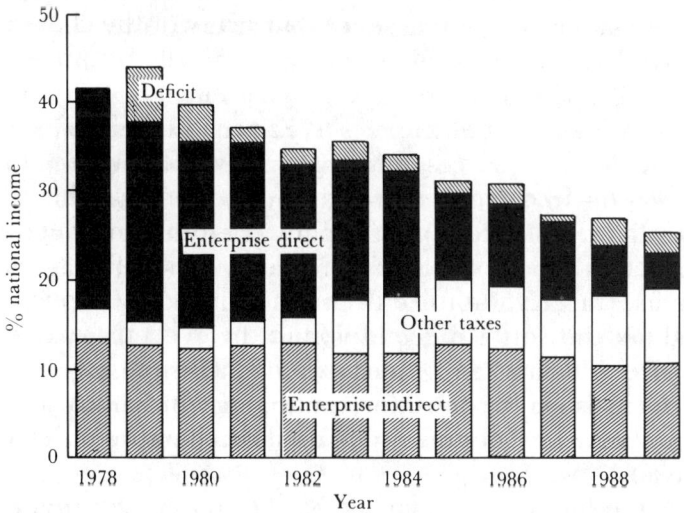

Figure A.1. Composition of Chinese government revenue

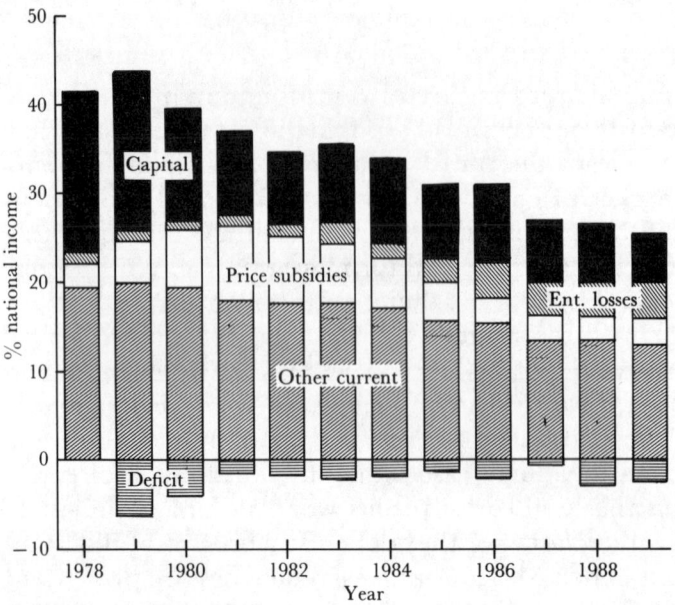

Figure A.2. Composition of Chinese government expenditure

enterprise losses) required the government to cut its expenditure dramatically, and to a remarkable extent (compared to the USSR, for example) it succeeded in doing so. Nevertheless, given the inevitable lags in adjusting government expenditure, the budget was in (modest) deficit throughout the period, with the almost inevitable trade deficit, a growth in foreign debt (again, to modest levels) and in domestic claims (in the form of highly liquid wealth).

Not only were the macro balances in deficit, but many of the chosen tax instruments have had perverse micro incentive effects. It appears that the environment facing enterprises in China has much in common with that of bureaucratic socialist economies of Eastern Europe. Taxes and subsidies, along with resources more generally, are subject to bilateral negotiation, which, given the limited information available to the centre, leads to an inability to commit to future actions, and hence to soft budget constraints and poor incentives. One of the key first steps in systemic reform in Hungary was the creation of a uniformly applied, non-arbitrary legal tax code, as a precondition to the decentralization of investment finance. Without the predictability which such a system provides, banks cannot assess the credit worthiness of enterprises, and bankruptcy becomes an arbitrary and rarely used mechanism (at least for large enterprises).

Hussain and Stern argue that as it may be hard to reduce consumption, macro balance will require reduced investment, which in turn might best be achieved by credit rationing and raising the debt-equity ratio of enterprises, to reduce their ability to borrow from banks. If the experience in Poland is a guide, it may also be necessary to think of ways of restricting trade credit between enterprises, which has allowed large firms there to avoid (or at least postpone) bankruptcy despite a massive fall in demand.

In their discussion of the labour market, the authors argue that the combination of decentralized wage setting which responds to increased profitability, together with little insecurity of employment for the bulk of the non-contract labour force, and a strong sense of equity or parity, makes for an explosive inflationary mixture. The market solution is to harden budget constraints, reduce demand, and hence precipitate bankruptcies. This would create unemployment and a downward pressure on wages. The alternative adopted by many Eastern European economies in the days of guaranteed employment was a resort to baroque structures of penal excess wage taxation, but this rapidly distorts the factor markets even further and undermines the attempt to move towards a decentralized market guided economy.

What to do? The authors argue that the excess liquidity should be reduced by the creation of alternative less liquid assets. Shares in privatized SOEs, at least as direct holdings, seem improbable – even in developed market economies few own shares directly. Indirect holdings as pensions may be an attractive way of dealing with the political problem of how to privatize with least damage to the fisc,[1] but presupposes a wider system of state-funded pensions than China has. If unemployment or the risk of unemployment is likely to increase, then households will need higher precautionary liquid balances anyway, and may not wish to spend them (as we see in the former GDR). The obvious asset attractive to a significant fraction of households is the house itself, but this requires the reduction of housing and rent subsidies, as well as the creation of legal property rights. Even Hungary, with its longer history of intelligent and gradual reform, has found this a difficult task. One suspects that money holdings will be dealt with by inflation, as in Poland. Fear of that might encourage massive real investment by small entrepreneurs using family funds – desirable in the reform process but likely to exacerbate inflationary pressures in the short run.

This leads the authors to conclude that the government should increase taxes on personal income and/or consumption as far as politically expedient, and cut government investment which may have doubtful social value. Perhaps instead one should encourage the government

---

[1] As argued in Newbery (1991).

to reallocate its funds to infrastructure, particularly those communications facilities which enable complementary small scale private investment – roads so that private trucking ar.d passenger transport can prosper and serve as an outlet for enterprise and savings, and telecommunications to facilitate private and foreign business. Given the difficulties of freeing up the labour market and creating a system of unemployment insurance in a poor densely populated country like China, the key question for the continuation of the reform process is whether hardening budget constraints on enterprises via tougher credit policies, together with the elastic supply of labour associated with the large, dominantly rural economy, will allow creeping commercialization and continue moves towards a price-guided market economy in the industrial sector.

General discussion

A number of panellists were concerned about difficulties in reforming the system of microeconomic incentives. There was discussion of incentives for saving: Edmond Malinvaud doubted whether shares in state enterprises could be an adequate alternative to holding money for the household sector. Even with a well developed stock market to ensure liquidity, there was likely to be insufficient confidence in the future profitability of state-owned enterprises. Vittorio Grilli added that the financial system as a whole was underdeveloped, causing particular difficulties for floating government debt. Moving on to incentives for enterprise management, John Black said that the large positive net worth of corporate enterprises might be irrelevant, since corporate assets did not constitute collateral unless there was a way for creditors to liquidate the assets. Restructuring firms' balance sheets to incorporate debt might have no effect on lending for unprofitable projects. He also thought that restrictions on freedom of movement might make it hard for profitable enterprises to expand employment. Damien Neven stressed the importance of considering the role of competition in product markets; in its absence, improved managerial incentives might just lead to the exploitation of monopoly power.

Restrictions on aggregate investment were next discussed. Paul Seabright said that the macroeconomic balance was not *per se* a reason for restricting investment; socially profitable investment could always be financed by foreign borrowing. Axel Weber wondered what scope there might be for foreign direct investment. Richard Portes said that a great deal of investment was not socially profitable because of bottlenecks; foreign capital goods were no solution because there was often inadequate infrastructure to utilize them properly.

Portes also pointed out the significance of the dramatic decline in public expenditure (unlike in the Soviet reforms, for example). Sweder van Wijnbergen said it was important not to overlook the considerable successes of the reform programme. A number of Latin American countries had had several years of reform programmes, all of them accompanied by low economic growth. Why had China been able to enjoy much higher growth than these countries? At all events, he and other panellists were agreed in thinking that, daunting though the transitional difficulties might be, China was in a much better position to face them than were many other countries facing similar reforms.

References

Blejer, M. I. and G. Szapary (1989). 'The Evolving Role of Fiscal Policy in Centrally Planned Economies Under Reform: The Case of China', IMF Working Paper.

Easson, A. J. and Li Jiyan (1987). 'The Evolution of the Tax System in the People's Republic of China', *Stanford Journal of International Law*.

Granick, D. (1990). *Chinese State Enterprises*, Chicago University Press, Chicago.

Guesnerie, R. and K. Roberts (1984). 'Effective Policy Tools and Quantity Controls', *Econometrica*.

Hussain, A. (1990). 'The Chinese Enterprise Reforms', *China Programme Paper No. 5*, STICERD, London School of Economics.

Komiya, R. (1987). 'Japanese Firms, Chinese Firms: Problems for Economic Reform in China', Part I and II, *Journal of Japanese and International Economies*.

—— (1989). 'Macroeconomic Development of China: "Overheating" in 1984–1987 and Problems for Reform', *Journal of Japanese and International Economies*.

Koo, A. Y. C. (1990). 'The Contract Responsibility System: Transition from a Planned to a Market Economy', *Economic Development and Cultural Change*.

Lin, C. (1989). 'Open-ended Economic Reforms in China', in V. Nee and D. Stark (eds.) *Remaking Economic Institutions of Socialism*, Stanford University Press.

Liu Guoguang (1989). 'A Sweet and Sour Decade', *Beijing Review*.

McMillan, J. *et al.* (1989). 'Impact of China's Economic Reforms on Agricultural Productivity Growth', *Journal of Political Economy*.

Naughton, B. (1990a). 'Inflation: Patterns, Causes and Cures', mimeo (to appear in U.S. Congress Joint Economic Committee (ed.), *China's Dilemma in the 1990s*, U.S. Government Printing Office, Washington, D.C.).

—— (1990b). 'Monetary Implications of Balanced Economic Growth and Current Macroeconomic Disturbances in China', in Cassel *et al.* (eds.): *China's Contemporary Economic Reforms as a Development Strategy*, Nomos Verlagsgesellschaft, Baden-Baden.

—— (1990c). 'Macroeconomic Obstacles to Reform in China: The Role of Fiscal and Monetary Policy', mimeo, University of California, San Diego.

Newbery, D. M. (1991). 'Reform in Hungary: Sequencing and Privatisation', *European Economic Review*.

Nolan, P. (1988). *The Political Economy of Collective Farms*, Polity Press, Oxford.

Perkins, D. H. (1988). 'Reforming China's Economic System', *Journal of Economic Literature*.

Portes, R. (1989). 'The Theory and Measurement of Macroeconomic Disequilibrium in Centrally Planned Economies', *International Studies in Economic Modelling Series*.

Portes, R. and A. Santorum (1988). 'Money and Consumption Goods Market in China', in B. L. Reynolds (ed.), *Chinese Economic Reforms – How Far, How Fast* (Reprint of a special issue of the *Journal of Comparative Economics*), Academic Press, New York.

SSB (1982). *Statistical Year Book of China 1981*, State Statistical Bureau, Beijing.

—— (1986). *Statistical Year Book of China 1985*, State Statistical Bureau, Beijing.

—— (1987a). *Statistical Year Book of China 1986*, State Statistical Bureau, Beijing.

—— (1987b). *Zhongguo Guding Tuozi Ziliao 1950–85* (Fixed Investment Statistics of China 1959–85), State Statistical Bureau, Beijing.

—— (1988). *Statistical Year Book of China 1987*. State Statistical Bureau, Beijing.

SSB (1989). *Zhongguo Tongji Nianjian 1988* (Statistical Year Book of China 1988), State Statistical Bureau, Beijing.

—— (1990a). *Statistical Year Book of China 1989*, State Statistical Bureau, Beijing.

—— (1990b). *Zhongguo Tongji Zhaiyao 1990* (Summary Statistics of China 1989), State Statistical Bureau, Beijing.

Summers, R. and A. Heston (1988). 'A New Set of International Comparisons of Real Product and Price Levels Estimates for 130 Countries, 1950–1985', *Review of Income and Wealth*.

Takahashi, W. (1989). 'Recent Developments in the Chinese Economy – Economic Reform, Its Success and Problems', mimeo, Research and Statistics Department, Bank of Japan, Tokyo.

Tidrick, G. and Chen Jiyuan (eds.) (1987). *China's Industrial Reform*, Oxford University Press for the World Bank, Oxford.

Vogel, E. (1989). *One Step Ahead – Guangdong Under Reform*, Harvard University Press, Cambridge, MA.

Weitzman, M. (1974). 'Prices vs. Quantity', *Review of Economic Studies*.

—— (1980). 'The "Ratchet Principle" and Performance Incentive', *The Bell Journal of Economics*.

World Bank (1988). *China – External Trade and Capital*, World Bank, Washington, D.C.

—— (1990a). *China – Macroeconomic Stability and Industrial Growth Under Decentralized Socialism*, World Bank, Washington, D.C.

—— (1990b). *China – Country Economic Memorandum, Between Plan and Market*, World Bank, Washington, D.C.

—— (1991). *China – Financial Sector Review: Financial Policies and Institutional Development*, World Bank, Washington, D.C.

Economic Policy   April 1991   Printed in Great Britain

The British electricity experiment

John Vickers and George Yarrow

Summary

Privatization of the British electricity supply industry has been accompanied by a series of far-reaching structural and regulatory reforms. Whereas traditional solutions to market failure problems in electricity supply rely on high degrees of vertical and horizontal integration or collaboration, the British reforms have included the vertical separation of transmission from generation and (partially) of distribution from supply, together with horizontal de-integration in generation.

The comparative radicalism of the reforms should yield considerable information about a set of generic issues that confront policymakers, not only in electricity supply, but also in other industries where major questions of competition policy arise. These issues include efficiency tradeoffs between markets and hierarchies, problems of tacit collusion, the significance of entry conditions, the role of regulators, and the interactions between regulation of market power and other controls, such as environmental regulation.

Initial evidence indicates that, as intended, significant new entry is occurring in both electricity generation and supply. Many issues remain to be resolved, however, not least in the area of environmental regulation, and it is far from clear whether, ultimately, the reforms will be judged a success in terms of their impact on economic efficiency.

The British electricity experiment

John Vickers and George Yarrow
Oxford University

1. Introduction

The privatization of the electricity supply industry (ESI) in Britain, which began in 1990, is in itself an unremarkable event: much of the ESI is privately owned in several European countries and in the US, and the UK privatization programme has embraced utilities since 1984, when British Telecom was privatized. The thing that *is* remarkable about recent policy towards the industry is the radical nature of the regulatory reform accompanying privatization. A vertically integrated, administered generation and transmission structure was replaced overnight (on 31 March 1990) by one that is de-integrated and market-based: generation and transmission have been separated, and there has been an attempt to establish competition in generation. A number of countries have been moving gradually in the direction of encouraging competition, but nowhere else have such dramatic changes been implemented so quickly.

Given the importance of the industry, these reforms are of great interest for their own sake, but, we suggest, for far more than that. The experiment promises to be highly informative for policy-makers elsewhere who are currently assessing options for regulatory reform, not only in the energy sector, but in a wide range of industries. Indeed, being subject to a variety of market failures ranging from natural monopoly to environmental externalities, and with its 'vertical' and

This research is part of the project on The Regulation of Firms with Market Power under the ESRC initiative on The Functioning of Markets. Financial support from the ESRC and the Office of Fair Trading is gratefully acknowledged. The views expressed in the paper are entirely our own, and we are responsible for any errors. We are very grateful to Billy Jack and Kaiser Kabir for their research assistance, and to David Begg, John Black, John Mayer, Nick Morris, Jean-Charles Rochet, Paul Seabright, Tony Venables, Nils-Henrik von de Fehr and seminar audiences at Harvard and MIT, for their helpful comments and suggestions.

'network' characteristics, the ESI provides a rich case study in public policy towards industrial organization. The radicalism of British reform brings into sharp focus a combination of pervasive issues about ownership, competition, entry conditions, vertical integration, contracts, investment incentives, price regulation, quality assurance and environmental protection.

With these generic issues in mind, we aim in this paper to give an interim review of the competitive and regulatory regime that has been established for the British ESI. We shall identify strengths and weaknesses of the new regime, and the key factors – including future regulatory policy – on which its success is most likely to depend. In addition we shall link our analysis to questions facing European energy policy more generally, and draw conclusions relevant to policy issues in other industries that share some economic characteristics with the ESI.

Section 2 contains a brief outline of the key economic features of electricity supply, and Section 3 describes recent developments of policy towards the industry. The next five sections are devoted to a series of generic issues that arise in various industries: vertical supply arrangements (Section 4), oligopolistic competition and collusion (Section 5), entry and access terms (Section 6), price regulation (Section 7) and environmental regulation (Section 8). The final section summarizes potential lessons for energy, competition and regulatory policies.

2. Economic characteristics of electricity supply

For the purposes of economic analysis, key features of electricity supply may be summarized as follows.

(1) To a first approximation, electricity is non-storable; and demand fluctuates considerably by time of day, by season and randomly.

(2) Supply occurs through distinct vertical stages: (i) fuel inputs, (ii) generation, (iii) transmission through the high-voltage grid, (iv) distribution through regional and local networks and (v) supply – acquisition of electricity and its sale to customers. An indication of the relative significance of each of these stages in the late 1980s is given by Table 1.

(3) Environmental externalities are associated with the main fuel inputs – emissions of carbon dioxide, sulphur dioxide and nitrous oxides with fossil fuels (coal, gas, oil); toxic radioactive wastes with nuclear power; and ecological damage with hydro stations.

(4) Capital-intensity, sunk costs and long lead times are features of generation technologies.

Table 1. UK electricity prices: components of the final price (%)

Fuel	Generation	Transmission	Distribution	Supply
42	29	6	19	4

Source: Estimates based upon Corporation Reports and Accounts.

(5) To ensure reasonable security of supply – i.e. an appropriately small probability of supply failure – the industry must operate with excess capacity in most periods.

(6) Coordination between generation and transmission is vital to ensure the integrity of the supply network. Electrical equilibrium – market clearing in the sense that supply and demand balance – must be maintained continuously at every node in the network, otherwise non-localized supply failure may occur. Since random supply and demand shocks can happen very suddenly – faster than agents could conceivably respond to price signals – equilibrium requires some central control.

(7) The 'transportation' services of transmission and distribution (in a given area) are characterized by natural monopoly cost conditions.

(8) Energy losses and constraints in the network imply that transmission costs can be extremely sensitive to where power is supplied in the system.

(9) The business of supplying large final customers is not naturally monopolistic. Generation is not naturally monopolistic if it is separated from transmission, but it is less clear whether or not generation-plus-transmission (in a given area) is a natural monopoly (see Section 4).

(10) Electricity pricing can significantly affect income distribution.

Thus, the industry is characterized by its multiproduct nature (outputs are individuated by time, by location and by contingencies such as weather conditions), its vertical structure, sunk costs, uncertainties, and monopoly and externality market failures. Most specifically, fully decentralized market transactions cannot meet the technological need for continuous electrical equilibrium.

A number of these features are shared by other industries, most obviously other network utilities (telecommunications, gas and water). In electricity, however, the list of potential market failures is a particularly long one, providing an excellent opportunity to examine the policy implications of interactions among such failures.

3. The development of policy towards the industry

3.1. The pre-privatization structure

Before privatization, the ESI in England and Wales had two parts, as shown in Figure 1. The Central Electricity Generating Board (CEGB) ran generation and the high-voltage transmission system, the National Grid. Twelve Area Boards distributed power to customers in their respective regions. Thus, the CEGB had a monopoly over the wholesale market, and the Area Boards had regional monopolies over retail supply. In Scotland there were two vertically integrated companies – the South of Scotland Electricity Board (SSEB) and the North of Scotland Hydro Board.

The 1983 Energy Act tried to introduce some competition into generation and supply by liberalizing third party access to transmission and distribution networks, and by requiring Area Boards to buy from non-CEGB sources on terms reflecting avoided costs. But the Act had virtually no effect, in large part because it failed to guarantee new entrants protection against anti-competitive behaviour by the CEGB (see Vickers and Yarrow, 1988).

3.2. The new structure

The new structure, which came into being on 31 March 1990, is summarized in Figure 2. The CEGB has been split both 'vertically' and 'horizontally'. Transmission has been separated from generation, and is carried out by the new National Grid Company (NGC). The NGC is responsible for despatching power stations in accordance with arrangements for the power 'pool', the new wholesale market for power (see Section 3.4). The company is owned jointly by – but is meant to be operated at arm's length from – the 12 distribution companies created from the old Area Boards. Thus, the de-integration of generation and transmission

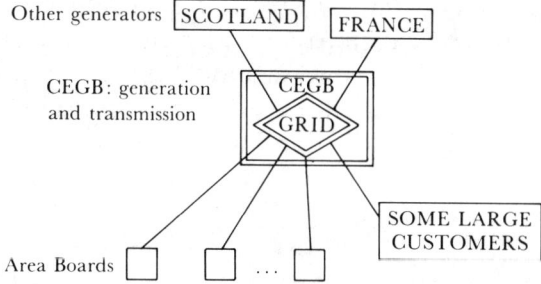

Figure 1. The old structure of the industry in England and Wales

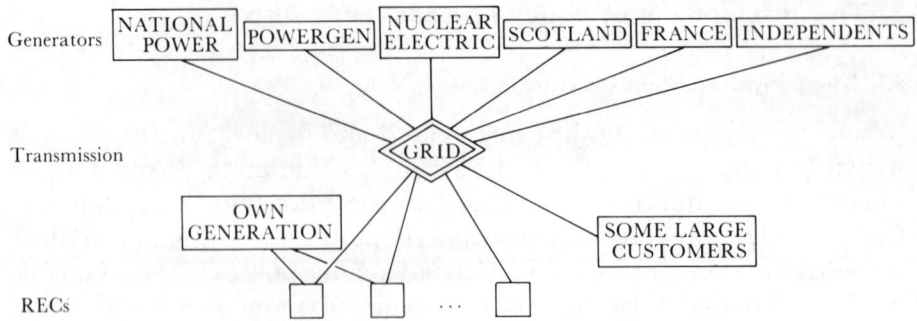

Figure 2. The new structure of the industry in England and Wales

has been accompanied by the integration (at least in terms of ownership) of transmission and distribution.

The CEGB's generation activities have passed to three new companies. Two are scheduled to be privatized in 1991: National Power, which has about 52% of CEGB generating capacity in England and Wales, and PowerGen, which has about 33%. They have fossil fuel stations in the main, and a few hydro stations. All nuclear capacity, about 15% of the total, is now with Nuclear Electric, which will remain in public ownership (the original plan in the 1988 White Paper, Department of Energy, 1988, was for nuclear capacity to be privatized as part of National Power).

On the distribution side of the industry the changes have been less dramatic. The twelve Area Boards were renamed Regional Electricity Companies (RECs) and privatized in December 1990. While future mergers between RECs will, in principle, be allowed, any proposals along these lines can expect to attract close regulatory scrutiny. Integration between distribution and supply is permitted (as is integration between generation and supply), and RECs can enter generation to a limited extent.

In Scotland, vertical integration between generation, transmission and distribution has been retained. The SSEB, now called Scottish Power, and the Hydro Board, now called Hydro Electric, are to be privatized. However, the SSEB's nuclear power stations will remain in the public sector. In what follows we shall focus on the more radical reforms, involving vertical separation, in England and Wales.

3.3. The regulatory regime

The broad framework for regulation is contained in the 1989 Electricity Act, but the main vehicles for regulation are the licences under which firms in the industry operate. The Act set up the Office of Electricity Regulation (Offer) to regulate the industry. Its head as the first Director General of Electricity Supply (DGES) is Professor Stephen Littlechild, who, in addition to his contributions to electricity privatization plans, was also actively involved in the earlier development of regulatory policies for the telecommunications and water industries. His main tasks are to ensure that reasonable demands for electricity are met and that licensees can finance their activities, to monitor licence conditions (including price controls), and to promote competition in generation and supply. Licence conditions can be altered either by agreement with the licensee, or by the DGES successfully making a reference to the Monopolies and Mergers Commission (MMC), the UK competition authority. This institutional structure follows the model established for British Telecom in 1984, and later adopted for gas and water.

The thrust of public policy is to regulate the naturally monopolistic parts of the industry (transmission and distribution) and, initially, supply to smaller users, and to rely on competition in generation and in supply to larger users. Some of the main features of the licences are as follows.

3.3.1. Control of transmission charges. The average amount per kilowatt (kW) charged in a given year by the National Grid Company for the use of its system is capped. The average price cap evolves over time according to an 'RPI-X' formula of the kind first introduced for British Telecom (see Littlechild, 1983), with X initially set equal to zero.

3.3.2. Control of distribution charges. The average amount per kW charged by each REC for the use of its wires is capped in similar fashion. The formula for distribution charges takes the form of RPI plus X, and the X terms vary between RECs, ranging from zero to 2.5% (see Table 2).

3.3.3. Control of supply charges to smaller customers. Customers with peak demands of less than 10 MW are 'right-to-tariff' customers. This means that their local REC is required to meet their reasonable demands at published prices. Those prices are subject to RPI-$X + Y$ regulation. The X term in the formula for supply charges has been set at zero initially. The Y term reflects the cost to the REC of electricity purchases, transmission and distribution charges, and the fossil fuel levy (see below): there will be full cost pass-through of changes in these cost components. However, until 1993, changes in supply charges to customers with peak demands less than 1 MW will also be limited to changes in the RPI and the fossil fuel levy, giving small users protection against fuel price fluctuations in the short run.

Table 2. Allowable annual percentage changes in real average revenues

Company	Transmission	Distribution	Supply
NGC	0	—	—
Eastern	—	0.25	0
East Midlands	—	1.25	0
London	—	0.00	0
Manweb	—	2.50	0
Midlands	—	1.15	0
Northern	—	1.55	0
Norweb	—	1.40	0
South East	—	0.75	0
Southern	—	0.65	0
South Wales	—	2.50	0
South West	—	2.25	0
Yorkshire	—	1.30	0

Source: RECs' Privatization Prospectuses.

3.3.4. Deregulation of supply charges for larger customers. Users with peak demands greater than 10 MW are 'contract' customers. The prices that they pay for electricity are unregulated and will be determined by competition.

3.3.5. Retail competition and monopoly. Right-to-tariff customers will also be free to seek supplies from sources other than their local REC. (This is different from the gas market, where British Gas enjoys a monopoly franchise over tariff customers.) All users will have this freedom after 31 March 1998, but before then RECs will have monopoly franchises as follows. Until 31 March 1994, customers with peak demands less than 1 MW will not be free to seek competitive supplies – they can buy only from their REC. Between 1994 and 1998, customers with peak demands less than 100 kW will be confined to their REC. Thus, the monopoly franchise shrinks over time.

3.3.6. Limits on retail competition. The extent of competition to the supply businesses of the RECs from National Power and PowerGen has been limited by placing (weakening) quota limits on the generators' share of the market for an initial eight-year period.

3.3.7. Cross-subsidization. The regulated companies must have separate accounts for separate businesses (generation, distribution, supply, etc.) and must not engage in cross-subsidization.

3.3.8. Price discrimination. Generators' ability to engage in price discrimination is limited by the requirement that they offer comparable terms to comparable persons. This provision extends to dealings between their generation and supply businesses. Similar provisions apply to RECs.

3.3.9. Ring fencing of the transmission monopoly. The National Grid Company cannot buy and sell electricity on its own account, except in connection with its pumped storage business.

3.3.10. Network access. The wires owned by NGC and the RECs must be made available for use by third parties at regulated prices (see Sections 3.3.1 and 3.3.2).

3.3.11. Limits to vertical integration. RECs may generate their own electricity up to a limit of 15% of their requirements.

3.3.12. The 'fossil fuel' levy. RECs must buy a designated fraction of their demands from non-fossil (which means largely nuclear) sources. The extra costs entailed will be recouped by a levy on sales of electricity from fossil fuel sources. The main effect of this device is to protect Nuclear Electric.

3.4. The wholesale market for power

In addition to the above, there are regulations concerning the workings of the power pool – the spot market for wholesale electricity – which is the hub of the new system and the key point of departure from the old. To achieve the instantaneous coordination between generation and transmission that is essential for the maintenance of system integrity, the Pooling and Settlements Agreement, to which all the main players must belong, accords a central role to the National Grid Company. All sizeable generators must submit to central despatch by NGC, and NGC can secure various ancillary services (e.g. reserves on standby) from them.

Under the old centralized system, the grid controller would try to operate 'merit order' despatch of power stations on the basis of information about their operating costs. Under the new system, NGC will operate merit order despatch on the basis of bids made by generators. Each day, generators inform NGC of the availability and offer prices (i.e. prices at which they are willing to supply power) for each of their generating units for each half hour of the following day. On the basis of these offers, NGC ranks stations into a merit order. Together with demand estimates, knowledge of constraints in the transmission network, and a range of other factors, NGC works out a plan for the least-cost operation of the system. It also includes provision for standby reserves, etc. NGC can revise the plan in keeping with specified rules as events unfold.

The price per kilowatt hour (kWh) paid to generators for electricity supplied to the pool in a given half hour is the pool input price (*PIP*). It is the sum of two terms. The first is the system marginal price (*SMP*), which is the offer price of the marginal generating unit in that half hour (ignoring transmission constraints). In other words, it is the price at the intersection of the estimated demand curve and the industry 'supply curve' implied by the generators' bids. The *SMP* is intended to reflect short-run costs – fuel and operating costs. The second term is a capacity element, which is paid for all capacity that is declared available, whether or not the relevant sets are called upon to deliver power to the system. It is the probability of capacity being insufficient to meet demand because of a random shock – the 'loss of load probability' (*LOLP*) – multiplied by an amount intended to reflect the cost to consumers of a supply shortage – the 'value of lost load' (*VOLL*) minus the marginal cost of power as measured by *SMP*. Hence, $PIP = SMP + (VOLL - SMP)\,LOLP$.

VOLL has been set at £2 per kWh, though the justification for this number is far from clear. Incentives to build sufficient capacity in excess of average demand (to ensure adequate security of supply) depend on the *LOLP* and *VOLL*. Generators also get paid for services such as being on reserve. Electricity is purchased from the wholesale market at the pool output price (*POP*). This is the same as *PIP* except that, at certain times of day when demand is relatively heavy, an uplift is added to cover the cost of transmission constraints, reserves, and so on.

Thus, the pool is a kind of spot market for wholesale power. The NGC is like a Walrasian auctioneer matching supply and demand, but because of the continuous need for electrical equilibrium and transmission constraints, it has the more active role of issuing instructions for the despatch of power stations, albeit subject to the offer prices submitted (see Section 5.1).

Pool prices, and especially the capacity element, are likely to be quite volatile and, partly as a result, generators and distributors can be expected to enter into longer-term contractual arrangements. Since all physical trades of electricity are into and out of the pool, purely financial contracts may be suitable for many purposes. That is to say, rather than contracts specifying that actual delivery of electricity must take place, equivalent financial side payments can be made instead. For example, when *PIP* and *POP* are the same, a contract giving distributor D the option to buy 100 mn. kWh of electricity from generator G for £2 mn. is equivalent financially to a contract under which G pays D 100 mn. times any positive difference between the pool price (in kWh) and 2 pence. The latter, purely financial, contract has advantages in terms of transactions costs. Moreover, economic agents other than electricity companies could deal in such contracts. One possible development is the emergence of a market in electricity options.

Options are a natural form of contract because ownership of a power station itself resembles ownership of an option. Suppose that G's marginal cost is 2 pence per kWh. If G offers to sell into the pool at this price, its net profit per unit of capacity will be the pool price minus 2 pence in half hours when the pool price exceeds 2 pence, and zero in other half hours. By selling a call option with a strike price equal to its marginal cost, G perfectly hedges the risk in its returns. The fee for the option will go towards, and may exceed, the capital cost of the plant.

The wholesale electricity market will, therefore, likely consist of an intriguing combination of a short-term spot market overlain by various longer-term financial contracts. Whether or not this structure has good prospects of delivering both competition and coordination will be considered below.

3.5. Moves towards markets for power in other European countries

Although there have been moves in several countries towards encouraging competition in electricity supply, by and large these developments have been marked by their modesty and gradualism, even in the US where the deregulation of many other industries was pioneered (see Joskow and Schmalensee, 1983; and Joskow, 1989). International comparisons, then, serve to highlight further the radicalism and experimental nature of the recent British reforms.

In Europe there remains almost everywhere an absence of competition, and there are divergent views about the feasibility and desirability of trying to create competitive electricity markets. There is wide diversity in respect of ownership, vertical relationships and horizontal supply structures. France, Greece, Ireland, Italy and Portugal have nationalized generation-transmission monopolies, similar to the CEGB before the British reforms. There is public ownership at provincial and municipal level in many countries. For example, Austria, the Netherlands and Germany have regional or provincial generating companies, and municipal ownership is particularly common in distribution. In some cases, the regional or local utilities are both generators and distributors. Transmission grids are generally either nationalized or operated by producers' associations. In Belgium, Denmark and Spain, generation is mostly in private ownership, and in Germany there is mixed public/private ownership. Overall, there do not appear to be any simple relationships between comparative economic performance and industrial or ownership structures (Holmes, 1990).

Developments in regulatory policies toward the ESI reflect a range of different preoccupations. There are examples of privatization (Austria, Norway, Portugal), restructuring of generation to *increase* concentration (Belgium, Netherlands), separation of generation and distribution (Netherlands, Portugal), separation of generation and transmission (Norway) and contractual reforms (Germany). In nearly all the cases of ownership and structural reform the policy approach has been much more cautious than in Britain, although the Netherlands is something of an exception here: the Dutch restructuring plan has involved the separation of distribution from generation, consolidation of generating companies and reduction of the control exerted by generators over grid operations.

The generally cautious approach to regulatory reform is well illustrated by German Government decisions in 1990. Ironically, in East Germany generation, transmission and distribution were run by different companies, so that the vertical structure of the industry appeared ideal for an experiment in competition. More specifically, there were two generating groups, based respectively on brown coal and nuclear technologies, one transmission network group, and fifteen regional distribution companies. The President of the Federal Cartel Office, Wolfgang Kartte, pressed for the retention of this vertical structure, with some horizontal restructuring to create at least two generators using fossil fuels, and the implementation of measures to allow electricity transit and encourage independent generation.

Had President Kartte's arguments won the day, the resulting industrial structure in Eastern Germany would have closely approximated the new British system. In the event, however, the argument that prevailed was that the massive capital injection urgently required to upgrade the East German system would simply not be forthcoming under such a structure. The result is that the three leading West German utilities – RWE-Energie, Preussenelektra and Bayernwerk – have been allowed to acquire 75% of the transmission network and brown coal power stations, and 60% of the regional distribution companies.

3.6. European Community policy on competition in energy markets

The economic characteristics of electricity supply, and the extent of state involvement in the national industries, make it difficult to implement the aims of the Single European Act and the 1992 internal market

**Table 3. Exports, imports and net exports
(% of gross consumption), 1989**

Country	Exports	Imports	Net exports
Belgium	11.7	7.8	3.9
Denmark	6.7	35.9	−29.2
F.R. Germany	4.9	4.8	0.1
France	14.1	2.6	11.5
Greece	1.8	2.9	−1.1
Ireland	0.0	0.0	0.0
Italy	0.3	14.1	−13.8
Luxembourg	0.0	78.0	−78.0
Netherlands	0.5	6.9	−6.4
Portugal	4.8	9.1	−4.3
Spain	3.2	1.9	1.3

Source: Eurostat.

programme in the ESI. Nevertheless, the goal of an internal energy market is being pursued.

Intra-EC trade does take place at present, but, although the quantities involved are significant, much of it is accounted for by inter-utility transactions that are aimed primarily at load management. There has been some trend toward steadier, uni-directional flows in recent years (see Table 3), connected with developments such as the emergence of excess capacity in France. Again, however, this is dominated by trade between utilities operating at the same stage of production (reflecting cooperative rather than competitive behaviour).

In the summer of 1989 the European Commission published four draft measures on electricity: price transparency in non-tariff electricity sales; notification to the Commission of planned investments; coordinated planning of capacity expansion; and transit rights on large, integrated high-voltage grids. The last of these measures (transit) was agreed by the Council of Energy Ministers in Autumn 1990, but it can be noted that the rights will only be granted to existing operators of high-voltage grids: the transit agreement does not mean that local distribution utilities or large industrial consumers will be able to shop around for supplies.

Key issues for the future development of EC policy include terms of access to transmission facilities, system coordination, and the role of national industrial policies. Although some existing interconnectors are capable of handling considerably more trade than currently occurs (see Table 4), the access question is not just one of pricing. Without appropriate grid investment, competition in generation can be frustrated (see Section 4.2). Transmission constraints are obstacles to trade. The nature

Table 4. French and German interconnections

France to:	Capacity (MVA)	Germany to:	Capacity (MVA)
Belgium	3,170	Austria	9,799
Britain	2,000	Denmark	2,040
Germany	5,075	France	5,075
Italy	4,350	Luxembourg	3,460
Spain	3,030	Netherlands	4,320
Switzerland	5,520	Switzerland	10,943
	23,145		35,637

Source: Holmes (1990).

of electricity as a good – especially its non-storability and the need for continuous electrical equilibrium – mean that system coordination is essential. Prices cannot be relied upon to clear markets in all eventualities, and some form of centralized control is required.

These problems interact with the possible use of national industrial policies. For example, the subsidization of the German coal industry – by the Jahrhundertvertrag contract to buy coal and the kohlepfennig (coal penny) tax scheme – would be undermined by imports of cheap electricity from France. The scale of those imports is constrained by the capacity of the interconnectors between the two countries. There is no incentive on the part of the German authorities to strengthen capacity and remove the barrier to trade. German industrialists, on the other hand, have a strong incentive to acquire inexpensive imported power; and might even go so far as to build their own links to France, despite the presence of natural monopoly cost conditions in transmission. Whereas the EC could not at present require any Member State to strengthen its grid, it might be able to stop any attempt to thwart such 'bypass'.

3.7. Environmental policy and its implications

Political pressure for tougher environmental regulation is occurring at both national and international levels. Until recently the nuclear issue has been the main focus for public concern, and nuclear programmes have been halted or scaled back in many countries. Concern about acid rain (see Newbery, 1990) has also given rise to significant policy developments, the European Commission's Large Combustion Plant Directive of 1988 being a case in point. The Directive specifies reductions in SO_2 and NO_x emissions over time: the UK, for example, must reduce SO_2 emissions relative to the 1980 level, by 20% by 1993, 40% by 1998 and

60% by 2003. Similar constraints on carbon dioxide emissions have not yet been implemented, but could be introduced in the future.

Generators of electricity, therefore, face the prospect of rising costs associated with meeting tightening environmental regulation, and environmental policy will play a large role in determining the respective roles of the various technologies (coal, gas, nuclear, hydro, wind, etc.). Moreover, conservation measures are being promoted in many countries – for example, the EC THERMIE and SAVE initiatives on energy efficiency – which, if successful, will serve to depress demand. How electric utilities respond to these simultaneous cost and demand pressures will have a major bearing on the ESI's performance, and it can be expected that these responses will be heavily influenced by other (i.e. non-environmental) aspects of regulatory policy. Thus, the effectiveness of the new structure of the ESI in Britain is likely soon to be put to a relatively severe test by cumulating environmental pressures.

4. Vertical supply arrangements

The most radical features of the reform of the ESI in Britain are the vertical separation of generation from transmission, the creation of a market for wholesale power supplies, and the (partial) vertical separation of distribution and supply. These 'structural' reforms, which are aimed chiefly at promoting competition where competition is feasible, raise questions concerning the tradeoffs between 'markets' and 'hierarchies' (Williamson, 1975) in a particularly clear way. Consideration of vertical supply arrangements is, therefore, an obvious starting point for analysis of the ESI and, as we will show, it leads on naturally to questions of competition (Sections 5 and 6) and, where effective competition is not feasible, to questions of price regulation (Section 7).

Our discussion of vertical issues will be in two main parts. First, we shall abstract from network characteristics, by treating transmission as a homogeneous input to electricity supply, in order to focus on generic problems of investment, anti-competitive behaviour and contracting. Second, we shall examine some network economics of transmission, which have an important bearing on the question of vertical organization because of the difficulty of efficiently pricing transmission in a decentralized regime. These features are not unique to electricity – they arise also in other network industries – but they occur in their sharpest form in the ESI because of the nature of the product. Finally, we shall link these two sets of issues, and draw some implications for policy towards competition in generation.

4.1. Vertical integration

4.1.1. Investment problems. In respect of the relationship between a supplier and a buyer, consider the question of why they might wish to form a long-run relationship, or integrate completely, rather than deal spot. One important reason has to do with the hold-up problem that can arise when there are sunk costs (see Tirole, 1988). If the supplier has to invest in specific assets, which are much less valuable in other relationships, he faces the risk of being exploited by the buyer *ex post*. Confronted with that risk the supplier might not invest in the first place.

Of course, in this example it is not a very sensible institutional arrangement to give the buyer the power to determine price *ex post*. But the problem can arise also in other settings. For example, if price is determined by *ex post* bargaining, then the supplier will have an inefficiently low incentive to invest, because he will gain only a proportion of the extra value created by additional investment, but will pay all of the extra cost. The hold-up problem can be solved by integration between buyer and supplier, or by a contract that settles terms in advance (see Joskow, 1987).

The new structure of the ESI is of course much more complex than in the simple story above. There are sunk costs in both generation and transmission, there is regulation of transmission and distribution charges, and there is some competition on both sides of the wholesale market. Insights from the story are relevant nevertheless. For example, generators might be deterred from investing efficiently in plant with sunk costs for fear of exploitation by the grid downstream. Regulation seeks to alleviate this problem by controlling transmission charges, but there could still exist a monopsony problem further downstream – with the RECs – if they acted collusively. The more competition there is among RECs (and other suppliers) for wholesale power the smaller this problem becomes, because none can then hold the generators hostage. Put another way, competition reduces the specificity of buyer/seller relationships and serves as an alternative antidote to any under-investment problems.

A parallel issue is raised by privatization itself. Under state ownership investment and pricing functions are integrated. After privatization, investment decisions are made by private agents, but the state retains certain regulatory powers, especially concerning prices. The danger that a regulator or government in the future might tighten prices once investments had been sunk could be a deterrent to efficient investment: private sector discount rates will include a premium to reflect this risk. The question is how well the government can commit itself, and its successors, not to behave in such a way – see Vickers and Yarrow (1988), and Gilbert and Newbery (1988). Note that in the ESI the mix as well as the level of investment could be affected by these problems, which are greatest for plant that is capital-intensive and has long lead times (i.e. nuclear).

4.1.2. Risk sharing. Another reason for longer-term relations, including integration, between upstream and downstream parts of the ESI is risk sharing. This is not just a question of risk-aversion. A generator reliant on spot market sales runs the risk of bankruptcy (and its associated costs) if, for example, demand a decade hence turns out to be lower than expected. Supply companies, on the other hand, are well placed to bear these risks because they can often pass them on to consumers. Or, if they have contracts to supply consumers at fixed prices, they can avoid spot market risk themselves by contracting long-term with generators, or more simply integrating with them. In the new regime in Britain, the RECs can integrate backwards into generation, but only to the extent of 15% of their needs.

4.1.3. Anti-competitive conduct. The main problem with vertical integration is that it can facilitate anti-competitive conduct. (Long-term contracts can also be barriers to entry – see Aghion and Bolton, 1987 – but here we shall focus on full integration.) With integration between generation and transmission, the dominant firm might try to make access to the naturally monopolistic grid difficult or impossible for rival generating companies, thereby extending its market power from transmission to generation. A similar issue arises between distribution and supply. Vertical separation removes the incentive for such behaviour, which is of course the main idea behind the structural reforms in the British ESI.

4.2. Network issues

The points so far discussed would arise even if transmission were a homogeneous product. Further complexities, involving spatial pricing, result from the network characteristics of electricity transmission. With vertical integration of generation and transmission, the system can be optimized internally, but with separation it is necessary to have actual (rather than just shadow) transmission prices, and these will have real effects. Principles of optimal spot pricing for electricity are derived by Bohn *et al.* (1984), on whom we draw in the following. (See also Wilkinson, 1989).

   The four characteristics of electricity supply that affect optimal pricing in their analysis are (i) transmission losses; (ii) capacity constraints in the network; (iii) the need for continuous electrical equilibrium at each node; and (iv) the fact that electrical flows cannot be directed along particular lines – they get allocated by Nature according to Kirchoff's laws. As a consequence there are major externalities across space – the optimal price at node i can be much affected by events at far away node j.

The optimal spot price at node i has three components. The first is the cost of the marginal generating unit in the system (plus any premium needed to curtail demand to the available capacity). This term, which is the same throughout the system, is then grossed up (or down) by the second component, which reflects incremental transmission losses caused by demand at node i. The reason why this second factor might be less than one is that demand or supply at node i might reduce losses in the system as a whole. Third, terms reflecting transmission constraints are added – there are shadow prices for capacity on lines that are fully loaded, and the price difference between nodes is wider than it would be if spare transmission capacity existed.

Because power flows get allocated throughout the system naturally, the (optimal spot) transmission charge at any node depends on events throughout the network, and will vary over time and randomly as supplies and demands alter. It is entirely possible for the optimal charges at some nodes and times to be negative – i.e. for a generator to be subsidized for inputting power, or for a consumer to be subsidized for drawing power from the system.

These results have important consequences for competition between generators. Bohn *et al.* (1984, page 371) examine how much market power a generator has in terms of its ability to affect the price that it faces by varying its supply. They conclude that:

> 'At some times, a generator may have no effective competitors and thus considerable power to affect prices. At other times, the same generator may find itself competing with generators hundreds of miles away. The stronger the transmission system, the more effective competition will be.'

This last point bears emphasis. Transmission charges are a kind of transport cost. High transport costs reduce the geographic scope of rivalry. With a stronger transmission system, capacity constraints are less likely to bite, transport costs are lowered, and competition is made more effective. Policy implications of this 'pro-competitive externality' of grid investment will be discussed below.

4.3. Vertical arrangements: conclusions

The discussion of spot pricing can now be related to earlier observations about investment and anti-competitive behaviour. First, if transmission charges are regulated according to the principles of optimal spot pricing, and if the grid operator is a profit-maximizer, then there could be serious under-investment problems. Optimal prices fall as the grid is strengthened, and so the grid company would hold back on investment. This factor, together with the pro-competitive externality of grid strengthening for competition in generation, suggest that regulation of grid investment is important. Given the difficulties of regulating the investment of a private firm, this might be a reason for having the grid under public ownership.

Second, if vertical integration between transmission and generation is allowed, the grid company will have incentives for anti-competitive behaviour in its grid investment policy (even if grid pricing is regulated, e.g. according to marginal cost principles). The firm could shield its own plant from competition, and raise rivals' costs. A similar point applies to international competition. Grid investment (or rather under–investment) can be used as a means of protecting domestic suppliers. For example, a major bottleneck between France and Germany could limit the competitive threat of EdF to the German electricity (and coal) industries. This raises the question of whether a supranational Eurogrid is needed to have a truly competitive internal market.

5. Oligopolistic competition

Oligopoly and/or oligopsony characterize several stages of production in the electricity industry. Given, however, that the major structural reforms were motivated largely by a desire to increase competitive pressures in electricity generation, we shall focus here on competition in the wholesale power market. Very roughly, horizontal restructuring can be viewed as a means of creating immediate competition among incumbents, and vertical separation can be viewed as a means of reducing entry barriers. The discussion is, therefore, divided into analysis of competition among incumbent generators (this section) and of competition from (actual and potential) entrants (Section 6).

5.1. Competition and collusion

A full analysis of oligopoly issues must take account of a whole range of features of competition in the wholesale market. Nevertheless, it is useful as a first step to focus on a situation in which generators sell into a completely unregulated spot market with price-taking consumers.

Indeed, suppose for a moment that the industry is also perfectly competitive. Being unable to influence market prices, profit-maximizing generators will offer to supply power at the marginal cost of their

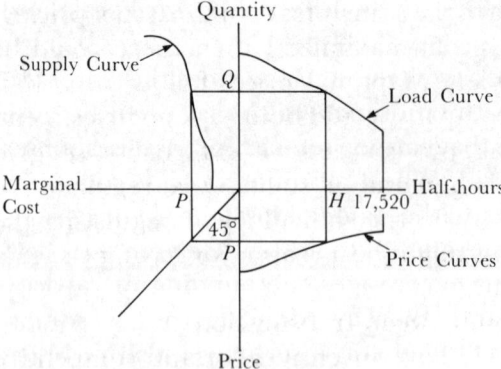

Figure 3. Electricity demand and price

generating units. The result of aggregating these bids will be an industry supply curve. Price is determined by the intersection of that curve with the demand curve. Figure 3 shows how price varies with demand in this situation. In the top-right quadrant is the annual load curve, in which half-hours are ranked in decreasing order of demand. Thus, demand exceeded Q megawatts during H half-hours in the year. The industry supply curve, derived from marginal costs as described, is shown in the top-left quadrant. In a half-hour when demand is Q, price will be P. A price curve corresponding to the load curve can be plotted in the bottom-right quadrant by reflecting off the 45% line as shown. Price exceeds P in H half-hours of the year. Figure 4 uses this price curve to assess the annual profit of a power station with marginal cost c. The station will run for J half-hours and its profit will be the shaded area. Over time there will be an incentive to invest in plant for which this profit, discounted over time, exceeds fixed cost. There will be

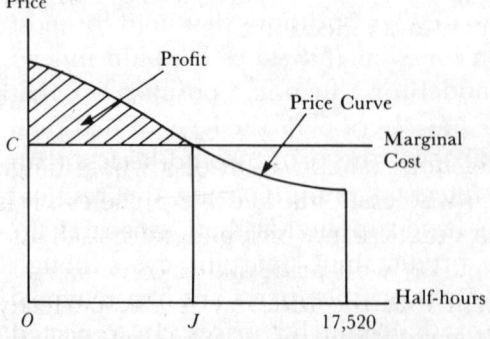

Figure 4. The profitability of a price-taking plant

incentives for the industry to invest to achieve the optimal scale and mix of plant.

In this model there is no 'capacity element'. How does this enter the picture? The answer has to do with rationing, which may occur because of supply and/or demand shocks that happen too fast for price responses to equilibrate supply and demand. When rationing occurs, consumer surplus is lost (this is the idea behind the 'value of lost load'). For periods when this might happen, it is appropriate to add an element to reflect the probability of lost load. This encourages the building of capacity and somewhat constrains demand, thereby reducing the congestion externality. Note that the capacity element is set by regulatory intervention, so the market is no longer completely unregulated.

Leaving aside these issues to do with rationing, let us now turn to the issue of market power on the supply side. Even the simplest oligopoly models suggests that this might be a serious concern in the circumstances of the ESI. Because prices rather than quantities are offered to the pool, Bertrand competition is a more natural initial approach than Cournot competition. With constant marginal cost level c and large enough capacities, the unique Bertrand equilibrium indeed has price equal to c. For example, if total capacity K is divided equally between n firms, and if demand when price equals c is $Q(c)$, then marginal cost pricing is the unique equilibrium if and only if $n > K/[K - Q(c)]$. In other words, capacity must be divided between a large enough number of firms for capacity constraints not to upset the marginal cost pricing equilibrium.

This kind of condition plainly does not hold in the British ESI in the majority of demand states. The analytical difficulty when capacity constraints bind is that equilibrium in pure strategies fails to exist (the way that demand is rationed between firms also needs to be specified). Mixed strategy equilibrium must be analysed – see Kreps and Scheinkman (1983), and Tirole (1988). The general conclusion is that high price-cost markups emerge from this one-shot model when capacity and demand parameters are set to correspond with the conditions that hold for most of the time in the ESI. Except in low demand states it would indeed be a dominated strategy in this model for a firm in a position like that of National Power to offer a price anywhere near the level of marginal cost. Even if it supplied at full capacity, the profit would be less than that achieved by a high-price strategy of monopolizing the residual demand left after the other firms have supplied at their capacities.

Note that these static models predict high margins even though behaviour is entirely non-collusive. In practice firms are in a dynamic relationship, with daily setting of (half-hourly) prices. In repeated game models, tacit collusion can be sustained by threats to revert to non-cooperative behaviour – see Tirole (1988) for an account of the main results. The degree of such collusion may be limited if the number of firms is large, if discounting is high, or if detection lags are long, but none of these things is remotely true of the British ESI, where, in terms of the models, dream conditions for collusion prevail.

Given that these models suggest that the prospects for competitive outcomes in generation are gloomy, it may be asked whether there exists any defence, other than (the threat of) direct regulatory intervention in the event of excessive prices, against the exploitation of market power. Several factors, absent from the models looked at so far, need to be examined.

5.2. Contracts, entry and regulatory intervention

The first is *contracts* (see Anderson, 1990). Suppose National Power were committed, via long-term contracts struck in the past, to supply a designated number of units of output at a designated price. Then the economic profit on the contract in any particular period would be equal to the specified output multiplied by the difference between the contract price and the pool price (the latter being the opportunity cost of supply). Since any move by National Power to raise prices in pool would depress the profit from the long-term contract, the existence of such a contract serves to reduce the incentives to behave restrictively.

When the new industry structure was introduced in March 1990, the government imposed an initial set of contracts (called 'contracts for differences') between the RECs and the generators – the most substantial of which are of three years duration – which do indeed reduce the incentives of National Power and PowerGen to raise pool prices. The fact that such contracts tend to diminish market power suggests that, once the initial government-imposed contracts run out, the generators might seek to limit the number of contracts that they sell. There are, however, pressures in the other direction, which, in addition to the factors discussed in Sections 4.1 and 4.2, could include the strategic motive of selling contracts to induce output contractions from rivals. And, unlike the daily repetitions of the spot market game, conditions for collusion in the contract market are distinctly less favourable: longer contracts reduce the relevant discount factor, and secret price cuts are much harder to observe. The relative ease of collusion, therefore, suggests that spot prices might be higher than contract prices.

The second key factor is *entry*, which will be considered in more detail in the next section. Import competition from Scotland and France is the main immediate threat, but it is limited by the capacity of the interconnectors. Given the time lags in constructing new plant, entrants

Table 5. Pool selling prices: comparison with the Bulk Supply Tariff (BST)

	Lowest price in the day, £/MWh	Highest price in the day, £/MWh
Pool, 22/8/90	11.31	24.53
Pool, 29/8/90	11.35	23.86
BST, summer rates, 1988/89	16.00	26.20

Source: Daily Telegraph; Handbook of Electricity Statistics (1989).

will take a while to establish themselves at a substantial scale, through the period required for the introduction of new combined cycle gas turbine (CCGT) plant is not long by past industry standards. Thus, a purchaser facing high spot market prices because of opportunistic behaviour by incumbent generators could enter a long-term contract with a new producer (or build its own plant) for supplies beginning, say, four years hence. That would threaten the generator with stranded capacity in the future. Put another way, the ability to strike long-term contracts gives new entrants the capacity to make pre-emptive (pricing) moves against incumbents, and may, therefore, serve to increase the competitive pressures that potential competitors exert on established firms. Purchasers, notably RECs, might also contract for new supplies to reduce the market power of the incumbent generators. However, free rider problems between purchasers could limit this, and it does not deter the generators from exercising their market power in the short term anyway. What might do the latter is fear on the part of incumbent generators that a reputation for short-term opportunism would jeopardize longer-term business. The strength of such a reputation mechanism is a matter for debate.

The third factor is the fear that the exploitation of market power in the short term would *trigger regulatory intervention.* This would be the worst of both worlds for the incumbent generators – the longer-term reputation loss would have been incurred for minimal short-term gain. (It would also be rather embarrassing for the Government's reforms, which are based on the idea of competition replacing regulation in generation.) The incumbents must strike a balance between short-term profit and the desire to avoid this risk. In the fear of regulation is an important curb on the exercise of market power, then there is a sense in which the wholesale market is subject to regulation after all. At any rate, it is not characterized by laissez-faire competition as normally understood.

There is some evidence about pricing behaviour from the first few months of the workings of the system – see Table 5. The evidence is limited, and it must be treated cautiously because the period in the run-up to privatization may not be representative of what happens later. For example, all sorts of strategic signalling might be going on between participants in the industry. That said, initial prices in the pre-privatiz-ation period do not indicate price-cost margins at the very high levels that are implied by duopoly models without contracts, entry threats, and the fear of regulatory intervention, although there is some indica-tion that the dispersion of time-of-day prices has increased. However, whether or not the generators behave strategically with respect to the capacity element in the pool price, for example by underdeclaring available capacity in order to raise the loss of load probability, remains to be seen (this is likely to be more of a problem in the winter).

Another important piece of evidence comes from investors' valuations of the incumbent generators even allowing for the incentive of the financial community to talk down the offer prices, it does appear very unlikely that the government will be able to sell either National Power or PowerGen at a price even close to their balance sheet (CCA) asset values. For what it is worth, this evidence suggests that the capital market does not perceive a large pot of monopoly profits on the generation side of the electricity industry in the long run.

5.3. Oligopoly: conclusions

The analysis of oligopoly is beset with many difficulties even in the simplest of settings. In the electricity supply industry further complica-tions arise from issues of capacity constraints, the mix of plant, the nature of dynamic interaction, contracts, potential competition and the threat of regulatory intervention. Given that conditions for collusion between the incumbent generators appear on the surface to be so favourable, at least in the short term, we believe this last factor to be very important. But it implies that the wholesale market is not really free from regulation. Rather, it suggests that a kind of limit pricing may operate, where the danger is entry by the regulator. Although price regulation is usually associated with monopoly or dominant firms, the regulation of oligopoly is not unprecedented: the UK salt duopoly is subject to price controls, for example (see MMC, 1986). It is, there-fore, conceivable that the question of wholesale electricity prices might eventually be referred to the MMC by the DGES, but whether or not this happens, the possibility of regulatory intervention is likely to be a constraining influence on the exercise of market power in the new electricity supply industry.

6. Entry and access

Given the question marks hanging over the effectiveness of competition among incumbent firms in the wholesale power market, it remains to be considered whether the reform of the ESI can be expected to lead to a substantial increase in competitive pressures as a result of lowering of entry barriers. Since the difficulties of entering the transportation activities (transmission and distribution) are very substantial because of natural monopoly conditions combined with sunk costs, we focus on generation and supply. We start with generation because this is the area where there is the greater scope for reducing costs (see Table 1), and because the most radical of the structural reforms (vertical separation of generation and transmission) was targeted chiefly on promoting competition in generation.

6.1. Entry into generation

At present the industry has excess capacity overall, but an inefficient mix of plant. The nuclear programme is effectively at a standstill due to high real interest rates, and following revelations about costs of waste disposal and decommissioning. Environmental measures (see Section 8) are likely to raise the relative cost of coal-fired stations. Technological advance has made combined cycle gas turbine plant much more efficient, and in the near term new generation capacity is, therefore, likely to be CCGT. Over the longer run the need for new capacity will depend on the rates of demand growth and the retirement of older capacity.

Consider first whether the main incumbent generators, National Power and PowerGen, have intrinsic cost advantages over potential entrants (strategic factors, for example arising from first mover advantages, will be examined later). Comparing the incumbents' existing plant with potential new plant, capital costs are to a large degree sunk in the case of the former. However, this is not entirely so. For example, existing coal-fired stations may require expensive investment in flue gas desulphurization (FGD) equipment. Moreover, much of the incumbents' existing plant has relatively high operating costs because of its age and mix. Environmental measures will further increase those costs. In addition, coal prices paid by the ESI have in the past been artificially high. This will continue in the short term, although the implicit subsidies to the domestic coal industry are being steadily reduced.

As for competition to construct new plant, where the track record of the incumbents is poor (see MMC, 1981), National Power and PowerGen do not have obvious advantages due to their scale, and their vertical integration with transmission has now ceased. The main potential competitors are themselves large international players – in the oil, gas, power equipment and construction industries for example – with no capital market disadvantages. Some of them have incentives for vertical integration (see Section 4), for example forward integration by fuel and equipment suppliers, and backward integration by RECs and large customers. Auto-generation has a tax advantage in that it is exempt from the fossil fuel levy, and combined heat and power (CHP) projects are also favoured. Without a wholesale market larger firms can provide a given supply security level with proportionately less plant than smaller firms because of the law of large numbers, but in principle the pool should remove any incumbent advantages on this score.

The cost advantages of the incumbents are more related to locational issues, where there are at least two problems. First, they have the great asset of existing sites with planning permission for new plant. Environmental objections are increasing the difficulty and cost of developing new sites (an example of conflict between competition and environmental concerns). Second, the present configuration of the transmission system is closely related to existing power station locations, and hence to the sites of the incumbents.

Turning to the possibility of strategic behaviour, the first question is whether the incumbents can credibly threaten to cut prices in the event of entry to a level that renders entry unprofitable. Capital intensity, durability, and asset specificity in generation suggest that this might be possible without the incumbents pricing below their variable costs. On the other hand, since plant is of many vintages and types, the variable costs of marginal plant can be high, indeed higher than the total cost of optimal new plant. Selective price cuts targeted against newcomers are impossible given the nature of the market, and sunk costs imply that it would be hard to make an entrant withdraw from the market once it had come in, though aggressiveness might still have reputational advantages for incumbents.

The next issue is whether incumbents will rationally pre-empt entry by building capacity ahead of rivals, rather as in the pre-emptive patenting literature (Gilbert and Newbery, 1982). The idea here is that competition will be greater, and hence industry profits will be lower, if a newcomer rather than an incumbent builds the next unit of capacity. With a monopolist or perfectly colluding incumbents, it follows that the incumbent(s) has a greater incentive to build the next unit, but this argument does not extend to non-colluding oligopolists because there are free-rider problems in entry deterrence between incumbents (Gilbert and Vives, 1986; Vickers, 1985).

Virtually all new power projects are for CCGT plant, thanks to the changes in the economics of coal versus gas (see Table 6). There are indications that the incumbents, National Power and PowerGen, have

Table 6. New power projects announced by October 1990

Location	Size/type	Lead company
Killingholme	900 MW CCGT	National Power
Rye House	680 MW CCGT	National Power
Killingholme	1,000 MW CCGT	PowerGen
Little Barford	680 MW CCGT	PowerGen
Roosecote	220 MW CCGT	ABB
Wilton	1,750 MW CCGT	Enron

Source: Power in Europe (1990).

been moving more quickly than most competitors into new CCGT construction. However, it is equally evident that there is a great deal of interest in entry, unlike in the period after the 1983 Energy Act. Firms seeking backward or forward integration – fuel suppliers, power equipment makers, construction companies, distribution companies, etc. – are particularly prominent. Imports from Scotland also appear to be expanding.

Finally, it can be asked whether entry, or the threat of it, may lead to excess capacity in the industry. This could happen for two reasons. The first is pre-emptive capacity building by incumbents, which has just been discussed. The second is that oligopolistic collusion on pricing, the subject of Section 5, could lead to high profits that are competed away by capacity building, with the inefficient result of over capacity in the industry.

6.2. Entry into supply

The entry problem in supply – the acquisition of electricity and its sale to final consumers – stems from the supplier's dependence on incumbent competitors. In a few cases suppliers can bypass the RECs by taking lines straight from the grid, but generally they must use REC wires. One response to the possibility that the regional monopolies in distribution will extend to supply would be complete separation: just as transmission was separated from generation, so distribution could have been separated from supply. However, that would entail the loss of economies of scope between the two activities, which, particularly for smaller loads, may be significant. An alternative approach, and the one that has been followed, is accounting separation accompanied by regulation: the RECs must keep separate accounts for separate businesses, and their distribution charges are regulated. There remain problems of monitoring (the fine detail of connection arrangements, etc.) to ensure that the RECs treat their own and their rivals' supply businesses equally. On the other hand, RECs might not go to great lengths to hold on to their initial dominant positions in supply, especially if competition squeezes margins, and may be content to focus on profit from their wires businesses (recall that, in terms of value added, distribution is a much more significant activity than supply).

In fact, public policy has sought to restrict the competition faced by RECs in supply, by means of the franchises and quotas limiting National Power and PowerGen described in Section 3. As in telecommunications, where British Telecom and Mercury were protected from competition in fixed link network operation, dominant incumbents have been shielded from competition in electricity supply. Such limitations on competition may enhance sales proceeds and may be attractive to the protected incumbent firms, but they are questionable on efficiency grounds.

The integration of generation and supply is a factor that might assist entry into supply by generators, but hinder competition from others, if generators are able to operate a vertical price squeeze. Such a strategy involves raising the wholesale price of electricity on the spot market, thereby increasing the costs of competitors in supply, and to undercut them in the retail market. Again, accounting separation and regulation against cross-subsidy are intended to cope with the problem, and the alternative policy of rigidly separating generation and supply would have removed an important source of competition to RECs in supply.

Indeed, National Power and PowerGen achieved a very rapid rate of market penetration at the large-load (chiefly industrial) end of the market once competition in supply was opened up. By the end of May 1990, just two months after the new regime came into being, they had captured 9% of the market formerly held by the RECs. Scottish Hydro also won a contract to supply 12 sites of BOC, one of the UK's largest industrial consumers with a maximum demand of about 250 MW. Hydro has also contracted to supply RECs directly. Its strategy is especially interesting because its share of capacity on the interconnector between Scotland and the English/Welsh system is limited, so that it will have to buy from the pool to meet its commitments. Nevertheless its entry into supply has not been deterred.

More generally, Table 7 shows the market shares captured by second-tier suppliers – including RECs supplying outside their own areas, as well as companies like National Power, PowerGen and Scottish Hydro – in the first three months of the new regime. These data make it clear that significant competition in the supply of electricity is already a reality.

Table 7. Percentage market shares of second-tier suppliers, 1 July 1990

Region	Non-franchised market	Total market
Eastern	16.0	3.5
East Midlands	19.2	5.7
London	39.0	7.0
Manweb	49.0	25.0
Midlands	33.0	9.9
Northern	57.0	26.0
Norweb	36.7	10.9
South East	44.4	8.7
Southern	32.2	6.7
South Wales	71.0	36.0
South West	62.6	13.6
Yorkshire	42.5	18.7

Source: RECs' Privatization Prospectuses.

6.3. Entry and access: conclusions

In the short time since regulatory reform took place in the UK electricity supply industry, there has been a good deal of evidence of new entry in both generation and supply. This contrasts with the disappointing results of liberalizing generation in the 1983 Energy Act, and it is interesting to ask why this is so. Part of the reason is that technological advances, factor price changes, and environmental policy have made CCGT plant very attractive, and entrants as well as incumbents have been taking that investment opportunity. However, the reformed regulatory framework has been an essential condition in our view. The weakness of the 1983 Act was the lack of regulation for competition, in particular regulation of access terms. That deficiency has now been made good, and it is the effects of (actual and threatened) new entry on plant construction costs and fuel input costs that are likely to represent the most significant source of benefits from the recent regulatory reforms.

7. Price regulation

As already noted, the scope for increasing competition (actual or potential) in the naturally monopolistic activities of transmission and distribution is highly limited. In respect of these activities, therefore, the emphasis of the policy reforms accompanying privatization has been on the development of new methods of controlling prices so as to prevent abuse of monopoly power.

As explained in Section 3, RPI-X regulation applies separately to transmission, distribution and supply to smaller consumers. The general merits of RPI-X regulation and its relation to rate-of-return regulation have been much discussed elsewhere – see, for example, Vickers and Yarrow (1988), and the symposium on price cap regulation in the *Rand Journal* (1989). Here we shall focus upon both the specific implications of RPI-X regulation for the electricity market and the issues that regulation of the British electricity supply industry has highlighted, but which are potentially also of importance to other industries.

7.1. Transmission charges

The analysis of price regulation usually assumes that the firm maximizes profit subject to regulatory constraint. In the case of the National Grid Company, however, a distinction must be made between the profit from its own activities and the profits of its owners, the 12 RECs. Because of NGC's key position in the market and its access to commercially sensitive information from all major participants, there are restrictions on the extent to which its owners can control its behaviour. Moreover, the transmission licence gives NGC some quasi-regulatory duties, such as the duty to facilitate competition, which will sometimes conflict with the RECs' objectives. However, we shall begin by supposing that NGC's objective is to maximize profit from its transmission activities, as if it were an independent entity.

Because of its high degree of both spatial and temporal differentiation, electricity transmission provides some graphic illustrations of the difficulties of price regulation in multiproduct industries. For example, should regulators focus on constraining some relatively simple overall price index, leaving detailed aspects of the price structure to be determined by the regulated firm itself, or should regulators attempt to control the structure as well as the overall level of prices? The first option risks the introduction of pricing distortions as the firm seeks to minimize the impact of the regulatory constraint on profits, whereas the latter runs the risk of distortions due to flawed regulatory decisions as a result, for example, of limited information.

The initial tariff structure for the privatized National Grid in England and Wales represents an *ad hoc* mixture of different approaches (Table 8 gives an outline). The main distinction is between charges for connection to the grid and for the use of the system. The former are intended to cover the costs (mostly capital costs) incurred in providing points of entry, where generators connect to the grid, and points of exit, where RECs and other electricity suppliers draw power from the grid. Entry and exit capital is frequently specific to one or a small number of generators or suppliers. Thus, while entry and exit charges for existing facilities are included within the overall price cap for transmission,

Table 8. Initial tariff structure for the national grid (£)

Average annual entry charge	1.25/kW
Average annual exit charge	4.00/kW
Proposed system service charge	3.37/kW
Suppliers' infrastructure charges (zonal)	5.96–8.50/kW
Generators' infrastructure charges (capacity)	0.00–3.10/kW
Generators' infrastructure charges (energy)	0.00025/kWh

Source: Holmes (1990), from NGC.

connection charges for users requiring additional facilities are excluded from the cap, and are separately regulated on a rate-of-return basis. The exclusion can be seen as an attempt to prevent price cap regulation from discouraging new investment in access facilities.

Use-of-system charges are regulated according to an RPI-X formula (with X set equal to zero) that specifies an upper limit on NGC's revenue per unit of (average cold spell) maximum demand on the system. Use-of-system charges include: a per kW system charge levied on all suppliers, which is claimed to reflect the benefit that all suppliers derive from the existence of the grid system; generators' infrastructure charges, levied on both power (per kW) and energy (per kWh), with variations in charge levels among 11 regional zones; and per kW suppliers' infrastructure charges, also zonally differentiated.

Since volume for the purposes of the pricing formula is defined as maximum demand on the system, profit maximizing behaviour implies NGC seeking to increase that maximum demand at least cost. This means encouraging location patterns of incremental demand and supply that do not require major new investments in reinforcing the system. While it may be argued that this will encourage optimum use of existing transmission assets, the incentive system can go too far in this direction. Consider, for example, two power station projects of equal size, located at different points of the grid, one in the North and one in the South. Suppose that the North is a net exporter of power, that the North to South flow is limited by transmission constraints, and that the incremental demand giving rise to the requirement for new power projects lies in the South. Finally, let the incremental generation and transmission costs be G_n, G_s, T_n, and T_s, where $T_n > T_s$ and $G_n + T_n < G_s + T_s$. That is, incremental transmission costs are higher for the power station in the North, but the overall cost of delivered power is lower, and so efficiency is higher, if the Northern location is chosen.

Now a profit-maximizing transmission company subject to RPI-X regulation of the British type will prefer the less efficient project. That is because the revenue implications of the two projects are the same, but the transmission costs associated with locating the power station in the South are lower. The grid company might, therefore, seek to discourage new generation investment in the North directly, by quantitatively limiting access to the system, or indirectly, via a charging structure with similar effect. The general point is that there is a bias – resulting from a vertical externality and pushing towards regional autarky – built into the type of price control formula under discussion. As well as potentially leading toward short-run resource misallocation, this could clearly also have adverse long-term effects on the state of competition in electricity generation.

Thus far, the analysis has been based upon the assumption that the transmission company maximizes profits, but it might be argued that suboptimal project selection would raise the costs of RECs, and that the latter would, therefore, have every reason to use their influence as owners of the grid to discourage the distorted pricing structure. The strength of the point is weakened, however, by the facts that (i) the value to RECs of cost savings is limited by the cost-pass-through provisions of the pricing formula for the franchise market, (ii) there are 12 RECs and there may be conflicts of interest among them in respect of particular grid reinforcement investments, and (iii) as well as facilitating additional competition in generation, grid reinforcement might increase competition in supply, to the detriment of the RECs' own supply businesses. For example, from the perspective of RECs, the construction of additional transmission links to France might be viewed as a two-edged sword: on the one hand it might increase competition in generation, to the benefit of RECs, on the other hand EdF might win business from RECs in supplying the non-franchised electricity markets.

In our view, the fact that is most likely to modify the distorted incentives implicit in the RPI-X formula is the prospect of regulatory intervention. Among the more obvious limitations of the existing structure are the following: (i) there is no tariff component which reflects the costs of transmission losses (see Section 4.2), (ii) the degree of spatial differentiation in charges appears to be significantly less than the corresponding differentiation in costs, (iii) the system service charge is not closely linked to an identifiable category of costs, and (iv) there is no temporal disaggregation of charges (for example, a generator with given capacity would pay the same transmission charges whatever the time profile of its supply).

Unsurprisingly then, the Director General of Electricity Supply has already indicated his desire to see changes made, and his first report outlined a timetable which sees revised transmission charges being phased in from April 1993 onwards. The initial pricing structure for the grid must, therefore, be regarded as something of a holding operation. It is likely to be changed in the not too distant future; but how it will be changed is unclear. The regulatory uncertainty that exists in the meantime complicates investment planning – especially location decisions – in both generation and transmission.

7.2. Distribution and supply

An important innovation of the electricity privatization exercise was the distinction made, in PES licences, between the distribution and supply businesses of the RECs. As noted in Section 3.3, the two businesses are subject to differing price-cap formulae, and the supply business of any REC must purchase electricity transportation services from its own distribution business, on terms similar to those available to a competing electricity supplier. This approach – which aims for accounting/business separation of naturally monopolistic distribution from potentially competitive supply – is in marked contrast to the regulatory decisions taken at the time of the gas privatization in 1986 (when accounting separation between the carriage and supply of gas was not imposed). Because it will facilitate public monitoring of the terms on which competing suppliers will have access to the wires of the RECs, the innovation represents a significant improvement in the implementation of regulatory policy.

Since electricity distribution is similar to transmission in that it is a 'transport' activity, many of the issues raised by the regulation of distribution charges are similar to those surrounding the regulation of transmission rates (and the criticisms cited in Section 7.1 also apply to the structure of distribution charges). We will, therefore, focus here on questions concerning the regulation of supply charges to smaller customers.

In respect of supply, a key point to note is that the value-added contributed by REC electricity supply businesses amounts to something of the order of only 4% of the final selling price. The remainder is accounted for by the RECs' purchase costs, which comprise the purchase costs of bulk electricity, the fossil-fuel levy, transmission charges and distribution charges. To a large (but not total) extent, these purchase costs are beyond the control of a REC's supply business. Thus, for example, when there is a major hike in fossil fuel prices, RECs will find it almost impossible to avoid large increases in their purchase costs.

In the above circumstances, a substantial degree of 'pass-through' or purchase costs can be justified. Linking price changes to (marginal) cost changes is generally good for allocative efficiency, and the loss of cost-reduction incentives will be limited if the relevant cost components are genuinely beyond the control of the firm. Where, however, the regulated firm has more influence on the relevant cost items, it will tend to be more efficient to allow only partial indexation of prices: allocative efficiency is sacrificed to improve overall efficiency by strengthening incentives for cost reduction.

In England and Wales each REC will be allowed to pass through 100% of changes in its own bulk electricity purchase costs, the fossil-fuel levy, distribution charges and transmission charges (all of which are included in the Y-factor in the pricing formula). However, this was not always the intention of the government. In the first published versions of the draft PES licences in early 1989, pass-through of bulk electricity purchase costs was linked to a yardstick formula which implied that pass-through would be greater (less) than 100% if an individual REC was more (less) successful than other RECs in restraining its bulk purchase costs. In this way, it was intended that RECs would face strong incentives to strive for lower bulk electricity prices, and thereby increase the pressures on generators to improve upstream efficiency.

In principle, yardstick regulation is a potentially effective way of making use of relevant economic information to improve the trade-off between allocative and cost efficiency. However, the attempt to turn general principle into regulatory practice was not particularly well thought through. It was never clear, for example, why only bulk electricity purchase costs were singled out for the yardstick treatment when cost components over which RECs had more influence were not. The yardstick proposal was also linked to plans envisaging a relatively complex contractual structure linking suppliers and generators. These plans were later abandoned.

It can be argued that the simplicity of the final arrangements for purchasing bulk electricity, and in particular the availability of supplies from the pool, means that there is little ground for concern about the incentives effects of 100% cost pass-through, particularly as RECs come under increasing competitive pressures in their supply businesses. The blunting of incentives to reduce costs by the application of effort – the effect analysed in many applications of principal-agent theory to the regulatory problem – is not, however, the only negative consequence of the cost pass-through provisions. Difficulties also arise as a result of interactions between price regulation and vertical integration in the industry, which in some circumstances might provide RECs with incentives to raise costs.

Recall that each REC owns a stake in the National Grid Company and, under the terms of its licence, is allowed to generate up to 15% of its own electricity requirements. As explained in Section 7.1, it is possible to envision circumstances where RECs would prefer higher generation plus transmission costs because (i) the profits of transmission activities are increased as a result and (ii) the higher overall costs can be passed forward to consumers. Similarly, an REC could find it beneficial to have higher bulk purchase prices if it can participate in the higher generation profits that this implies (see Helm and Yarrow, 1988). The general point here is that vertical integration can hinder effective regulation by making it more difficult to prevent adverse spillover effects of price controls.

7.3. Price regulation: conclusions

The general problem with regulation is that, although its purpose is to redress market failure problems, it can induce distortions of its own – in pricing, cost reduction and investment decisions. Early theoretical work on US rate-of-return regulation suggested dangers of over-investment, among other problems. In the UK, RPI-X price cap regulation was partly intended to overcome some of these perceived problems. However, depending on the information available for regulation, RPI-X might not be very different from rate-of-return regulation (with long lags). Moreover, it faces problems of its own, for instance the risk that policy credibility problems may lead to under-investment. This is an example of a problem that can occur in the simplest of settings with a single homogeneous good, but we have seen how it can be important also in the complex circumstances of the electricity supply industry.

The importance of the *structure* of regulated prices is illustrated by the question of grid pricing. The average price cap might introduce distortions that in turn affect investment decisions in generation as well as transmission. This is not to say that there are alternative easy answers – quite the reverse is true – but we hope to have indicated that the value of designing more efficient schemes is potentially very great. Above all, the vertically de-integrated electricity supply industry illustrates the important point that price regulation at one stage of the supply chain (e.g. transmission) can have major effects on competition at another stage (e.g. generation).

8. Environmental regulation

Perhaps the most important issues facing the electricity supply industry in the coming years have to do with environmental protection. Environmental regulation has been analysed elsewhere (see Newbery, 1990), and the main concern of the current paper is with the industrial organization of the ESI. However, the issues are closely related, and in this section we will examine two specific linkages: (i) possible investment problems induced by environmental regulation (which are particularly acute with nuclear power) and (ii) the 'fossil fuel levy' and its relation to the problem of carbon dioxide emissions and the greenhouse effect.

8.1. Investment issues

Intertemporal considerations affect environmental regulation because of investment problems of the kind already discussed in other contexts. A firm making sunk investments faces the risk that subsequent changes in environmental policy may require additional investments, such as the retrofitting of FGD equipment, which, if anticipated at the outset, would have rendered the project unprofitable. This type of risk is present even if the product markets into which the firm sells are unregulated. However, additional problems arise when, as we have argued is implicitly the case for bulk electricity, product prices are subject to regulatory influence. Thus, policy-makers may find it difficult to make credible commitments that future expenditures required by a tightening in environmental standards will be reflected in higher allowable product prices. In these circumstances, firms might face the prospect of falling profits as a result of political unwillingness to allow recovery, from consumers, of the costs of environmental protection.

Nuclear generation in the US provides a good example of the type of effect just described. Although it was not the only factor at work, the additional costs imposed by more stringent environmental regulation in the wake of events such as the Three Mile Island accident revealed the vulnerability of profitability to policy changes. Regulatory Commissions were unwilling to allow the escalating costs of nuclear power – to which cost over-runs and higher interest rates were also contributory factors – to be passed through to consumers. As a consequence, there was a large scale abandonment of nuclear projects, including power stations already under construction.

The threat of radiation release, such as occurred at Three Mile Island, is only one of the environmental considerations relevant to investment in nuclear generation capacity. More important in the UK has been the problem of disposal of nuclear waste. The safe disposal of such wastes imposes liabilities on generators that are highly uncertain and, more important here, whose value is highly susceptible to future public policy decisions as to what are and are not considered to acceptable methods of disposal. The result is another major policy credibility problem, which adds to the perceived costs of electricity produced from privately-owned nuclear power stations. In the event, initial plans to privatize nuclear generating capacity in the UK, set out in the 1988 White Paper, were abandoned in 1989, and the future nuclear programme (excluding the station currently under construction at Sizewell) has been frozen.

8.2. Greenhouse gases and the fossil fuel levy

At first sight it may appear ironic that the nuclear power programme has been mothballed at a time when increasing concern about global warming is anticipated to lead to environmental measures aimed at limiting atmospheric emissions of carbon dioxide. One of the possible regulatory instruments that might be applied in connection with this problem is a 'carbon tax' levied on fossil-fuels, which will tend to raise the costs of generating electricity from some of the main technologies competing with nuclear stations, particularly coal.

In fact, as part of the privatization exercise, the government has introduced a 'fossil-fuel levy' which will be applied to electricity generated by coal, oil and gas-fired power stations. The proceeds of this levy will be paid to Nuclear Electric, thereby simultaneously taxing power from fossil-fuel stations and subsidizing nuclear power. The levy originated from a long-standing government commitment to nuclear power that had more to do with a desire to avoid heavy reliance on domestically produced coal – where security of supply has been disrupted by industrial action in the past – than to environmental concerns, although the latter have been used as an *ex post* justification for the levy. And, although the levy might be viewed as a rough, first approximation to a carbon tax, there are a number of important differences. For example, the levy bears down only on fossil-fuel used to generate electricity and its base is the unit of electricity produced, not the amount of carbon dioxide emitted in producing that unit (which is lower for gas than for coal or oil).

That the fossil-fuel levy proved inadequate to make the privatization of nuclear power a viable proposition reflects in part the strength of the policy credibility problem for a technology as capital-intensive and politically sensitive (for environmental reasons) as nuclear electricity generation. For example, simply raising the magnitude of the levy would not have disposed of the problem, since it would have been difficult for the Government to commit to maintaining the levy over long periods.

Of the principal technologies used to generate electricity in Britain, the one most favoured by tightening environmental regulation is CCGT. Policy credibility problems, and the more general uncertainties surrounding the introduction of the new market and regulatory structures, tend to favour CCGT because it is less capital-intensive than nuclear, coal or oil. In addition, the risks posed to investors by changing environmental policies are rather lower than for coal and oil. If, say, a carbon tax were introduced at some point in the future then, because it produces less carbon dioxide per kWh generated, such a tax would increase the cost of CCGT technology by less than the costs of existing coal and oil technologies.

8.3. Environmental regulation: conclusions

The major policy reforms surrounding the privatization of the ESI in Britain were not developed with a view to tackling environmental problems. Nevertheless, there can be little doubt that environmental regulation will have a strong influence on the future conduct and performance of the industry. Indeed, such regulation is increasingly identified, worldwide, as the most important challenge facing the electricity industry in the 1990s.

The growing priority assigned to environmental protection raises major questions about how the new regime will function alongside environmental regulation. Answers must await evidence on how the experiment works in the post-privatization period. Meanwhile, however, it is safe to conclude that much work remains to be done in understanding the interactions between regulation of market power and regulation for environmental protection, an area of analysis that is still very much in its infancy.

9. Concluding remarks

Solutions to the multiple market failures that occur in electricity supply have traditionally involved high degrees of both vertical and horizontal coordination, whether by common ownership or by collaboration among independent firms. Although one or other version of the traditional approach is still predominant in virtually all countries, there has been increasing interest among policy-makers in moving away from integrated structures, at least to some degree. Whereas this process has been cautious and gradual elsewhere, Britain has just taken the radical step from nationalized monopoly to a privatized, vertically de-integrated structure with competition in both wholesale and retail supply.

Policy interest in de-integration is not, however, confined to electricity supply. Competition policy more generally is concerned with just such questions, and one of the major issues that arises in many industries is the effect of vertical relationships on horizontal competition. At EC level, for example, special regulatory provisions exist in relation to vertical contractual arrangements in the supply of beer, of petrol and of motor vehicles (see Whish, 1989). All three of these industries have also been the subject of recent major UK competition policy investigations, but whereas vertical agreements were given a clean bill of health in petrol supply (MMC, 1990), the MMC recommended that similar agreements be weakened in beer supply (MMC, 1989).

How then does analysis of the British electricity experiment help us to understand better these difficult issues of 'markets' versus 'hierarchies'? In the first place, it illustrates the point made in Section 4 that vertical integration and long-term contracts may themselves be market responses to failures and inefficiencies surrounding spot contracting. Public policy that seeks to restrict these responses, therefore, risks the reintroduction of the underlying market failures, which take the form of vertical and horizontal externalities. This general risk, common to many markets, is particularly acute in electricity because of economic characteristics of transmission grids (Section 4.2).

The main argument *for* vertical separation is that it may promote horizontal competition. In respect of supply of electricity to the non-franchised market, the partial separation of supply and distribution has indeed led to a surge in competition for the accounts of large end users (Table 7). The supply business, however, accounts for only a small fraction of final electricity prices, and it requires little in the way of capital to enter: the much more important issue concerns the effects of the policy reforms on electricity generation. In respect of generation we have argued that, in the absence of regulation, the market conditions created will be conducive to non-competitive pricing behaviour, including tacit collusion (Section 5). Implicit regulation of the bulk market is, therefore, likely to persist.

One possible conclusion from this is that the reforms were not radical enough: they should have gone further in promoting horizontal competition by, for example, splitting the CEGB into a larger number of generating companies. Since the creation of the National Power and PowerGen duopoly was largely dictated by the desire to privatize nuclear power, and since nuclear power was eventually dropped from the privatization programme, *ex post* there is indeed little rationale for the existing market structure. However, given some of the key characteristics of the industry (including investment lags, a highly replicated price game for wholesale supplies to the pool, massive spatial and temporal product differentiation through the network), while more radical proposals – such as splitting the CEGB's non-nuclear generation activities into five companies, each of similar size – might have diminished the severity of the problem of collusion, it is far from clear that they would have been sufficient to create really effective competition in the pool.

Where the reforms are likely to have more beneficial effects on competition is via their impact on entry conditions (Section 6). Lower barriers to entry in generation will have two main effects: (i) current arrangements whereby the ESI has been used to protect the domestic coal industry will be undermined, and (ii) there will be downward pressure on power station construction costs, where past industry performance has been poor.

The importance of entry conditions for competition is a message that has long been stressed in the industrial organization literature, but, accepting the general policy goal of reducing entry barriers, it is not clear that the objective is being achieved in the most efficient way. Protection of the domestic coal industry could have been simply and easily ended by, for example, liberalizing trade in coal. Bidding schemes for new power station construction offer one of several alternative approaches to reducing capital costs by promoting competition. Evidence in favour of the British 'structural' approach is the contrast between the entry that is occurring now and the absence of new entrants following the Energy Act 1983. On the other hand, the unfavourable comparisons between past UK power station construction costs and those elsewhere in the world might be interpreted as showing that much greater cost efficiency can be achieved without radical restructuring: as already noted, the countries with costs lower than the UK continue to rely on integration and collaboration in electricity supply. This latter view would suggest that the British electricity experiment may be a case of taking a sledgehammer to crack a nut.

Regulatory reform has not, of course, been directed exclusively at attempting to increase competition: new arrangements for regulating the naturally monopolistic transmission and distribution networks have been put in place. In these areas, the general lessons to be learned concern the relative effectiveness of regulated private monopoly and public monopoly, an issue that has arisen throughout the course of the UK privatization programme, and one that is relevant to utility industries everywhere.

We have stressed the regulatory complexities that arise from the spatial and vertical characteristics of electric networks (Section 7). These characteristics, and the resulting regulatory problems, are, like the monopoly positions themselves, not fundamentally changed by privatization. Initial attempts to deal with many of the problems of price regulation have an explicitly interim aspect to them. However, the laudable, longer-term intention to improve upon relatively crude intial tariff structures necessarily comes into conflict with the objective of providing stable incentive structures.

This is another problem of vertical relationships: the regulator is like a monopsonist with unilateral powers to vary price (see Section 4.1), and one of the dangers of this arrangement is inefficiency in investment.

The problems can be countered either by public ownership – a form of vertical integration between regulator and firm – or by a long-term regulatory 'contract' or 'bargain' (implicit or explicit), both of which are to be found elsewhere in the world. Britain has abandoned the first solution, but, in effect, has not yet fully embraced the latter. The spectre of policy instability, which proved so damaging to the ancien regime, still lurks.

Finally, we have addressed some questions surrounding the environmental regulation of the ESI (Section 8). Once more, there is a general, vertical dimension to the problems: the environmental regulator can unilaterally determine the terms on which firms will have access to environmental 'services', an important input so far as electricity generators are concerned. Familiar policy credibility and under-investment issues therefore arise, with perhaps the best example being the problems faced in attempting to reconcile nuclear power programmes with private ownership.

As a result of increasing public policy concern about the effects of atmospheric emissions of waste gases, and as in many other industries, this particular contractual boundary between the ESI and its regulators is likely to become increasingly important over time. Indeed, environmental regulation can be expected to be *the* major issue facing the ESI, worldwide, in the 1990s. Since the new regulatory framework in Britain was not developed with environmental problems in mind, there is a danger that, at the international level, it will come to be treated as a mere sideshow to the main (environmental) event. If so, that would be a pity; for, as we hope we have shown, the information the experiment promises to yield will be relevant in many contexts, not least in the context of environmental regulation itself. The reforms may not be widely copied, but they do merit close scrutiny.

Discussion

Jean-Charles Rochet
University of Toulouse

It is always interesting for economists to witness large-scale experiments, but I must admit to a feeling of relief that this particular experiment is not taking place in my own country.

Is it possible to explain the radicalism of this reform by the failure of the 1983 Energy Act to encourage new entry into power gene ration? The idea that competition might be fostered without introducing vertical disintegration of the incumbent was applied to the telecommunications industry only a year later. The telecommunications reform regulated transmission charges and the right of access; it was the failure to regulate these that undermined the Energy Act. The irony is that in the present reform, vertical disintegration has occurred in precisely the sector in which vertical coordination is most crucial, because of the characteristics of electricity as a good.

The hub of the new system is the spot market for wholesale electricity. How efficiently will this function? My main concern is about the risk of supply failures when demand exceeds available capacity. There are two elements in the price: the System Marginal Price, that equates supply and demand, and a correcting term (a capacity element) involving a 'Loss of Load Probability' (*LOLP*). What matters is how the *LOLP* is computed and revised, and whether it can provide correct incentives for generators to build enough capacity. Under a centralized system this capacity element was completely under control. Now it has become strategic and the probability of manipulated excess demand is not negligible. Since rationing electricity is more complex than for other goods, the welfare implications of this will depend crucially on who bears the costs of a cut-off.

The Vickers and Yarrow analysis illustrates how there is no such thing as complete deregulation. Even in this extreme experiment, new regulations have had to be introduced, particularly to deter abuse of market power by the monopsonistic grid. Transmission charges are to be regulated by a complex mixture of price cap and rate of return considerations. Given that rate of return regulation has been heavily criticized elsewhere, it would be interesting to know why it has been introduced here, and the extent to which the deficiencies of rate of return regulation can be avoided.

The idea that potential reregulation might discipline incumbent firms in the same way that potential entry does in models of contestable markets is an interesting one. But given the economic and political costs of reregulation I doubt its practical relevance. The more significant effect of political uncertainty on firms' behaviour is likely to be systematic underinvestment in all activities for which environmental costs could become important in the near future.

The evidence from pool prices in its first months of operation seems to suggest the following patterns of change:

a more than negligible reduction in average prices;
an increase in the variance of prices (which is good for incentives but bad for risk-averse consumers;
deregulated prices exceed regulated prices only at peak hours.
It is early days, but at least these trends are reasonably encouraging.

Anthony Venables
University of Southampton

I approached this paper wanting to know two things. The first concerns the operation of the new system. How are the problems of vertical coordination of such a complex system going to be solved, and can we be fairly confident that the lights will not go out? The second issue relates to the economic efficiency of the system. How is the potential market power of some of the new companies going to be controlled? Will economic efficiency within the industry be achieved, or might incentives created by imperfect competition distort investment decisions and destroy productive efficiency?

The paper does an excellent job in informing the reader about the new organization of the industry, and about the structures that are intended to coordinate the system. The new structure of the industry, especially of the wholesale power market, is set out extremely clearly. But I wonder how some of the longer-term contracts, and in particular options contracts, might work. Who is going to trade electricity options, and what are the likely benefits? There seems to be a fundamental problem in that a few agents (the generators) can control the spot price of electricity. What do we know about options markets when the spot price is subject to control in this way? Could the generators destroy the options market by manipulating the spot price? Would they want to?

The second issue concerns the economic efficiency of the system. The downstream activities of the industry are to be regulated by means of price controls of the RPI-X type. But the highly concentrated generating sector is left largely unregulated. What is the likely outcome of this? To address this the authors review oligopoly theory, which suggests that the likely outcome will be far away from perfect competition. The authors then argue that the tendency towards high price-cost margins might be offset by the presence of long-term contracts; by the possibility of entry; and by fear of triggering regulatory intervention.

I have two comments on this section of the paper. First, I would have been interested to see the application of oligopoly theory to this industry developed more fully. The industry is quite unusual in that market rules (or at least some of them) have been set by the operation of the power pool. We know that generators are not playing a game in either prices or quantities; instead they have to offer supply curves to the grid controller who then acts as a Walrasian auctioneer. What does oligopoly theory predict in this case? It would have been interesting to see the literature on supply function equilibria applied here. My second comment concerns the effect of long-term contracts. It is not evident to me that the existence of long-term contracts will reduce collusion.

Deviations from collusive behaviour can still be swiftly punished by price cutting in the spot market. Once again, the interaction between options contracts and spot markets in an imperfectly competitive environment seems to merit further research.

Economic efficiency concerns are important not only because of the price-cost margins set by the industry, but also in the choice of technique decisions made by generators, and hence the productive efficiency of the industry. Monopolies and perfectly competitive industries will choose techniques of production to minimize average costs. However, firms in an imperfectly competitive environment may choose techniques which are not cost minimizing, but which strengthen their competitive position *vis-a-vis* rivals. I would argue that inefficiencies due to this might be particularly severe in the electricity generating industry, for two reasons. First, there is a range of techniques available with widely differing marginal costs. This range arises because of the age structure of the capital stock, and suggests that we might expect to see scrapping decisions being distorted for competitive reasons. Second, the fact that demand varies during the day puts a high premium on having plants with low marginal cost – since these are the ones which will run all day. These considerations may, therefore, create incentives for firms to scrap plant too soon. There is a kind of idle capacity dumping game going on. There is a private return to me from shifting the idle off-peak capacity from me to you – although the social return to this is zero. It is possible then, that in addition to inefficiencies created by monopoly power in pricing, the new system may also have built in incentives for productive inefficiency to be introduced by premature scrapping of equipment.

General discussion

David Newbery pointed to the difficulty of valuing the electricity companies. PowerGen had been valued at £5.5 bn., but the bid from Lord Hanson had been for only £1.5 bn. Replacement cost was an inappropriate valuation concept, for most power stations would not in fact be replaced. In particular they faced a large liability for retro-fitting of flue gas desulphurization.

Newbery also discussed barriers to entry due to the opacity of pricing in the gas market. This made it hard for potential entrants to justify the profitability of their entry strategies to their financial backers. The theme of potential inefficiencies due to imperfect competition, in both the output and the input markets, was taken up by a number of other panellists. Damien Neven thought electricity had a number of the characteristics of models of spatial competition, where the inefficiencies of competitive outcomes were well known. Michael Burda thought the spot market potentially very vulnerable to manipulation.

Nicholas Crafts wondered about the rationale for the structural changes. Where were the welfare gains to come from, and how large were they? Paul Seabright said that the old merit order system had made the Central Electricity Generating Board a fairly efficient allocator of demand between power stations. If anything the new imperfectly competitive structure would make demand allocation less efficient than it had been before. The gains, if any, were likely to come in lower costs of power station construction. George Yarrow and David Newbery agreed, and both cited anecdotal evidence to suggest that construction costs were coming down substantially. Yarrow reiterated that the restructuring of the industry might well be considered taking a sledge-hammer to crack a nut; there might have been other ways of achieving a similar end. However, the ending of the contract for purchase of British coal at higher than world prices perhaps indicated that private ownership was a politically necessary condition of at least some aspects of efficient management.

References

Aghion, P and P. Bolton (1987). 'Entry Prevention through Contracts with Customers', *American. Economic Review*.

Anderson, R. W. (1990). 'Futures Trading for Imperfect Cash Markets: A Survey', in L. Phlips (ed.) *Commodity Futures and Financial Markets*, Kluwer, Amsterdam.

Bohn, R. E., M. C. Caramanis and F. C. Schweppe (1984). 'Optimal Pricing in Electrical Networks over Space and Time'. *Rand Journal of Economics*.

Department of Energy (1988). *Electricity Privatisation*, HMSO, London.

Gilbert, R. J. and D. M. Newbery (1982). 'Preemptive Patenting and the Persistence of Monopoly', *American Economic Review*.

—— (1988). 'Regulation Games', CEPR Discussion Paper No. 267.

Gilbert, R. J. and X. Vives (1986). 'Entry Deterrence and the Free Rider Problem', *Review of Economic Studies*.

Helm, D. R. and G. K. Yarrow (1988). 'The Regulation of Utilities', *Oxford Review of Economic Policy*.

Holmes, A. (1990). *Electricity in Europe*, FT Business Information, London.

Joskow, P. L. (1987). 'Contract Duration and Relation-Specific Investments: The Case of Coal', *American Economic Review*.

—— (1989). 'Regulatory Failure, Regulatory reform, and Structural Change in the Electrical Power Industry', *Brookings Papers*: Microeconomics.

Joskow, P. L. and R. L. Schmalensee (1983). *Markets for Power*, MIT Press, Cambridge, MA.

Kreps, D. and J. Scheinkman (1983). 'Quantity Precommitment and Bertrand Competition Yield Cournot Outcomes'. *Bell Journal of Economics*.

Littlechild, S. (1983). *Regulation of British Telecommunications Profitability*, HMSO, London.

Monopolies and Mergers Commission (1981). *Central Electricity Generating Board*, HMSO, London.

—— (1986). *White Salt*, HMSO, London.

—— (1989). *The Supply of Beer*, HMSO, London.

—— (1990). *The Supply of Petrol*, HMSO, London.

Newbery, D. M. (1990). 'Acid Rain', *Economic Policy*.

Power in Europe (1990). Financial Times Business Information, London.

Rand Journal of Economics (1989). 'Symposium on Price-Cap Regulation'.

Tirole, J. (1988). *The Theory of Industrial Organization*, MIT Press, Cambridge, MA.

Vickers, J. S. (1985). 'Pre-emptive Patenting, Joint Ventures and the Persistence of Oligopoly', *International Journal of Industrial Organization*.

Vickers, J. S. and G. K. Yarrow (1988). *Privatization: An Economic Analysis*, MIT Press, Cambridge, MA.

Whish, R. (1989). *Competition Law*, Second edition, Butterworths, London.

Wilkinson, M. (1989). 'Power Monopolies and the Challenge of the Market: American Theory and British Practice', Kennedy School, Harvard University, Discussion Paper E-89-12.

Williamson, O. E. (1975). *Markets and Hierarchies: Analysis and Antitrust Implications*, Free Press, New York.

Economic Policy   Issue 10   Erratum

Trading systems on European stock exchanges: current
performance and policy options

Marco Pagano and Ailsa Roell

p. 75 Table 3 and related text should be replaced by the following:

Table 3. Continental stocks traded in London (SEAQ International) (a) (b)

	Jan.–Oct. 1987	Jan.–Dec. 1988	Jan.–June 1989
As % of total domestic turnover in the respective national markets			
Paris	8.6	6.74	12.07
Frankfurt	N/A	6.70	8.02
Milan	—	—	1.39
Madrid	N/A	0.04	0.8
As % of turnover for the same stocks in the respective national markets			
Paris	20.64	13.72	25.08
(no. of stocks)		(24)	(29)
Frankfurt	N/A	12.65	16.21
(no. of stocks)		(13)	(15)
Milan	—	—	6.52
(no. of stocks)			(9)
Madrid	N/A	0.53	6.15
(no. of stocks)		(2)	(4)

Sources: The data for Paris in 1987 are drawn from Conseil National du Credit
(1988), Annexe XV; the data used to construct all the other figures have been
supplied by SEAQ International, the Societe des Bourses Francaises, Dresdner
Bank, Euromobiliare S.p.A., the CONSOB and the Banco de Espana.
Notes: (a) All percentages in the table are averages of monthly figures. Dashes
(—) indicate that no stocks from that market were traded on SEAQ International. Figures for Paris in the top panel are based on turnover in the *marche
a reglement mensuel*. The number of companies is meaured in June of the
relevant year. (b) To enhance comparability across the markets, we have
divided SEAQ volumes by two, because on SEAQ each trade between final
holders is intermediated by a market maker and thus gives rise to two separate
transactions – or even more than two, if it generates intra-market maker
trading. However, note that on auction markets trades may sometimes be
intermediated by professional speculators as well. Because of double-counting,
German volume data have also been divided by two.

The volume of business lost by Milan to London, beside being high
relative to the comparable figure for Madrid, has increased at an
impressive rate: looking at monthly figures (not reported in the table),
one finds that in June 1989 London trading on Italian stocks amounted
to 9.7% of the Milan turnover for the same stocks, up from 2.7% in
January.

PUBLIC FINANCE/FINANCES PUBLIQUES

International Quarterly Journal founded by J. A. Monod de Froideville
Revue Trimestrielle Internationale Fondée par J. A. Monod de Froideville

Publisher / Editeur
Foundation Journal for Public Finance
Fondation Revue de Finances Publiques
(Stichting Tijdschrift voor Openbare Financien)

Editorial Board / Comité de rédaction
M. Frank, A. J. Middelhoek, A. T. Peacock
Managing Editor / Editeur Gérant: D. Biehl

Volume XXXXIV/XXXXIVième Année
No. 3/1989

The articles published in English, French, or German are followed by summaries in the three languages.
Annual subscription rate (3 issues): DM 142,50.

PUBLIC FINANCE / FINANCES PUBLIQUES
c/o Institut für öffentliche Wirtschaft, Geld und Währung
Johann Wolfgang Goethe-Universität
Postfach 111932
D-6000 Frankfurt am Main 11
Federal Republic of Germany